P9-ECL-864

Nonprofit Mergers and Alliances

Nonprofit Mergers and Alliances

SECOND EDITION

WITHDRAWN

Thomas A. McLaughlin

WILEY

John Wiley & Sons, Inc.

Copyright © 2010 by Thomas A. McLaughlin. All rights reserved.

Published by John Wiley & Sons, Inc., Hoboken, New Jersey.

Published simultaneously in Canada.

No part of this publication may be reproduced, stored in a retrieval system, or transmitted in any form or by any means, electronic, mechanical, photocopying, recording, scanning, or otherwise, except as permitted under Section 107 or 108 of the 1976 United States Copyright Act, without either the prior written permission of the Publisher, or authorization through payment of the appropriate per-copy fee to the Copyright Clearance Center, Inc., 222 Rosewood Drive, Danvers, MA 01923, (978) 750-8400, fax (978) 646-8600, or on the Web at www.copyright.com. Requests to the Publisher for permission should be addressed to the Permissions Department, John Wiley & Sons, Inc., 111 River Street, Hoboken, NJ 07030, (201) 748-6011, fax (201) 748-6008, or online at http://www.wiley.com/go/permissions.

Limit of Liability/Disclaimer of Warranty: While the publisher and author have used their best efforts in preparing this book, they make no representations or warranties with respect to the accuracy or completeness of the contents of this book and specifically disclaim any implied warranties of merchantability or fitness for a particular purpose. No warranty may be created or extended by sales representatives or written sales materials. The advice and strategies contained herein may not be suitable for your situation. You should consult with a professional where appropriate. Neither the publisher nor author shall be liable for any loss of profit or any other commercial damages, including but not limited to special, incidental, consequential, or other damages.

For general information on our other products and services or for technical support, please contact our Customer Care Department within the United States at (800) 762-2974, outside the United States at (317) 572-3993 or fax (317) 572-4002.

Wiley also publishes its books in a variety of electronic formats. Some content that appears in print may not be available in electronic books. For more information about Wiley products, visit our Web site at www.wiley.com.

ISBN-13 978-0-470-601631

Printed in the United States of America
10 9 8 7 6 5 4 3 2 1

To Gail, Paul, and Emily

Contents

Acknowledgments

Even more than the first edition, this version has benefited tremendously from the contributions of many individuals. Since that first edition was published, I have consulted to more than two hundred nonprofit mergers and alliances, and virtually every single one provided an important insight or a fresh perspective.

I carried out my first mergers for Dr. Yitzhak Bakal at what is now known as the North American Family Institute, although I would not have said that's what I was doing at the time. It was on this initial base of experience that I later built a successful consulting practice in nonprofit collaborations. I applied some of my early methodologies on behalf of Punky Pleten-Cross, Kathy Wilson, Dianne McCarthy, Geri Dorr, and Deb Ekstrom. Early on, a handful of individuals made valuable suggestions, challenged my concepts, or helped clarify parts of my thinking. Ginny Purcell, Jim Boles, Kitty Small, Bill Taylor, Jim Heller, Rob Hallister, and Sue Stubbs are among these.

I have had the benefit of working with many talented colleagues. For nearly a decade, Stacey Zelbow has supported and challenged me as we worked with various nonprofit collaboration clients too numerous to count. Her steady presence has been an enormous benefit, and her detailed comments on an early draft of this edition helped improve it far beyond what I could have achieved on my own.

Over the years, literally dozens of leaders in foundations, associations, nonprofit federations, government agencies, and academic institutions have given me the opportunity to speak to their members and constituents about collaborations in one way or another. I deeply appreciate these opportunities to hone a message that resonates with large numbers of nonprofit leaders.

My colleagues at the Nonprofit Finance Fund have been wonderfully receptive and accepting of this new kind of consulting capability that I have recently begun building on the excellent foundation they laid over the last twenty-nine years. Clara Miller, our founder and CEO, has been consistently supportive in many ways, as has Leon Wilson. Kate Saliba has become an indispensable part of most of my collaboration consulting teams, and Rodney Christopher has regularly shown me how one can blend compassion with clear-eyed business savvy. Bill Pinakiewiciz "got it" very early on and has been a valuable partner in many different ways. Kristin Giantris has ably cleared away countless administrative roadblocks, while Renee Jacob, Linshuang Lu, and Jenn McVetty have made major contributions to our collaboration analytical capacities.

At John Wiley & Sons, Marla Bobowick first signed onto this project at a time when for many people the tems "merger" and "nonprofit" didn't belong in the same sentence. Susan McDermott has competently taken over responsibility for this edition.

Most important of all, I must thank my wife, Gail Sendecke, for the time and attention from me that she sacrificed to help make this second edition a reality.

Introduction

I t is time for systematic, structural innovation in the nonprofit sector. For decades, innovation in this field has almost always been synonymous with innovation in programs and services. Changes in society, the economy, and government have meant that nonprofits have had to spend much of their organizational energies on new and innovative forms of services. Today, much of that demand has subsided. For better or worse, we have established most of the major models of service that the nonprofit sector will supply for the foreseeable future. Programs and services that were once considered alternatives have become mainstream. And now the demand for innovation is shifting to the way those programs are managed.

This is why, for nonprofit organizations of all kinds, considering mergers and alliances will be the new strategic planning for the twenty-first century. Nonprofit service systems in areas ranging from the arts and health care to social services and advocacy are on the verge of significant change. Nonprofits in many parts of the country have already entered into a period of rapid change in the way they are structured and managed. Most others will follow. This book is an attempt to explore the choice that many of them will be making.

To some in the nonprofit field, the idea of mergers is scandalous and distasteful.

Decades of media coverage of Wall Street mergers have permanently linked the idea to images of human suffering caused by heartless downsizers whose designer suits are more valuable than their ethics. Inflicting the same fate on nonprofits seems cruel and unnecessary.

Yet the same restructuring is occurring in newspapers, banking, financial services, retailing, bookselling, and many other fields. There is no reason to think that nonprofits will—or should—be immune from it simply because of their tax status. The reality is that mergers among nonprofits are necessary. In many parts of the country today, there are simply too many nonprofits. This situation is caused by many factors, including the best of intentions, but the plain fact is that having an excessive number of nonprofit organizations actually weakens the collective power of the entire field. Organizations that should be serving a mission must instead spend disproportionate amounts of resources worrying about how they are going to fund it, manage it, and perpetuate it.

That said, we must emphasize that nonprofit mergers are different from those in the for-profit sector. A fair amount has been written about the latter. Very little has been written about nonprofit mergers, probably because the widespread adoption of the technique is relatively recent. Consequently, board members and nonprofit executives considering a merger or some form of strategic alliance often can find little specific guidance. More insidiously, transposing the for-profit merger experience and related techniques to the nonprofit sector is often frustrating and ineffective. Nonprofit collaboration of this kind requires different expectations, processes, and techniques. We hope that this book will help fill that gap.

Encouragingly enough, nonprofits have many structural advantages that can allow them to enter into mergers without repeating the same behaviors as some of their Wall Street counterparts. We will cover these in some depth, because managers and board members who understand these dynamics will be able to make the process work for their missions and their consumers, and it is to them among others that this book is addressed.

We have two goals for this book. The first is to describe a context for nonprofit mergers and alliances, including a discussion of the forces helping to shape nonprofits' use of mergers and alliances. It is important that nonprofit managers and board leaders be aware of both the similarities and the differences in their sector's merger patterns and techniques. Ultimately, a nonprofit sector that knows well how to collaborate will be far more effective in the pursuit of its public-spirited mission.

The second goal is to provide concrete guidance based on actual nonprofit collaborations. Ultimately, the information presented here will become common knowledge among some nonprofit managers and the inevitable cadre of merger specialists that the trend will create. Some of it will likely be proven wrong, while undoubtedly a few strategies and tactics that no one has even thought about yet will become routine. For the present, it is hoped that this material will be a creditable start.

The book includes a discussion of reasons to collaborate; a description of the C.O.R.E.™ model, a merger/alliance analysis framework; partner selection; structure choice analyses; and a section each on the processes of mergers and alliances.

It is worth noting that, while the author has worked in nonprofit collaborations virtually across the board, many of the examples in the book are drawn from a handful of fields, such as hospitals, arts organizations, and social services. The reason for this is twofold. First, most people are likely to be at least somewhat aware of mergers and alliances involving hospitals because they are large, highly visible nonprofits. Second, thanks to earlier waves of change, there have already been a significant number of mergers and alliances in these three fields. In ten years, this situation may very well be different. For instance, as the book was going to print, there was a sharp spike in interest in collaboration among community development corporations. If sustained, this spike may produce greater familiarity with collaborations with this type of organization.

Similarly, the attentive reader will notice more references to mergers than alliances. There is a disarmingly simple reason for this tendency too—there are far more mergers than alliances. A secondary reason is that many people equate a brand name with a corporate entity and they conclude, wrongly, that if a merger occurs, it means at least one brand name will go away. Therefore, if a brand name persists after some form of collaboration occurs, it must have been an alliance or, at least in their view, a "nonmerger." Truth be told, it also derives partly from a personal preference for the definitiveness and coherence of a well-done merger over the inherently fragmented alliance approach. Still, let it be said that either mergers or alliances can be perfectly valid forms of collaboration. Thus, the title.

Different readers will treat this book differently. All readers can be expected to gain something from the first few chapters. Board members, executives, funders, government officials, nonprofit advisors, and academics can profit from all sections, while managers may wish to concentrate primarily on Chapter 15 onward.

As prevalent as they are likely to become, collaborations are not a panacea for all the challenges facing the nonprofit sector. Carried out poorly, they can create as many problems as they solve. Nor do they always work. There is much we must all learn about both the process of merger and alliance development and how to manage the new entities that they create. But there is no doubt that it is time to begin this grand restructuring of society's most under-recognized and underappreciated sector. Let the rebirth begin.

Nonprofit Mergers and Alliances

CHAPTER 1

A Valid Strategic Option
for the Future

The best time to consider a merger or an alliance is *before* it is necessary, when coming together with another organization will mean combining strength with strength, and when the collective energies and creativity of the two or more entities can be used proactively instead of being sapped by the demands of crisis management. Without an external market mechanism to prod and enforce these kinds of strategic decisions, many nonprofits wait until the time comes when an alliance is not viable and they must choose between merging or going out of business. At that point, it is too late. An alliance will be a waste of time, and a rescue merger will be far more difficult and probably less effective than a merger made in less desperate circumstances. One of the primary objectives of this book is to make the case for nonprofit mergers and alliances as a preferred strategic option, not as a last-minute decision made in despair.

The single most compelling reason to merge nonprofits or to consider developing an alliance is to tap into complementary strengths. Many times, two different organizations come together and in the process discover unexpected sources of strength in the other: the ballet company with excellent administrative systems merges with a dance troupe with high public recognition; a small clinic that owns its own building merges with a larger set of clinics that needs to diversify its asset base; a chief executive with good "outside" skills brings her organization together with another whose chief executive officer is excellent at overseeing operations; and so on.

Note: Why Mergers Have a Bad Name

One of the reasons why mergers may have a negative connotation for nonprofit board members and managers, aside from the botched for-profit mergers the media have covered so thoroughly, is because of when they occur. In any industry experiencing consolidation, weaker players will always be the first to merge or go out of business. What the casual observer does not realize is that whatever bad things may happen to such an organization after a merger, such as services being shut down or people losing jobs, would almost certainly have happened without a merger, and probably worse would have occurred.

Good leaders read the signals of their environment, and nonprofit leaders are no exception. For many decades, nonprofit board members and senior managers have been astutely reading the messages sent by funding sources, government regulators, and social leaders. Universally, these signals said, "Grow. Expand your services. Create more organizations. Innovate and grow."

Nonprofits responded. Beginning in the mid-nineteenth century with voluntary child welfare and mental health organizations and continuing throughout the past century with the modern hospital, symphony orchestras, economic development groups, museums, civic leagues, associations, and charter schools, the nonprofit form of organization has witnessed a tremendous growth in scope and application. Today, the voluntary sector is a crucial—and increasingly acknowledged—element of the American economy.

Along the way, something subtle but very important occurred. Nonprofits by nature are intermediary organizations, serving as private buffers between the individual and government. While acting as an intermediary for a particular part of society, they serve as the proving grounds for social values and as vehicles for interpreting potential changes in those values. Consequently, nonprofits as a class invariably reflect the times in which they were created. On a practical level, this happens because they must solve most of the same economic challenges that any business must solve: assuring a demand for their service or product, selecting and hiring staff, overseeing operations. At a higher level, it happens because nonprofits represent one way in which society attempts to prevent or mitigate what could be a major dysfunction.

Thus, the mayor of an early-twentieth-century mill town invited an order of nuns to create an orphanage for children whose parents were killed or maimed by unsafe manufacturing processes; a major national advocacy organization mobilized an unprecedented campaign of fundraising and research to eradicate polio; and nonprofits have joined the burgeoning effort to find environmentally responsible answers to the fossil fuel dilemma. What all of these and countless other programs had in common is that they were the product of a unique mix of social, economic, cultural, political, legal, and other forces.

The individuals who lead these programs must negotiate an individualized balance of all these forces in order to be successful. It is an underlying theme of this book that the way that balance is achieved is on the verge of changing dramatically. Put simply, the way to be successful as a nonprofit organization will be very different in the twenty-first century than it was in the past 50 years.

Government's Retreat

The starting point for this difference is a central reality. For nearly 30 years, government at all levels of our society has taken a step back from its traditional role in responding to social needs. The New Deal and the Great Society were two vivid examples of government taking unprecedented initiative in key areas of society's needs, and the 2010 passage of the health care law was notable for its uniqueness.

In the meantime, as government was shrinking its area of responsibility, nonprofits were growing both in size and numbers. The growth trajectory over the past 20 years has been more consistent and more positive than that in many for-profit industries. As a result, in many areas, the nonprofit sector now has both the opportunity and the responsibility to assume some of that leadership role. It is well positioned and well experienced to do so.

In recent years, there has been a steady stream of messages from business leaders and others that there are "too many nonprofits." In this view, nonprofits have proliferated to the point where there are costly redundancies and overlapping services. Funders grumble that more and more nonprofits are pursuing the same philanthropic dollars, and civic leaders have begun to wish out loud that there would be what they delicately term "consolidations."

These are well-intended observations, but they miss the point. The reason that there is a surplus of nonprofits is not because there has been mindless growth but because for many years the prevailing philosophy of funders and government officials has been "Let a thousand flowers bloom." In the 1960s, certain kinds of foundation funding was implicitly based on the notion that if a human services program could produce three to five years' worth of success, the federal government would fund it permanently thereafter. For two or three decades, there was widespread innovation and experimentation, so it made sense to try many different approaches to see what works.

Today, however, in most parts of the nonprofit sector, we cannot sustain a thousand flowers anymore. Instead, we need a few dozen oak trees. We now know what works as a response to most dysfunctions, and the task is to set about doing it on as large a scale as is necessary and sustainable. The problem is not with the effort and the public spiritedness and the energy that lies within those hundreds of thousands of nonprofits; the problem lies in the way they are structured, particularly their capital structure. But after years of growth, those mature parts of the nonprofit sector now have substantial resources locked up in aging program models and out-of-date corporate structures. Those resources are both financial and human, and we must find a way to tap into them as never before. Nonprofit collaboration through mergers and alliances is a crucial means to make this happen.

For many parts of the nonprofit sector, mergers and alliances must be one of the primary strategic choices of the future.

The Freestanding Nonprofit
and Other Rugged Individualists

It may not have seemed so at the time, but IBM symbolized the true beginning of the Information Age in the mid-1980s with a simple change in its advertising. For the first few years of its existence, the IBM personal computer (PC) had used the lovable tramp created by silent movie star Charlie Chaplin as its logo. In many ways this was a good choice. Charming and funny, the little tramp was designed to be as engaging in print and television advertising as the company needed its personal computers to be.

But with the introduction of newer and more powerful versions of the PC designed to be linked together in networks, the company had a problem. The lovable tramp, for all his endearing and nonthreatening qualities, was the ultimate individualist. If the future was in networking, as IBM correctly foresaw, the company needed a completely different theme. And what better way to bring alive the idea of computers in a team than to appropriate the single best-known team in America at the time—the medics of *M*A*S*H*, the wildly popular movie and television series. Did IBM make this switch with as much deliberation and foresight as we have implied? Perhaps it did. Perhaps not. It really does not matter. The point is that the changeover from stand-alone to team has been planted in our collective public consciousness for longer than we realize.

Why Nonprofit Services Are Fragmented: A Story

The three youth-serving organizations, part of the same name-brand nonprofit federation, were each located in different large cities within 15 miles of each other. Surrounding the cluster of cities was an expanded ring of suburbs and exurbs. Each organization had been founded within a few years of each other, and together they covered a sizable percentage of the metropolitan area. Each city was notoriously culturally isolated from the other. None of those cities liked each other very much, and the sniping was legendary.

Were it not for the imperatives of twenty-first-century electronic communications, the story might well have ended there. But those three cities and their related suburbs were all part of the same media market. The bits and bytes of data sharing and high-definition television had reduced the friction and mixed interests of those separate municipalities to a story of second-order magnitude. When business needed to be done, when the region needed representation in the state capital, when the economy needed some help—those rivalries faded in the face of the overriding common interests of the locations.

A parallel story was unfolding among the three organizations. Their carefully drawn turf based on county lines was increasingly meaningless because volunteers from one city wanted to volunteer in the other. Donors routinely mailed checks to the wrong organization, while corporations and foundations were frustrated by not being able to support the cause more readily. A merger seemed in order.

The resulting organization was among the largest of its kind in the nation. Carefully, it drew up plans to keep fundraising resolutely local—except when targeting region-wide givers—and service provision coordinated centrally with heavy local volunteer recruitment. After only two years, fundraising and number of youths served had increased substantially, and costs were cut by a double-figure percentage.

This story illustrates the barriers that must be overcome among nonprofit board members and their executives if they are to position their organizations for maximum effectiveness in the twenty-first century. The natural tendency to focus services in a narrowly defined geographic area, the lack of an inherent motive to spur growth, and the inability to raise large amounts of capital are powerful elements that tend to keep nonprofits isolated from each other and fragmented in service delivery.

Yet the rise of globalization (and its cousin, regionalization) is pushing nonprofits together, like it or not. Mergers and alliances lower those self-defined barriers that tend to make services fragmented and inefficient. Some of those barriers are institutionalized through revenue sources. Nonprofits generally are forced to spend a lot of time focusing on their revenues and expenses and virtually no time streamlining their economics. Funding sources give money as if it were a stack of wood that they insist on being burned in a stove of their own specifications. The result is that a growing nonprofit is like a multistory building heated entirely by a basement filled with stoves, each dedicated to a room or two, instead of a single central heating system.

Competition, the Mother of Collaboration

There is a wonderful irony in matters of competition, and it can be summed up in a single observation:

The more competitive an industry's participants are, the more collaborative they have to be.

This is an ironclad rule that applies to for-profits as well as nonprofits. As the companies in a given industry compete with each other, over time they will be forced to find ways of collaborating with each other as well. Often a level of government takes the role of indirectly forcing collaborative action through regulations and standard setting, but in the American economy, competitors themselves are forced to find ways to compete on one level while collaborating on another. This is how trade associations get formed, and it is why large software companies routinely participate in thousands of business alliances. Rugged individualism may work for cowboys, but it does not work for companies.

An Illustration

Immigrants typically require a variety of types of assistance, including language instruction, job search, housing support, legal advice, adjustment counseling, and so forth. Most immigrants need at least one of these services over a period of time, and many need more than one. Foreign Neighbors Institute (FNI) is a $2.3 million recently merged nonprofit organization dedicated to helping its city's Vietnamese immigrants. Its revenues come from a variety of sources, including state and city government, a legal services corporation, private and public English-language classes, and a small amount of special-events fundraising. Its single largest revenue source is private English-language instruction services.

FNI's smorgasbord of services is paid for by a comparable smorgasbord of funding sources. City and state education monies pay for language instruction, legal funding sources pay for legal advice, mental health and social service funders pay for adjustment counseling, and so on. The private instruction classes, however, are paid for by immigrants in their twenties and thirties who hold some type of job in the nearby urban area. These are Vietnamese immigrants who are moving up the socioeconomic ladder. They need the instruction not for basic activities of everyday life but to polish their social skills as they make their way through corporate America.

In the traditional view, FNI presides over a dizzying array of programs and services, or stovepipes, each of which must stand

Note: The Nature of Nonprofit Competition

Culturally, nonprofit executives can now speak more readily of competition between their organizations. Externally, the media and the general public are beginning to realize that the absence of a profit motive does not mean the absence of competition. And since competition is the bedrock of our economic system, the increased sense of competitiveness among nonprofits is generally applauded. Yet it still confuses and annoys many people who equate competition with wastefulness or unsavory business practices.

Part of the answer lies in the nature of competition in the nonprofit sector. When major consumer product companies compete, it is for millions of buyers. Companies that make cars and refrigerators and flat-screen TVs compete in the consumer market where a small number of suppliers are all that are needed for millions of buyers. By contrast, when 40 nonprofit child service organizations of all sizes and sophistication levels compete in the same geographic area for program funding that comes largely from one or two government agencies, they represent a large number of suppliers to a very small number of buyers.

Competition in this type of setting—which is typical of most nonprofit situations around the country—is not competition as in a consumer setting. Rather, it is more like competition between different mom-and-pop–size departments of the same large company: possibly intense, but ultimately having more common interests than differences.

on its own with respect to its funders. But immigrants using these services do not compartmentalize their needs in the same way, so usually FNI staff act as de facto case managers to ensure that the immigrant in need gets the appropriate services. In effect, FNI's real value is as a provider of a modest continuum of services to a carefully drawn market. What makes all of these programs work is the unrestricted income from the private classes' revenue that funds a significant part of its infrastructure.

FNI's chief strategic vulnerability is the always-present possibility that a for-profit language instruction provider would cut into its private language instruction market. With each program having a dedicated revenue stream but equal or greater costs associated with it, the broad-based language program is the only thing providing unrestricted funds and a bit of capital for the larger organization.

In FNI's case, its solution to the stovepipe problem is entrepreneurial. Not all organizations are lucky enough to be in this position. To be sure, there are strategic weaknesses in its model, but via its merger, FNI found a way to partially overcome the stovepipe problem.

A Nonprofit's Economics Are Part of Its Strategy

Board members, nonprofit managers, and advocates all must begin making nonprofit economics part of their long-term planning processes, and one of the simplest ways of doing that is to consider the role of economic size in its field. Let us begin with a threshold definition:

> An organization has achieved its economic size when it can operate over a period of years without substantially reducing its net assets.

There will probably never be a statistically reliable way of predicting economic size for any given organization because the factors that determine it are so particular and not always under the nonprofit's direct control. Still, it is possible to identify some of the elements that combine to determine the economic size. Here are some of the more common ones:

- Industry
- Government regulation
- Labor markets

- Geography
- Use of capital

Net assets are the nonprofit organization's equivalent of net worth, or accumulated surplus. When an organization incurs a deficit in any given year, it reduces its net assets by the amount of the deficit. Over time, a string of deficits will reduce net assets to zero or below, and the organization will be functionally bankrupt. As with a for-profit company, successive yearly deficits in a nonprofit mean that current management is using the built-up net assets of previous managers to stay afloat—in short, it is spending its future.

At base, economic size has to do with the ability of the organization to cover its fixed costs, which are expenses that will be incurred regardless of the volume of service the nonprofit provides. Fixed costs typically are things such as a chief executive's salary, occupancy costs, accounting services, depreciation on assets, and interest payments. For labor-intensive operations such as nonprofits, compensation and benefits often act very much like fixed costs, since labor is such an essential element in providing services.

Put all of these costs in a budget and there is not much room left—most of the remaining costs that will go up or down depending on the volume of service are small amounts. Fixed costs simply limit a manager's discretionary spending, and when they get to an unsupportable level, the organization either finds outside funders to pick up the difference or eventually goes out of business. As the demands on nonprofits continue to increase and funding continues to be cut or restricted, more and more will experience a financial crunch. In fact, a failure to achieve economic size is already one of the primary reasons for nonprofits merging or restructuring in the early part of the twenty-first century.

Industry

The nature of the nonprofit's field determines a great deal about its economic size. The economic size for a museum is considerably different from the economic size of an assisted-living facility for elders. Furthermore, the distinctions between certain types of organizations can blur over time, thereby altering the nature of the economic size. For instance, most hospitals were stand-alone facilities until at least the 1980s. Whereas the term "hospital" in the last century meant a stately looking brick building, today the word has effectively been replaced in business contexts by more conceptual phrases, such as "health care system" or "health provider networks."

Government Regulation

Next to industry type, the single greatest determinant of economic size of most nonprofits is the degree and nature of its governmental regulatory environment. The formula is simple: The greater the degree of governmental regulation, the lower the economic size. This phenomenon has occurred in industries as diverse as airlines and public utilities. An obscure but elegant example of government regulation in the nonprofit field is in antitrust policy. Antitrust actions are the responsibility of the Department of Justice and the Federal Trade Commission. As hospitals merged in the 1990s and into the next decade, federal interventions in proposed mergers roughly paralleled the dominant ideology of the party holding the presidency. Antitrust actions brought by the government to prevent mergers were more prevalent in the Clinton years, much less so in the George W. Bush era.

Government as regulator is not the same thing as government as payer. Government actions as a payer only influence the transactions with which they are involved, while government action as a regulator influences all transactions over which the government has jurisdiction.

Labor Markets

As mentioned briefly, labor expense in most nonprofits is a fixed cost over short spans of time. Any service that is open 24 hours a day or that must meet minimum staffing standards of some kind has to deal with costs that are predetermined within a relatively narrow range, no matter what the revenue may be.

Another aspect of labor that cements it as a fixed cost is collective bargaining. Labor cost is particularly intractable because of the nature of the collective bargaining process but also because the "political" characteristics of nonprofits (see Chapter 3) can easily become political in the electoral politics sense of the term. One major nonprofit institution trying to merge with a public entity needed more than two years to make the idea work because neither labor nor management could agree on terms for a very long time.

The changing nature of labor markets also complicates this aspect of economic size. Not only do segments of nonprofit service delivery have natural life cycles—mental health clinics are a mature type of entity, for example, while most environmental groups are still very young in their cycle—but local labor markets can fluctuate widely too. During recessions, nonprofits typically face soft labor markets (i.e., it is easy to hire employees), while prosperity brings hard labor markets because the labor force has other options.

Note: Life Cycles of Nonprofit Organizations

Nonprofit organizations can be said to have distinct life stages just like any type of business organization, and the place where each type of nonprofit finds itself says a lot about its readiness to collaborate. Here is one framework for analyzing the life stage of groups of nonprofits:

Formless. In this stage, there are not enough comparable nonprofits to constitute a recognizable type. Different groups respond to similar social needs and economic realities in similar ways without necessarily understanding why or even communicating with each other. Affiliations of any kind are virtually out of the question.

Growing. There is at least a general recognition that the particular nonprofit service is needed but most energies are devoted to building capacity and solving operational problems.

Consolidating. At this stage, the general type of organization is recognized and accepted by society and the nonprofit sector itself. Some organizations take on a leadership role while others struggle to come into being in order to cover geographic gaps left by the early types. The groups create formal associations and other support entities, and a recognizable national identity begins to emerge.

Peaking. As a field and as individuals, these nonprofits enjoy newfound acceptance and growing influence. The pace of new entrants slows, but those already in existence experience previously unimagined success in areas such as operations, public relations, financial, and political. Mergers occur for strategic purposes when strong players take over the few weak ones, which falter.

Maturing. Maturing nonprofits have long ago hit their peak and are beginning to lose some of the strategic momentum they had earlier. The services they offer are now being offered at least in part by others or are no longer perceived as necessary. No one can doubt their collective influence, but some are beginning to doubt their future.

Refocusing. Once past maturity, some nonprofits find they must reinvent themselves in order to survive. Some do; others fade gradually away or merge what is left of their services with compatible groups at an earlier stage of development.

Hard labor markets can force employers to pay proportionately more for staff, which can increase the pressure on agencies' fixed costs. This is what happened during the dot-com recession.

Geography

Geography shapes economic size. When an organization must cover the entire nation, a physically large state, or just a sizable rural area, travel costs are inescapable. Rural groups that must do any kind of outreach inevitably find that it takes longer and therefore is costlier than the same service in an urban area. In some instances, it simply may not be feasible to deliver a service. Service providers that depend on a certain volume or cultural organizations that need a concentrated market are examples here.

Use of Capital

Any time a nonprofit has to invest in capital assets to provide a service—typically buildings and equipment—it increases its fixed costs. Not only does it commit to paying back loans it may have obtained to buy the asset in the first place—a classic fixed cost—but large assets require upkeep and specialized staff to maintain. These things all raise the minimum economic size for the acquiring organization.

Tip: How to Know if You Are Keeping Up Your Capital Investment

To find out if your nonprofit is keeping up its capital investment level, try this test. Find the organization's total accumulated depreciation and divide it by the depreciation charge for that year. The result will give you your "accounting age" of all property, plant, and equipment measured in units called "accounting years." The higher this number, the lower your investment in replacing old assets. See whether the number of years makes sense in the context of your overall strategic direction. Better yet, calculate the same ratio for a handful of comparable nonprofits.

Capital requirements are some of the most important forces determining economic size for nonprofits. Especially because non-profit corporations cannot raise capital through selling shares, an increased need to make major investments in new buildings and equipment puts greater pressure on management. If the minimum investment level rises high enough, some nonprofits are forced to exit the field. High capital requirements are also the reason why, at extreme points, for-profit companies with their far greater access to low-cost capital will have a distinct advantage. This is what happened when Blue Cross/Blue Shield plans and certain hospitals sold their assets to publicly held companies and instead became private foundations (also known as conversion foundations).

Note: Need More Benefits?

Sometimes it is helpful to be able to cite other potential benefits of a merger or alliance. Here is a laundry list. Some may apply in your circumstances, others will not. Take the ones that fit.

- Acquire intangible assets (e.g., a prized board member or a brand name).
- Acquire tangible assets (e.g., a building).
- Add breadth and depth of services to meet consumer need.
- Assist in repairing a damaged brand.
- Capitalize on a chief executive's departure.
- Change the organization's name.
- Change staff compensation patterns.
- Create more varied career options for employees.
- Create operational efficiencies.
- Ease the transition from a founder-led organization.
- Expand the programming continuum.
- Gain cost savings in order to add program resources.
- Gain greater visibility in the community.
- Gain market share.
- Gain more clout with the national office (federated organizations only).
- Improve fundraising.
- Improve prospects for a new service.
- Increase political clout.
- Rejuvenate the organization.
- Make it easier to satisfy lender requirements.

Economic size often increases faster than the rate of inflation. As a consequence, nonprofits may have to increase profitability a bit faster than the rate of inflation just to stay ahead. With governmental and many private sources of funding plateauing or declining in many service sectors, growth is no longer just a matter of hiring the right proposal writer or making contact with a foundation or two. In fact, significant growth in most mature or near-mature nonprofit sectors will be virtually impossible for the foreseeable future *except* through mergers and alliances.

A word about growth. There is a prevailing sentiment against bigness in much of the nonprofit community, and for good reason. A great deal of what nonprofits have done well in the past has been firmly rooted in local areas with all the responsiveness and grass-roots characteristics that that entails. Many nonprofit leaders reject growth itself, arguing that it will dilute the culture of the organization. For some types of nonprofits, they are undoubtedly right. But there is no intrinsic reason why the majority of organizations could not grow significantly larger and still maintain faithfulness to their mission and their roots. Moreover, the absence of growth can lead to the kind of stagnation and tiredness that society cannot afford in its intermediary organizations. A component of achieving economic size is, therefore, learning how to grow strategically and not simply quantitatively.

Mostly, it would appear that opposition to "bigness" in the nonprofit sector is a function of comfort level with one's immediate social environment. There is some literature to support this notion, particularly Dunbar's Number, sometimes known as the Rule of 150. This anthropological concept argues that the maximum comfort level of human beings is in groups of approximately 150 or fewer, the premise being that physiological characteristics of the human brain bias us in favor of such a size. Whether the number is larger or smaller is literally academic because there is functionally a predisposition on many people's part in favor of limited size.

What most researchers do not recognize, however, is that this notion refers to social immediacy and is reliably linked to physical communities. The takeaway here is that the physical setting in which most people work is what determines their most immediate social connections, not the size of the sponsoring corporation. Since most nonprofit programming takes place in small physical sites, the bigness question tends to be more about inferences and fears than the actual day-to-day realities of a service-providing organization. Bigness should be measured in immediate people-related, client service factors, not corporate terms.

CHAPTER

3

Logic of Integrated
Service Delivery

Consider a common scenario. A new homeowner receives a property tax bill she considers to be based on an error by the assessor. She goes to the assessor's office in town hall that is responsible for valuing real estate but is told that she must first speak with the tax office that sent out the bill. That office explains that they are powerless to change any entry on the tax rolls because the tax information is now more than 60 days old (notwithstanding the fact that she only received the bill 10 days ago). To begin a request for an abatement, she must first file a written request for an abatement form with the treasurer's office. By the way, that office is now located across the courtyard. While standing in the treasurer's office, she completes a form requesting the abatement document, only to learn that the form must be notarized by a notary public not connected with town government.

This mythical albeit plausible scenario is repeated many times in many industries around this country every day. In all likelihood our heroine would refer to her experience as "the runaround." We will use the more exalted term "fragmented service delivery."

Fragmented service delivery is so common that we barely even think about it. Yet it does not have to be that way. Services do not need to be broken up into artificial segments called departments or bureaus or divisions the way they used to be. Online information management technology and our refined knowledge of how systems work allow us to integrate services to a degree never before possible. Moreover, we cannot afford fragmented service delivery anyway. Breaking down a process or flow into small packages always costs more than keeping it all together. Most important of all, fragmentation impairs quality.

To be sure, reasons other than simple slowness to adapt or an inability to make investments in computerized technology create fragmented service delivery. For instance, in our small-town example, one incentive that might inhibit more streamlined service is a policy of holding onto cash as long as possible, even at the expense of a little voter discontent. And in the nonprofit world, there is less capital available for investing in things like information technology. Nevertheless, the movement toward more integrated service delivery is widespread, and it occurs on all levels of our economy.

Applications of Integrated Service Delivery

Integrated service delivery will be a central goal of the next generation of nonprofit managers. The drive toward integrated services is already under way, although it is not always called that. Most levels of governments have experimented to one degree or another with online information delivery in lieu of the old paper forms that could only be mailed or picked up in person. More important, whole areas of service are being consolidated. In health care and the social services, there is an increasing trend toward using intermediaries for administrative tasks. For instance, Medicare has always integrated much of its insurance and payment functions through private sector insurance companies and administrators. This intermediary level simplifies what otherwise would be a hugely fragmented task of dealing with literally hundreds of thousands of service providers.

Elements of Integration

Integrated service delivery has its own special logic. When a variety of services are put together in an integrated fashion, things happen differently. Crude analogies with the physical world are instructive. City planners, for instance, have long known that less is more when it comes to street design. In certain instances, adding more roads to a congested traffic pattern can actually worsen the flow. Fiber optic cable networks can add a fourth city to a planned three-city network and use fewer miles of cable.

The recession of 2008 prompted many nonprofits to examine how to increase productivity by getting together in networks and administrative service organizations. This will be a long and slow process lasting a generation or more. At the same time, it is possible to see the roughest of outlines appearing to guide us in the journey. Some of the elements that will be present include:

- Trust
- Information as a strategic tool
- Massive investments in information technology
- Standardized services

Trust

Trust is probably the least appreciated engine of economic success in the world, yet it has a profound impact on the way all organizations conduct their business. For quick evidence of its role, look no further than the difference between industrialized countries and non-industrialized societies. What is the rational response to the demands of doing business when trust is generally absent from the larger society? Make the family the prime business unit, not the corporation. Unfortunately, as an economic unit, the family is severely limited. There are a limited number of members, there is no good basis for ensuring their fitness for employment (let alone their ability to get along), and the amount of capital it can raise is constrained. A society that cannot figure out how to trust non-family members is doomed to a second rate economy at best.

Our appetite for litigation notwithstanding, the United States is actually a high-trust economy. Nonprofits in particular benefit from this dynamic as fundraisers and as recipients of tax-exempt status for presumed publicly beneficial activities. No one, attorneys general and the Internal Revenue Service included, plays a widespread and systematically proactive enforcement role with public charities. Boards and their management are simply expected to adhere to high standards of accountability, and in the vast majority of instances they do just that. Contrast the United States with the recent history of the former Soviet Union, where years of political leadership purposefully attempted to wipe out intermediary organizations perceived as competing with the state, such as organized religion and nongovernmental organizations. When the Communist party lost power, the resulting vacuum was for some time partly filled by organized crime.

Of course, it is one thing to have public policies built on trust, and it is another to run systems based on trust. The latter is much harder. One of the reasons why one health care entity never accepts a referral from another without doing its own intake is because, on some level, they do not trust the referral source, a posture supported by a rich body of convention, regulation, and laws. As a consequence, each clinical organization spends a certain percentage of its professional resources doing steps that have already been done.

This is why the first few weeks and months in any merger or collaboration initiative must be spent in developing trust among participants. It is also why the best partners are often the ones that know each other and have worked together in some way in the past. After all, integrated services are still new as a widespread phenomenon in nonprofit fields. Ultimately there are no guarantees that any individual project will work, so it makes sense to be comfortable with those with whom one is taking a leap of faith—even if the leap is a small one.

Information as a Strategic Tool

Dramatic and continuing advances in computer technology are putting comparable advances in productivity within reach of the average nonprofit. The first use of information technology is usually to do existing tasks faster. Frequently this happens by clearing away needless work steps or by doing by computer what formerly could be done only by hand. The next step is to integrate those tasks with each other, and the third step is to automate entire processes. Nonprofits are just beginning to get comfortable with the first step and to explore the second. The holy grail of information technology is to be able to use information strategically, not just as an operating tool. Marketing and political campaigns have developed this practice into as high an art form as currently exists. Processing vast quantities of data, strategists are able to identify pockets of support and resistance. On-the-ground workers can then target supporters or potential consumers far more efficiently. In recent years, presidential campaigns have developed this technique into a highly refined function.

Investments in Information Technology

Integrating all those services requires a lot of computing capability, and this changes many nonprofits' management style, for two reasons:

1. Nonprofit managers are not accustomed to using technology very much. They can even be technology averse on a personal level, though less so than in the past.

2. Technology investments will be continual. For the foreseeable future, information technology represents our single best hope for leveraging productivity gains. Older systems will be replaced, not so much because they are worn out or broken (as has been the case with equipment in the past) but because the next generation of technology offers proportionately greater gains in productivity.

The other not inconsiderable fact about the need for information technology is that it will take capital, and probably lots of it. Many organizations are already on their third or fourth major generation of technology and can expect their future systems to have shorter useful lives. The increase in integrated services will be paralleled by—in fact, be facilitated by—an increased degree of integration in information technology.

The need for investment in information technology will have two effects:

1. It will boost the minimum economic size in virtually all fields, which in turn will put more pressure on groups to merge and find new ways of collaborating.
2. It will make it likely that for-profits will enter or expand their positions in fields where nonprofits have traditionally been active. For reasons discussed earlier, nonprofits cannot raise significant amounts of capital, and this will handicap their ability to respond to the demand for integrated services.

Networks of nonprofits may offer the best hope in this regard because the expense of developing a system from scratch is prohibitive for most organizations. Voluntary groupings, either as alliances formed for that purpose or as part of a more ambitious attempt to align corporations, offer a way to spread the cost and risk that a single organization usually could not afford.

Standardized Services

Many nonprofit organizations are fiercely dedicated to their local communities, which is appropriate and helps fundraising. But those same characteristics break up service delivery into thousands of little groupings between which there is usually little or no sharing of information or accomplishment. As a result, most programs operate not only in their own silos in their own organizations but with little meaningful connection or reliable means of information exchange with their peers on what works best and how proven practices can be adopted to improve quality.

Mergers or well-run alliances can break down some of those walls. One of our alliances' individual members realized after several months of working together that virtually all of the participants were planning to pursue a certain type of certification during the next year. This certification was a long and complicated process and typically involved individual organizations studying the requirements, hiring a consultant, doing self-studies, gathering data, and writing policies. Why not, they reasoned, approach the certification process as their first big program-related joint venture? It took less than two months for them to develop a strategy and solicit and hire a consultant. At that point, they had not only saved a few dollars over what it would have cost them individually, but they had gone through an important confidence-building exercise.

Pitfall: Integration Is Harder Than It Sounds

Just as revenue sources operate through stovepipes, so do most administrative systems. Take a small example in operations. A new employee in a large nonprofit must give his or her name to the human resource person upon being hired. Payroll will ask for it a second time, and it is not out of the question for that same employee to have to furnish that same information at least one or two more times to others, ranging from the pension plan, to the dental benefits administrator, and even to the parking lot manager. Why can the employee not give the information once and expect all pertinent details to be transferred automatically to appropriate others? There is no particularly good reason, except that it has never been done that way. What would it take to make it happen? In truth, it would take much more powerful and sophisticated software than currently exists, plus some managerial commitment to use it. Guess which will come first.

Still, the primary purpose of integrating services is not for the internal benefits it brings but because users of the services will benefit from service integration. Nonprofit managers and board members who believe otherwise should look at modern economic history. Standardization alone is enough of a service that it handsomely rewards whatever groups can achieve it. Entrepreneurs who could produce large quantities of reliably high-quality commodities, such as heating oil, soap, or hamburgers, not only survived in their industries but dominated them. Why should we expect it to be any different in fields traditionally served by nonprofits? Mergers and alliances of related nonprofit organizations are the best hope for achieving the economic benefits of greater size while preserving the localized character of nonprofit services.

CHAPTER 4

Deciding to Collaborate

Looking back on a successful merger or alliance, it can be difficult to pinpoint exactly when the momentum started. Was it the first phone call between the two chief executive officers (CEOs)? The impromptu coffee break at that conference? That first meeting between the board chairs and the CEOs—the one at the farthest table of the restaurant 10 miles from both organizations? Or was there no real point when the decision was made, just the slow but steady buildup of trust and interest?

Looking back, there is a very good chance that participants would say that the original decision to collaborate was not a formal choice made in a formal setting. Instead, the process is more like the collective accumulation of positive signals and pleasant discoveries that amounts to a growing sense of mutual interest. Taking each next step is just the formalization of the trust that develops.

Reader Warranty

The most unfortunate aspect of mergers is that they readily spawn jokes and innuendo around the metaphor of mergers resembling marriage. The tone of the conversation thereafter deteriorates, and the speaker inevitably finds himself in a place from which there is absolutely no dignified retreat. Motivated by reader compassion, we hereby warrant that there will be no comparisons drawn between mergers and marriage in this volume.

There are only two broad logical pathways to a decision to collaborate. The first is inherently negative. A nonprofit looks at its current financial state and finds that it can no longer deny it is in poor financial health. A few hurried meetings ensue, board leaders and executives huddle, and out of the quiet frenzy comes a decision to seek a partner.

The second is the polar opposite of the first. A nonprofit looks at its current financial state and finds that it has adequate financial health and a growth plan that can be fulfilled only by carrying out a series of mergers. Board leaders and executives huddle, and out of the deliberations comes a decision to build an internal capacity to identify, design, and carry out mergers.

It is easy to see in these two common scenarios the crucial differences between the two approaches. The first is a decision to collaborate born out of haste and panic brought about by years of denial around the organization's declining fortunes. The decision to collaborate is a last resort, and it is undoubtedly made amid great apprehension. The second is a long-term commitment to a defined strategy backed up by good execution, including creating new systems to support the long-term goal.

As we stated earlier, the best time to consider a merger is when it is not absolutely necessary. If there is no real alternative to a merger, the declining organization has almost certainly already damaged its programs and compromised much of its ability to make a difference in the lives of those it serves. Moreover, it will make decisions based largely on short-term expediency, and the inherent pressures of falling financials can erode staff stamina, quality, and commitment— not to mention cause staff to make bad decisions under stress and even motivate them to leave.

Rescue Mergers

To mangle a famous observation, "Successful nonprofits succeed in many ways, while failing nonprofits all look the same." My colleagues Paul Bennett and Garrett Brinckerhoff have spent considerable effort trying to pinpoint the exact nature of how nonprofits fail. On one level, their results are predictable, almost trivial: Nonprofits go out of business when they run out of cash. But the full picture is far more revealing. After researching many nonprofit organizations, they identified a few key patterns. Perhaps more important, they have told the story of failing nonprofits.

That story is simple yet consistent and powerful. By tracking the total cash and investments available to an entity over several years, they identified some key patterns. These patterns are readily visible in Exhibits 4.1 through 4.3.

Initially, all three organizations had two types of cash available to them: cash in their checkbook and an investment account or accounts. Look at the way the invested amount disappeared first. One can envision the anguished board meetings when the decision was made to convert some liquid investments (the darker color at the top) to ready cash. Look also at the fact that overall cash balances declined steadily. This pattern of overall decline is, paradoxically, the most striking yet it is the one most likely to be ignored. Note that each of these failed organizations showed at least six years of decline in this indicator. Years of chronic fiscal problems led to a quick "crisis." Financial train wrecks occur in slow motion.

The abrupt upward bump in overall cash may seem to be good news but is almost certainly not. As the groups' liquidity declined, they had no choice but to liquidate other assets. Most likely, at least some of the assets that the groups sold were buildings.

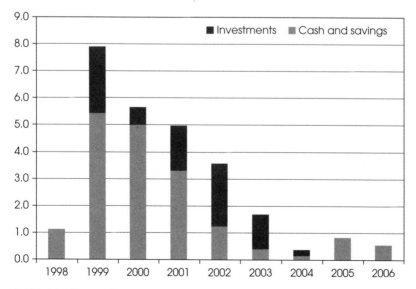

Exhibit 4.1   Museum: Months of Expenses Covered by Cash and Investments at Fiscal Year-End

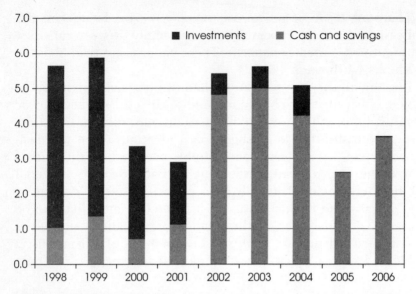

Exhibit 4.2   Theater Company: Months of Expenses Covered by Cash and Investments at Fiscal Year-End

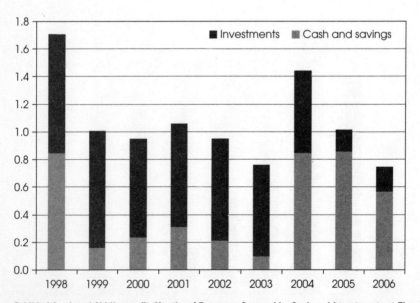

Exhibit 4.3   Legal Aid Nonprofit: Months of Expenses Covered by Cash and Investments at Fiscal Year-End

Accepting as a fact that a large number of nonprofits will be inclined to delay an inevitable decision to seek a merger or collaborate, we offer to board members and executives a quick guide to determine if your organization might be in serious financial decline.

Indicators of Financial Decline

	Yes	No
Our total days in cash and investments declined over the last several years.	—	—
We have sold some or all of our investments (endowment) in the last several years.	—	—
We have sold one or more buildings and held onto the proceeds as cash.	—	—
Our line of credit is maxed out.	—	—
We have recently missed one or more current obligations, such as a payroll, a payroll tax payment, a key insurance premium, or a key creditor payment of some kind.	—	—

The farther down this list the answer is yes, the more dangerous the nonprofit's situation. Admittedly, struggling nonprofits should seek a radically different course of action well before their financial situation makes it inevitable. But we have found that it is far easier and much more likely that nonprofit leaders will recognize the signs of fiscal distress than they will acknowledge failing programs, a fatally damaged brand, a broken model of service, or any of the other numerous sources of failure.

The key is to seek a merger or collaboration well before answering yes to the lower questions in the table. Once an entity has missed one or more fiscal obligations, it very likely will go into fire alarm mode. When that happens, there will be a cascade of crises. Management's attention will be distracted, they will have little time and less inclination to spend effort on developing a relationship with a potential merger partner, and often board and staff resignations further undercut capacity. Most important, programming suffers. The financial pressures may lead to staff layoffs or pay cuts, and management's pervasive sense of anxiety tends to give program staff a bunker mentality. At that point, the programs have already suffered what may be permanent damage. Left unsupported, the programs may reach a level of dysfunction from which they might never recover. In combination with the corporate financial losses, the entire organization may be too damaged to be valuable to a stronger entity.

Merger from Strength

Ideally, nonprofit board members and their executives will entertain a collaboration strategy from strength. Note that the term "strength" here does not necessarily mean that the organization expects to take over another nonprofit, a perception that almost always derives from comparing the total revenue of the two merger partners. It means that the organization sees itself and its value clearly and has made a considered decision to seek a merger or alliance in order to create something new that could not happen without the compatible strengths of a merger partner.

For example, one special education provider sought to become part of a larger organization for three distinct reasons:

1. The board and the CEO felt that they had reached the limits of their ability to provide access to a comprehensive range of services for the youth attending the program.
2. Special education policy makers in their state were clearly trying to integrate special education more tightly with public education and with social service providers.
3. The CEO was nearing retirement age and wanted to ensure the continued health of the program she had created.

The smaller organization began to research potential partners in a structured, fact-based manner and developed a list of potential groups.

The organization decided to open discussions with a larger entity serving adjudicated youths, which the year before had made a corresponding decision to enter the special education field. The two organizations were in complementary though not overlapping geographic areas, and each had minimal knowledge yet positive views of the other. During their discussions, the respect between the two organizations was evident, and the smaller organization was able to dictate the pace and depth of the explorations, especially after the larger entity discovered that a happy fluke of regulatory policy would create little pockets of profitability in several of its existing programs.

In this situation, there was an obvious size imbalance between the two organizations, yet the smaller group more than held its own in the give-and-take. Each organization offered value to the other, and the fact that the smaller one had approached the larger one probably preempted the normal sense of domination that it might have otherwise felt. This is a good example of two nonprofits each offering value to the other, truly a merger of strengths.

Deciding to Collaborate as a Function of Larger Forces

Typically, there will be different attitudes and behaviors toward collaborations, especially mergers, depending on the socioeconomics of the larger environment. In any geographic region, the first collaborations likely to be attempted are rescue mergers, as weak organizations seek relief by becoming part of a larger entity. Of course, these often do not work since one party is too wounded to be a source of complementary strength. Nonetheless, this class of mergers tends to be the first one to arise. Often one or more larger nonprofits carries out a series of rescue mergers—or near-rescue mergers—to build a much larger-scale operation than the area has seen before. These entities will be regarded with an equal measure of respect and fear, as smaller groups fear being gobbled up by the new giant. While perfectly understandable, this trend has the unfortunate side effect of suggesting that collaboration comes only from parallel stories of strength and failure.

Once the initial wave of rescue mergers subsides, the idea of collaboration as an effective response to strategic challenges will have been established, albeit only as an inherently imbalanced proposition. At that point, the remaining organizations are free to make a more clear-eyed determination about collaborating. This is where strength can seek out strength. Pure revenue size is less of a factor at this stage than is the value that can be derived from the collaboration. In short, the mission compatibility and the business elements of the combination can more reliably be the determining factors. Strength never fears strength.

Tip: Conduct a Mini-Brainstorming Session

To get a merger or alliance process started with a board of directors, try this simple exercise. Ask all members present at a meeting scheduled for the purpose to write down a handful of ideas about why they might want to collaborate with another nonprofit. One by one, take one idea from each director and write it on a piece of poster paper on the wall. Do the same with reasons why they might fear or be concerned about a merger or alliance. Summarize and synthesize the ideas listed. (Chances are there will be about 15 to 25 raw ideas of each type.) These are now your interests in a merger or alliance. If the positives can be achieved and the negatives either avoided or mitigated, the board should feel confident about approving the collaboration.

5

Preserving Identity

If there is a common concern voiced by organizations considering a merger, it is lost identity. This fear is nearly universal, especially with smaller organizations. Usually it is expressed in terms like "We'll get swallowed up" or "We'll get lost in the shuffle." The underlying theme is a fear of undesired assimilation. In order to properly speak to these fears, it is crucial to be clear about what "identity" means. Doing this is not as easy as it may seem because we humans frequently transfer the bedrock human instinct for individual self-preservation to corporate structures. The resulting confusion needs to get sorted out.

To get at what identity means in a practical context, let us unpack the common elements of the term. We begin with a simple equation:

$$one\ program = one\ site = one\ corporation$$

For many people, volunteers and especially employees of small nonprofits, these three elements are so fused together that it is pointless to separate them. In this view, a single program is operated on a single site by a single corporation. In fact, the first two elements are typically the only important ones in the equation since most people give little thought to the corporate status of nonprofit programs.

When large groups of nonprofits start up to deal with a social dysfunction, they usually follow this pattern. There is an appealing integrity to it, and the sense of unity that it conveys to those involved in a struggling new operation can be compelling. But success changes all that. Adding a second program or a second physical location for the same kind of program forces a rethinking of the comfortable initial model. Now the organization must hire new people for the expansion, or move people from the initial site, or both. The result is that the formerly compact identity becomes more complex, the social ties between fellow workers get at least slightly more difficult to maintain, and the overall sense of unity may follow the same path.

Nonphysical Components of Organizational Identity

What is really happening is that the sense of identity is beginning to derive a little less from physical things, such as a fixed site or a program sign, and more from shared concepts. To be meaningful, an identity must now rely more and more on things like shared values, a common language, and an intellectual acknowledgment of important common goals. This is a common evolution, but it can be difficult to make because only the initial state of one program on one site run by one corporation makes the identity experience easy and near visceral. Add in the possibility of a founder-led small organization and the close relationships that often go with it, and you have the equivalent of social cement. Moreover, a merger makes it virtually certain that the identity experience will never be as simple as it was before. In fact, in some cases, the identity experience will be much more complicated and potentially more unsatisfying than before.

But we must ask an impertinent question: So what? Why should it matter that people in merged entities have to work a little harder to achieve the same sense of identity that they did in smaller start-ups?

Part of the answer to this question is that they do not have to work harder; they just feel as if they do. Implicit in the one program = one site = one corporation model is the fact that the immediate environs are quite manageable. When one program is carried out on one site, the experience is gut level and immediate. When other programs and other sites are added, the visceral aspect of the initial model does not necessarily change. People who worked in a single program on a single site before the merger in all likelihood will continue doing so, and except for some possible cosmetic differences, nothing much will change because of a merger or an alliance.

What does get changed by the merger is the amount of learning, extrapolation, and inference that everyone needs to do in order to become knowledgeable about the newly combined entity. This is the hard part, and the thing that program staff will fear the most even if they do not say it this way. When one culture and set of values combines with another, no one really knows what will happen, and this is what causes program staff's negative reactions.

By definition, then, a merger—like any kind of rapid growth— almost automatically makes the identity experience less gut level, more conceptual, and therefore less satisfying. Add to that the preconceptions developed from decades of breathless media coverage of irresponsible corporate mergers, and it is little wonder that losing identity is such a big concern.

Federated Affiliates' Identity Advantage

The affiliates of federated organizations—which is the way most of the best-known nonprofit brand names are organized—have an advantage in discussing mergers. Although they are structured much like associations, with a national office and hundreds of locally based nonprofits, federated affiliates share a brand name. Often the local affiliates' names will include a reference to a neighborhood, town, city, or region, but the national name is the real trademark. In these cases, much of the concern about identity is alleviated, and sometimes the newly merged entity can adopt a new and broader geographic reference in the title, such as "XXX of the North Valley." This change can aid fundraising and brand development by broadening the boundaries of its local appeal.

What Is *Not* Part of "Identity"—and What Is

In no meaningful way is a corporate structure part of organizational identity. Nor are any of the trappings of corporate structure, nor any common administrative tools, such as software or management processes. The components of identity vary by distinct groups in a nonprofit. Board members tend to think of identity as the sum total of excellent programs and services and the positive associations that people in the community have for the organization. Theirs tends to be an outward-facing sense of identity. The corporate name is important.

Executives of a nonprofit have a duplex view. They tend to share the outside focus of board members, seeing the organization's identity reflected in the eyes of stakeholders. They also have an internal focus driven by programs and services and the staff who work in them. Managers usually think of identity in terms of the program or programs for which they are responsible, plus their colleagues. Direct service employees more often think of an identity that derives from their consumers, coworkers, and the physical work environment. The name of the overall corporate entity may or may not be important to them.

All of these differing views of identity have one thing in common: *None of them needs to change automatically as the result of a merger.* In fact, in cases where the identity of an organization has developed sufficiently so as to be recognized as a brand name, changing the identity may not be a good thing.

Collaboration planners would be wise to recognize that identity in the most meaningful sense of the term for staff and board members does not need to be threatened. Valuable brands and the social capital that has been built up over the years do not and should not need to be squandered as a by-product of the process. Corporate names that have value can be continued as either corporate or program names. Whether this actually occurs or not is a separate question that should be considered on the merits. Losing identity is not an inherent aspect of a merger.

CHAPTER

The Role of Funders

Funders such as private foundations, governments, and even large donors often anguish about the proper role to play in collaborations. Should they take a passive role and watch as their grantees pinball through the process, lurching inexpertly from step to step while racking up cost overruns? Or should they take a hands-on role and risk alienating the very people they are trying to help?

Taking a completely hands-off approach arises from a perfectly understandable funder instinct. At the opposite end of the spectrum, government officials and foundation funders that try to insert themselves into a merger of two independent nonprofits probably will not want to do so a second time. Actively intervening tends to mean they will achieve something between mischief and mayhem, and no funder wants to be in that position.

We seek a more balanced way. To put it succinctly, funders should encourage and fund mergers and alliances, not manage them. Nonprofits are an ingenious delivery system for social development, and they should be treated like the marketplace of solutions that they are. Part of the back-and-forth of solution development is offering the full range of choices, good and bad. Funders should shape and influence, not manage and control.

What Funders Can Do

That said, there are several things that funders can do to encourage collaboration in their communities. Happily for funders, most of them cost little or nothing. What they do require is the willingness to be a step ahead of their communities and to be willing to take the criticism and the applause that is likely to accompany such a stance. A few concrete things funders can do include:

- Give permission
- Hold harmless
- Do not replace; merge

Give Permission

The most important thing that foundation leaders and individual donors can do is to give permission to talk about collaboration. While the economic downturn that began in 2008 gave more credibility to the whole notion of mergers and alliances, there is often still a sense that a merger implies failure on the part of one of the entities. Funders operate at an enormously powerful crossroads of resources and respectability that gives them a unique position to publicly promote the strategy—without advocating for it in any given case.

Giving permission consists of obvious tactics, such as funding specific collaborations and publicly approving of the choice generally. It also means encouraging dialog and education on the subject, convening conferences, and sponsoring training sessions on the topic. It could mean defending organizations choosing to explore a merger when the media or a group of stakeholders objects.

In keeping with funders' justifiable desire to maintain a neutral stance, they could insist on giving organizations time and space to consider specific collaborations even when others seem intent on foreclosing the option. A strong form of permission giving is taking stands on behalf of the approach, especially if other funders in the area disagree or have not made up their minds.

Hold Harmless

Most nonprofits' greatest premerger fear is that publicly acknowledging that they are considering a merger with another organization could be enough to persuade a common funder to cut back on its historic donation levels. If organization A gets $50,000 from the local United Way and if organization B gets $50,000 from the same United Way, the nonprofits' enduring fear about a merger is that the United Way will decide to fund the newly merged entity at $50,000, giving the other $50,000 to an unrelated organization. In practice, this happens only rarely, but that is not the point. The concept has become a kind of urban legend among some board members and fundraising types, and funders could go a long way toward supporting the merger choice if they swiftly and demonstrably rejected this practice in advance.

"Do Not Replace; Merge"

Perhaps the single most powerful message that funders could send their grantees and potential grantees is "Do not replace; merge." This simple, powerful idea communicates a smart leadership response to normal executive attrition. This phase is when most organizations go through some period of introspection. As a result, they may be more willing to rethink old assumptions.

Of course, this is also when organizations engaged in a merger discussion may feel most vulnerable. Often their first response to the suggestion of a merger is to acknowledge the sensibility of the option—and then to propose a delay in discussing it until they replace the chief executive officer (CEO). Naturally, hiring a new CEO effectively quashes any merger discussions. In response to this and similar situations, interim CEOs have become a mini-industry in the nonprofit sector. These individuals, often former nonprofit CEOs, managers, or consultants, take on temporary assignments in the top seat and can be instrumental in maintaining consistency while the organization ponders a merger. Board members, in certain situations, can fill the same kind of role.

Funding Collaborations

All of the preceding ideas have the very considerable advantages of being both smart and cost neutral. But the main business of foundations is to provide funding to assist nonprofits' worthy ventures, and mergers and alliances certainly qualify on that count. So it follows that many foundations, especially in economic downturns, will look for ways to fund collaborations. In doing so, they will encounter a subtle but major difference in the objective and the nature of the funding necessary. The vast majority of foundation work consists of funding programs, but mergers and alliances are management activities. They must be evaluated and funded differently from traditional programs, and the bulk of the grant development work is likely to involve a different kind of person from those whom foundation staff typically encounter.

The implications of this difference are multiple. Collaboration processes are very different from program development or replication. Managers with generic skills, such as financial management or human resource management, will do most of the funded work instead of program people. Programs tend to be one of a kind, highly specialized, and aimed at an external constituency. Most collaboration work is done by and for insiders. And some merger-related decisions ultimately have to be made in a legal and regulatory context.

Another difference between foundations' traditional program funding and collaboration funding has to do with the long tail of most foundation funding. Funding proposals is a slow-motion game. Partly this is because of the legal requirements of being a foundation, partly it is the nature of societal change, and partly it is related to sector culture. Recipients experience this firsthand as grant cycles covering months and even years. Proposals sometimes work their way through a foundation's process and some projects are accepted for funding but are asked to wait for a future grant cycle. And some of today's unfunded proposals may nonetheless be favorites of the foundation staff, who know that for one reason or another, the internal prospects for funding will be better in a year or two. In sum, foundations rarely are without promising ideas that just need a bit of work to get them to where they need to be. These are all components of the long tail of foundation funding. Collaboration funding is not usually part of that long tail because it is so time sensitive and the window of opportunity closes quickly. Moreover, the whole idea of collaborations, particularly mergers, has taken a long time to be acceptable to many foundations, and often there is a kind of urgency to them that does not characterize the usual projects. These factors combine to make collaboration funding very different from what foundations normally see.

Still, none of these differences is insurmountable. In fact, the generic nature of most functions being merged makes it a bit easier and more predictable than most programming functions. The foundation staff—or the individual donor—just needs to be aware of the differences and take steps to minimize the potential disruptions.

These kinds of distractions should not diminish the funder's ability to set the right tone and create centers of strength.

Models for Funding Collaborations

Implicit in the notion of collaboration as a tool for reshaping the voluntary sector is the assumption that collaboration must happen on a widespread basis. Those who see collaboration between and among nonprofits as the primary tool for organizational accomplishment in the early-twenty-first century know that we must move beyond a cute collaboration here or an interesting collaborative idea there. This means that funders who support the notion of collaboration must become quite serious about mass-producing it. The next section suggests three concrete steps foundation funders can take in their own markets to improve the quantity and quality of collaborations they fund.

Joint Funding Pools

With more than one million nonprofit public charities alone, the U.S. voluntary sector is enormous, and so any one collaboration in one geographic area will make little impact. What will make an impact is a large number of collaborations, which implies a scale well beyond that which most single foundation funders can even contemplate.

Joint funding pools are a powerful tool for extending impact, ensuring quality, and building support resources to help nonprofits merge. Joint funding pools (we have heard them called everything from critical juncture funds to catalyst funds to community innovation resources) are a logical way to aggregate resources for maximum impact. The fact that they embody the very collaboration among funders that they fund among recipients is an elegant touch not lost on grantees themselves.

The key elements of such funds are:

- Dollar commitments on a large scale (for the region) from multiple foundations
- A pool manager, which could be one of the foundations or another nonprofit
- Simple but compelling guidelines and processes

To understand how the dollars would be spent, consider the three logical stages we have found most successful mergers or alliances go through:

1. Feasibility determination
2. Implementation planning
3. Postmerger integration

Here is a brief description of each:

> *Feasibility determination.* This is the early stage of exploratory discussions. At some point, participants decide the collaboration idea has merit, and they move to a more formal basis. Often they refer to it as "due diligence," but usually it is a broader and more strategic discussion than that phrase implies. The feasibility stage ends with a joint understanding of the potential pluses and minuses of the collaboration and a sign-off from each board that the idea is worth pursuing.

Nonprofits Do It in the Right Order

For-profit companies, largely for legal and regulatory reasons, must decide to carry out a merger and then see if they can make it work. The actual decision-making process must be secret because premature disclosure actually could unfairly damage—or improve—stock prices and therefore the value of investors' holdings. Consequently, the discussions must be kept a tightly guarded secret within a manageable group of executives and consultants.

Once the merger is announced, the due diligence process begins—an exhaustive examination of the other organization to make sure that what has been represented in negotiations is in fact true. This process, plus putting the finishing touches on the merger, takes months. Planners often insert penalties for unwarranted withdrawal from the process to guard against bad-faith negotiations. The result is that the initial plans may or may not have been based on good information and may have to be reworked in a potentially contentious atmosphere.

Without Wall Street restrictions, nonprofits do not have to negotiate in total secrecy and can wait until each party's knowledge of the other is complete and thorough before making a final determination.

Implementation planning. The parties think through matters of governance, corporate structure, mission, program deployment, administration, and economics in this stage. The end result of a good implementation planning stage is a shared plan for how the collaboration will work and—in the case of a merger—a vote by both boards of directors to merge their organizations based on the plan.

Postmerger integration. In this stage, the newly merged entity's executives and managers operationalize the combination according to the implementation plan but almost certainly make adjustments along the way. Unlike the first two stages, which are so heavily rooted in the specifics of collaboration, postmerger integration tends to look more like plain old day-to-day management tasks: assigning and managing personnel, creating or modifying basic management systems, managing leases, changing insurance policies, and so on. Each of these distinct stages entails very different kinds of activities, and funding vehicles can vary accordingly.

Grants

Grants are an obvious choice of funding method for feasibility studies and for implementation planning. They are especially appropriate in these stages because often most of this work is done by outside consultants, a typical use for one-time grants. This is also a chancy period because there is no guarantee that anything will come of the effort, and the participants should be well aware of this fact. Grants are a logical funding mechanism because of their one-time nature and because professional grant makers have made their peace with the fact that grants do not always achieve their objectives. Grants can also be used for postmerger integration, although by this stage, many funders are experiencing merger fatigue and the prospect of funding something so invisible to most outsiders has a weaker appeal.

Program-Related Investments

Program-related investments (PRIs) tend to be better utilized in the postmerger integration stage. Unlike in feasibility determination or implementation planning, the integration stage can be heavy on asset management because buildings and equipment may need to be disposed of or renovated and computer systems or other equipment may need to be updated. Those involved in an integration process often think of it as composed of millions of little details, and surely it is. But the items with the biggest impact on the new organization are the capital asset changes because a single transaction can change the entire financial complexion of the organization.

Of course, foundations can do all of these things on their own as well as in a pooled fund. Why go to all that trouble just to coordinate the funding of a finite number of mergers or alliances?

The answer lies in the differences between mergers in the for-profit sector and those in the nonprofit sector. When a publicly held company decides it wants to be part of a merger, it has a distinct advantage over its nonprofit counterpart. The for-profit company knows that there is a proven pathway through a merger or acquisition because thousands of other companies have been through it before. The for-profit company knows that there are outside consultants ready to help with every phase of the merger or acquisition process. They know or could easily discover the names of the best law firms, the most experienced systems integration people, the most reputable pension plan consultants, and so on. They know all this because the merger and acquisition process is a well-known, well-trod, and predictably regulated path.

The nonprofit sector has none of these advantages. Culturally, nonprofit mergers in the first part of the new century are still subconsciously regarded as one-time, interesting but unfamiliar events. There is no infrastructure of companies and individuals with thousands of transactions to their credit in this sector, nor is there much delineation of legal or regulatory requirements. The result is that each pair of organizations considering a merger at some point realizes that they are on their own. The result can be a meandering, unsatisfying, expensive, and potentially unsuccessful experience.

Quality Assurance through Foundations

The primary nonmonetary contribution of foundations and donors to their service area's nonprofits is to ensure that a collaboration infrastructure emerges as quickly as possible, including proven methodologies and approaches and the empirical validation to prove it. This is not a common activity of most foundations. But what other organizations are in a better position to help shape and fund the planning infrastructure necessary to carry out large numbers of mergers and alliances?

Foundations can do so by applying some of the material in this book in a systematic way. They can:

- Insist that their fund recipients show their plans for feasibility determination, implementation planning, and postmerger integration.
- Devise and promote quality standards for mergers and alliances, whether the work is performed by consultants to nonprofits or by the participating organizations themselves.
- Fund training sessions for area consultants.
- Research and circulate information about successful mergers.

In short, foundations should seek to build community capacity.

Foundations and even individual donors are in a unique position regarding nonprofit collaborations. They must find innovative ways to fund these projects, but they also should embrace the opportunity to approach them in such a way that gets individual mergers done while building systemic capacity for the future.

7

C.O.R.E. Continuum of Collaboration

For years, the term "merger" has been frowned on by most non-profit managers and their boards of directors. Corporate America's excesses—and the media's treatment of them—combined with various structural disincentives for merging except as a last resort have created a strong negative perception of the practice. Because the strategy of merging and integrating services has been so offputting, there is an understandable neglect of even basic terminology. Finally, as with any emerging discipline, a few participants are doing genuinely new things for which there is no well-worn path, let alone words to describe it.

Consider the words "merger" and "alliance," which are emerging as two of the favorite descriptors of the kind of activity, which we will call collaboration. Attorneys and finance professionals use the term "merger" all the time, as in the phrase "mergers and acquisitions." Right away there are obvious problems translating the concept to the nonprofit field, for exactly how does one go about acquiring a nonprofit entity, which, by definition, no one owns? Technically, the best one can do is to control it, which gives the same results as an acquisition but for different reasons. Emotional connotations aside, there is not a good fit.

"Alliance" suffers a different fate. Unlike other terms, there is no such legal entity. A partnership, for example, is a legally accepted form of business operation. How does one create a partnership? Describe it in writing, sign it, and, subject to a few regulatory requirements, one has created a partnership. But what is an alliance? For that matter, what is an "affiliation"? Two groups acting together for a specific purpose? Dozens of groups deciding to cooperate in a general way? A way to avoid the dreaded "m" word? In all likelihood, it is all of the above and more. These terms have no legal content yet are used almost interchangeably to describe different and sometimes contradictory forms of collaboration. We need a common vocabulary in order to be able to help make good choices and move the art of collaboration forward.

Our Model

In this book we take a different approach. In order to give our terminology specific meaning, we lay out a conceptual model against which terms can be measured. Our model is based on the premise that different forms of collaboration affect different aspects of the nonprofit organization. The four aspects affected are:

1. Corporate
2. Operations
3. Responsibility
4. Economics

It is worth a few words to clarify exactly what each of these terms means. By *corporate*, we mean the legal entity of the nonprofit corporation. This is the business structure that has an official purpose, a board of directors, officers, by-laws, and all those other things generally recognized to be part of overseeing a corporate body. The corporate level is where the Internal Revenue Service lodges responsibility for financial accountability. It is typically headed by the president or chairman at the board level and by the chief executive officer as part of management. It may be freestanding or it may be controlled by another group; for our current analytical purposes, it does not matter. More concretely, the corporate level includes actions of the board and entity-wide management that shape matters of substance involving the organization as a whole.

Many collaborations will also affect the program or *operations* level of the nonprofit organization. Operations are the heart of the nonprofit's unique reason for being, whether those operations carry out research into molecular structure, care for preschool children, or develop the economy of a neighborhood. Often this level of activity is called programming. Whatever the terminology, the operations level is where the nonprofit delivers on its promise of serving the public good.

All of this corporate oversight and program activity requires someone to be responsible from day to day. Paychecks need to be generated, bills sent out, expenses paid, and myriad other back-office tasks need to be performed if a nonprofit of any size is to keep the doors open. We call this type of activity *responsibility distribution*—the backbone that makes the organization run.

Finally, collaborations can affect the *economics* of participating nonprofits. The outcome of collaborating to affect economics could be as simple as bartering free office rent in return for certain services or as complicated as establishing a jointly owned for-profit support services company.

Applying the C.O.R.E.

Exhibit 7.1 shows the C.O.R.E. concept visually. In this display, the areas with the greatest effect on the collaborating organizations are shown as four horizontal bars. Vertically, the graph represents a continuum from the earliest and easiest area of impact (economics) to the highest level (corporate). The highest and most powerful choice that takes the longest to achieve is for the participants in the collaboration to act as a single entity in their marketplace, as represented in the top right corner. The horizontal continuum represents the degree of integration of the chosen collaboration. "Integration" refers to the nature and intensity of the commitment that two or more nonprofits must make to each other in order to collaborate using their chosen model.

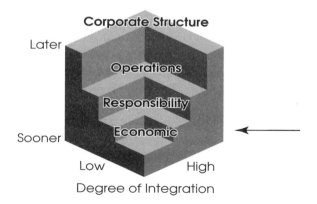

Exhibit 7.1   Continuum of Collaboration

Collaborations requiring very little mutual commitment would appear on the far left side; those requiring things like the exchange of money or signed contracts would appear on the far right side.

To illustrate the concept of integration at all levels, we will use economic collaboration. Economics is on the lowest, most readily accessible level because it is the low-hanging fruit of collaboration. Economic collaboration is perhaps the easiest to understand of the four vertical levels. It is nonthreatening, capable of an economic payoff, and does not demand much change from the participants. A simple exchange of certain information about a common supplier's practices, for example, might empower one organization to negotiate better business terms, but it does not necessitate any lasting connection between the nonprofits sharing the information. Because of this, information sharing requires very little integration, so it would appear on the far left. Creating a captive mutual insurance company for a defined group of nonprofits, however, would require a great deal of capital, along with legal commitments and executives' time. This is a high-integration undertaking, so it would appear on the far right.

In the last decade, there has been a subtle shift in attitude about economic collaboration. Whereas in the 1990s it was seen as a reasonable end in itself, in recent years it has also come to be seen a bit more as a possible starting point for a broader collaboration, including a merger. This is a positive development, with one caveat. Economic collaborations take time to create and even longer to provide benefits. Organizations that are trying to collaborate economically as a way of gaining savings quickly will be disappointed. This is largely due to the math of economic savings. Nonprofits typically spend the vast majority of their revenues on personnel. Moreover, outright spending on products and services is a much smaller amount of the revenue stream, say, 20 percent of the total. But that 20 percent includes many different types of products and services, each of which would have to be handled separately to gain economic leverage. Even lumping spending on a single product or service with that of other organizations only amounts to a small amount in total dollars. Assuming a quite respectable 10 percent savings on a single type of product or service, that translates into an overall savings no greater than a percent or two of total revenue—a lot of work for a small gain.

Collaborations operating at one level will probably affect levels below but rarely above. Also, there is no implied push up the C.O.R.E. Collaborations can form at any one level and stay there just as easily as they can expand to a higher level. One of the inescapable practicalities of collaborations is that, over time, they will go only as far as the participants want them to go.

The model can also help sort through common terminology describing various types of collaboration. The bold line between the Corporate and the Operations level makes a crucial distinction. Collaborations involving any one or all three of the O, R, and E levels are alliances. Those involving all four levels of the C.O.R.E. Continuum are a merger.

Mini-Glossary

So that there's no doubt about the terminology we'll be using in this book, here's a mini-glossary.

Affiliation. The lowest level of collaboration. Requires little more than meetings and good faith.

Alliance. Collaborations that entail change on any one or all three of the C.O.R.E. levels.

Collaboration. Our generic term for what happens any time two or more non-profits work together in some formalized way.

Merger. A collaboration that entails change on all four C.O.R.E. levels.

Network. Another name for an alliance, or a shortened reference to integrated service network.

Partnership. A legally binding agreement between two or more entities that is intended to produce economic benefit for both that is to be shared in some predetermined fashion. Partnerships can operate at any level of the C.O.R.E. continuum because they are simply legal vehicles for collaboration.

Much about the art of nonprofit collaboration has yet to be documented and agreed on, but the preceding models may help add some definitiveness for the purposes of this book. The next chapters take up the four levels of organizational impact, how they work and what they look like, starting from economics and working up the continuum.

CHAPTER 8

Economic-Level Collaboration

Chances are, few nonprofit organizations would seriously consider any type of collaboration if there were not economic pressures to do so. No matter how compelling the strategic, public interest, and moral arguments for nonprofit alliances might be, economic considerations are what move people. Organizations resist change for the simple reason that it causes pain, and usually the process of alliance building gathers momentum only when the present or anticipated pain of economic stress outweighs the pain of having to change.

Given the typical origins of alliances in economics, it is perfectly understandable that the details of day-to-day operations are usually the first area of focus. There is often plenty to do. Unlike for-profit organizations in which the owner or owners have a real interest in minimizing expenses so as to maximize profits, nonprofit managers do not have a direct incentive to keep expenses low.

Alliances created solely for the purpose of changing participants' economics are the loosest and least demanding kind. Since most of the simpler economic gains involve more efficient dealings with outside suppliers, it is easier to get unity against an external economic focus. This is helpful because, as all political leaders know, it is much easier to unite groups in opposition to a common enemy than any other way. By contrast, all the other levels on the continuum deal primarily with those inside the collaborating organizations, so a certain discomfort can always be present.

There are many ways to achieve greater efficiencies in nonprofit organizations. Happily, few of them truly risk interfering with the accomplishment of the mission, which is what many people

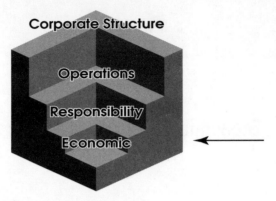

Exhibit 8.1   Economic Level of Corporate Structure

understandably worry about when attention turns to economics. In fact, anecdotal evidence suggests that, in some cases, it is entirely possible to save money and provide higher-quality services at the same time. The rest of this chapter is dedicated to describing a few distinct strategies for deriving economic gains from collaborations (see Exhibit 8.1). Most examples are keyed to alliances, since it is presumed that merged entities can accomplish the same results simply by taking advantage of their newly increased purchasing leverage, whereas alliances will have to work harder at the same thing.

Sharing Information

One of the quickest, least expensive, and most potent ways of making economic progress is sharing information. Although information can be shared about any number of economic areas in a nonprofit, in this section and the next ones we draw heavily on the area of supplies purchasing practices for our examples. We do this largely because vendor-provided services are so easy to quantify and so familiar to most people. Less commonplace services, such as benefits and professional services, may be equally promising candidates for comparative analysis.

There are many different levels of sharing economic information. The easiest kind of economic collaboration is to compare recent invoices or purchase orders from vendors of the same sort of product or service. A deeper approach would be to share copies of contracts and purchasing agreements along with accounting records. A more sophisticated technique yet would be to select one or more comparable items and track their price history side by side over a period of months or even years.

The advantage to information sharing as an economic strategy is that it is quick, easy, and inexpensive. The three disadvantages flow from the same facts:

1. There are no guarantees that any participant in the process will gain from the effort since it is left to participants as individual purchasers to act on the information gained.
2. There is no structured means of following up on any gains, so suppliers could eventually revert back to their old pricing structures without notice.
3. Any gains are elusive and hard to document. Opportunities for building momentum for collaboration and proving success can quietly slip away.

Bidding Jointly

Bidding jointly is a step up from the simple sharing of information. In this approach, participants go through a purchasing process together. They might design and issue a joint request for proposals (RFP), research the responses together, and interview bidders jointly. In the end, however, they negotiate separate deals.

This method has the advantage of reducing overhead slightly by sharing the costs of purchasing, and it may also encourage suppliers to be a bit more aggressive in their pricing, but there are no guarantees. Again, the risk is that unmonitored and independently structured arrangements can fall apart easily.

Pitfall: The Potato Chip Bag Trap

Purchasing analyses are not as easy as they sound. Sloppy analyses will lead to bad conclusions and may even result in spending more money. The key is to arrive at the same unit of measure for each item being compared and then to rigorously extract the price per unit from the inevitable jumble of vendor-related records. Vendors do not want you to do this sort of thing so they try to make it difficult. Ever notice the measurements on snack-size bags of junk foods? Vendors need to sell their bags at the same price as that of the competition, so their size varies wildly. Making comparisons between them is tedious and time consuming, which is precisely what the higher-priced manufacturers want.

Joint Purchasing

Joint purchasing is a favored strategy of alliances of all kinds, and for good reason. It can take many forms. In some cases, the alliance—frequently an association—simply researches and endorses a particular vendor. In this case, the association effectively becomes one of the vendor's sales representatives. Vendors gain when the association's endorsement drives more business to them, the members (presumably) gain from lower prices, and the association gains by earning a royalty or commission of some sort.

In other cases, the alliance creates a business entity expressly to carry out purchasing activities. Most joint purchasing initiatives operate on the same principle: Create savings for members and/or make money for the alliance by cutting out the last distribution point for the end user. Office supply superstores created a whole industry by doing the same thing. Office supplies used to be distributed to the consumer largely through small mom-and-pop stationery stores, which were in turn supplied by larger wholesalers. Office supply superstores effectively turn the wholesaler into the last stop for the consumer, thereby cutting out smaller and less-efficient retailers.

The more the alliance can act like a wholesaler, the higher the savings it will produce for its members. For example, if an alliance can buy large quantities of some commodity, such as paper, it can offer substantial savings for members in addition to some profit for itself. But this strategy requires an investment in appropriate storage capacity, a distribution system, security provisions, and so forth; in short, it requires the alliance to act like a true wholesaler. That is a responsibility that only the very largest and most sophisticated alliances are likely to take on, so most efforts probably will stop considerably short of this level.

Tip: Respect the Economics of Purchasing

Different products and services respond differently when purchased in quantity. Commodity products, such as paper or computers, behave predictably when purchased in bulk: The more you purchase, the lower the unit price is likely to be. Other things, such as insurance, are so complex and individually tailored that they defeat efforts to rationalize and bulk purchase them; in these cases, the primary advantage of joint purchasing is likely to be access to the product or perhaps a higher-quality product (because it has been designed expressly for the purchasing group).

Responsibility-Level Collaboration

The next step up the C.O.R.E. continuum is sharing responsibility for basic management and administrative chores, the backbone of administration (see Exhibit 9.1). Although obviously related to changes in economics, this area is considerably broader and less susceptible to quantification. Changing the locus of management responsibility happens automatically in a merger, but typically only after a great deal of trust has been established and some economic groundwork is laid in a network of service providers. Also, unlike economic change, shared management responsibility can be hard to see, not necessarily measurable, and subject to rapid changes.

More than any of the other three levels, collaborations at the Responsibility level require the same thing virtually across the board:

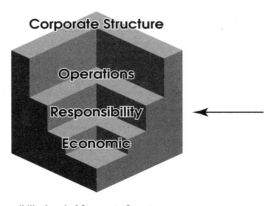

Exhibit 9.1   Responsibility Level of Corporate Structure

standardization, replicability, and scale. Most back-room functions, such as accounting, human resource management, information technology, and property management, are commodity operations: A function or group of functions must be performed over and over again in the same reliable way. The difficulty for most non-profits is that they typically are not standardized, or there is no appreciable scale even when combining two or more administrative systems.

The idea of shared administrative services got its start in the corporate world when executives of the early conglomerates realized that their far-flung and very different companies could be cheaper to run and more efficient to administer if they provided generic administrative services centrally. Shared services in this model were a tad easier to create because all of the participating companies were owned by the same parent corporation. Operating at a different scale, nonprofits do not have the same economic and efficiency advantages. Nonetheless, in select situations, the model can still be beneficial.

"Circuit Riders"

One of the simplest forms of Responsibility collaborations—and therefore one requiring the least integration—is a variation on the early American institution of circuit-riding judges. Especially in the rural West, judges would visit on a regular schedule locations that could not support a full-time judge. Today, particularly for small nonprofits, there are professionals such as accountants or technology specialists who act as circuit riders: Tuesday is the ballet, Wednesday the museum.

Pitfall: The Part-time Chief Executive

Ironically, sharing management staff may be healthy for nonprofits, but sharing the chief executive officer is not. We have no statistics to back this up—just lots of anecdotes. Nonprofits with part-time chief executive officers tend to suffer for it. The reason seems to be that the part-time chief executive always has at least one other focus for his or her professional energies, and this tends to dilute the person's impact on the organization. The real damage comes from the fact that the effect is insidious, hard to detect from day to day, and most often discernible over the long term as lost opportunities.

These professionals tend to work through a series of random, more or less unplanned relationships. One subtle difference between alliances and circuit riders is that, in the former, the initiative comes from the employing organizations, while informal circuit-riding arrangements are usually set up by the professionals. In any event, shared back-room staffing represents a valid, if largely informal, form of collaboration. One final note: Shared staff of this sort represent a good bridging step between two organizations on the way to a formal merger.

High-Integration Collaboration Models

Some of the more intriguing applications of administrative collaboration exist in the United Way system. In the latter part of the 1990s, national companies that had encouraged local branches or divisions to participate in United Way campaigns began to require that the organization had to establish a national electronic system for collecting and distributing campaign pledge forms. National companies with hundreds of local operations wanted a centralized system for running the campaigns and accounting for the contributions. This contradicted the ethic behind the approximately 1,200 fiercely independent local United Ways, but the demand was essentially nonnegotiable.

During a period of experimentation, at least two innovations arose from the United Way, both initiated and nurtured locally. One was an electronic system that provided standardized but locally branded campaign tools for participating United Ways. The other was a series of ultimately productive local experiments in standardizing pledge management and, eventually, back-room operations. Each of these innovations is what we would term an alliance on the Responsibility level of the C.O.R.E. Continuum.

More integrated back-room collaborations are also possible. A community health center and a local community-based organization collaborated around a shared back-room operation that provided most of the financial and technology supports each needed. Colocating with shared services is another way to create a more integrated Responsibility-level collaboration. In this model, nonprofits not only rent space in the same building but share administrative services, such as copying and information technology support. These situations also bring the added value of physical proximity for a group of like-minded organizations in a way that could result in serendipitous collaborations beyond the stated intent.

A Cautionary Note

During the initial stages of the reaction to the 2008 recession, there was a flurry of interest in administrative collaborations. This was a normal response to economic challenges. Nonprofit boards and administrators often seek to find savings in the least painful way, which usually means cuts in administrative spending.

Fair enough. The problem with this strategy is that it is guaranteed to fall short of the desired outcome. The reason lies in the mathematics of administrative spending. When two groups find savings in some item of administrative spending, it is likely to be modest—a 10 percent savings would be quite respectable most of the time. But a 10 percent savings on a line item that itself is likely to be no more than 10 percent of the total administrative spending amounts to a fraction of a fraction. Every ounce of savings helps, of course, but this is small reward for a big effort. Collaboration is a powerful tool, but the return should match the effort.

CHAPTER

Operations-Level Collaboration

In the end, nonprofits provide services, and any kind of meaningful integration must include program services, or the Operations level of integration in our C.O.R.E. Continuum (see Exhibit 10.1). In many ways, this is the level of integration that ultimately means the most for any merger or alliance of nonprofits because without success here, nothing else matters.

It is also the most difficult level at which to create alliances because relatively few such efforts have been widely accepted as successful and because program personnel tend to be indifferent or even overtly hostile to working together unless doing so is perceived as compatible with their mission. Conversely, because opportunities for professional interaction are hard to provide in settings

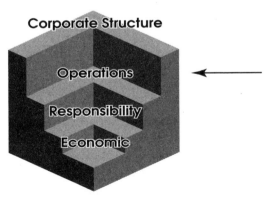

Exhibit 10.1   Operations Level of Corporate Structure

61

with a limited number of each type of professional, programmatic integration can be a very appealing process. One of the least recognized disadvantages of working in small nonprofit settings is that they can be tremendously isolating. Mergers and alliances can help provide a bigger pool of peers with whom to interact.

As with the previous levels, this level on the continuum of collaboration is itself a continuum. We have identified three different ways of increasing complexity and effective programmatic collaboration to illustrate the principle:

1. Shared training
2. Joint programming
3. Joint quality standards

Shared Training

Good managers of service providers know that, over time, the key to producing consistently high-quality service is training. In the American economy, we rely on high schools and undergraduate programs to educate future employees. Training is what their employers must give them. An unfortunate reality of budgetary politics in most organizations is that training budgets are the first to get cut. Like skimping on capital expenditures, the results of slashing training take a while to show up and are hard to quantify anyway, which makes them irresistible targets.

Still, training gets done. Often it is informal, ad hoc, and self-initiated, but it happens. Conferences are one way to get key employees trained, as are specialty meetings and orientation sessions. In merger situations, training policies tend to be driven by the merger partner with the strongest philosophy about training (for or against). Externalities such as regulations and funder requirements can have the same effect. In alliances, there is room for different approaches.

The simplest approach is to coordinate training programs. Similar to the low-end economic strategy of sharing information about vendors, this tactic is largely one of comparing calendars and attempting to coordinate efforts so that both parties get maximum coverage out of whatever training does take place. Participants might even try appointing a staff member to attend a class and then teach an in-house session for all agency staff who did not attend. (This is one of those ideas that always sounds like it ought to work much better than it does.) More formal attempts would involve the active commitment of all parties to invite staff members of other agencies to ongoing in-house training.

Joint Programming

The surest way to integrate programming is through mergers, when the control and accountability structures are reworked and the services that were formerly independent come under the same roof. Program-only collaborations, by contrast, would be considered alliances, and these are among the most difficult kinds of collaborations to manage. Here are some guidelines to keep in mind when planning a programming alliance:

- *Successful programmatic collaboration takes time.* Program collaborations often take a long time because most programming is not standardized between organizations so collaboration has to start with a blank sheet.
- *Trust underlies collaboration.* It is worth repeating that participants need to develop understanding and respect for each other, and this cannot be willed into existence.
- *Knowledge of your partner is essential.* When two collaborating organizations know each other well, the relationship tends to work better.
- *Flexibility is mandatory.* It is not uncommon for one or both organizations to lose key staff midway through an alliance. In fact, all alliances should expect personnel turnover among participating organizations. Successful collaborations find a way to adapt to these and other unforeseen events.

These simple lessons can be summed up in this thought: *Good programmatic collaboration requires excellent planning, patience, and time.* Participants need to develop mutual trust and respect over an extended period, understand a great deal about the other, and be willing to be flexible. Only then can the technical skills usually associated with programming get the fertile turf they need to flourish.

Joint Quality Standards

For an alliance in which members retain their independent corporate identities, the logic is to be so integrated programmatically that any one participant's services reliably meets the same minimum standards of quality. Theoretically, if one guarantees a minimum level of quality no matter which provider is chosen, then the choice of provider will be made on less dramatic grounds, such as price, geography, name recognition, and the like.

This is the same principle that has made everything from McDonald's hamburgers to an Ivy League education so successful. The consumer is guaranteed a minimum level of quality and a predictable experience, whether it is the consumption of a meal or the completion of a four-year educational program. What the deans of Yale or McDonald's Hamburger University understand is that the single strongest factor in consumer motivation is the desire to avoid risk. "Risk" in this context means everything from the risk of an unpleasant dining experience to inadequate preparation for adult life. By delivering services that effectively remove the risk of a bad "purchase," they can dominate whatever segment of the market they choose. To be sure, most consumer motivation rests on other factors too. But the integration of a large group of services around a single standard of quality will always be an extremely strong force.

And a frightening one. The truth is that the prospect of shared standards of quality is very threatening for most organizations. This is the heart of why service standards will be difficult in the nonprofit sector. In the absence of popular pressure, no industry will voluntarily subject itself to such action. The movie industry instituted a rating system only when pressured to do so. Japanese auto companies agreed to "voluntary" quotas only after the U.S. federal government appeared ready to impose import tariffs. Physicians steadfastly refuse to accept public disclosure of even the most rudimentary of performance data, especially in a time of instantaneous communication.

It is not that every participant within an industry fears accountability for standards of some kind. In fact, as individual organizations, many probably hope for such standards, or at least would be confident about working with them. But because they are acting in their own best interests as individual entities to resist them initially, pressures for quality standards have to come from a much more persuasive and reliable source, and that source can only be found in joint action of some kind.

11

Corporate-Level Collaboration: Merger

W e arrive now at the highest level of nonprofit collaboration, the level of corporate change (see Exhibit 11.1). No value judgments to be made here: We refer to Corporate Structure as the highest level not as tribute but rather as the point on the collaboration continuum that experiences the most profound level of change. The corporate vehicle is the legal fiction that we overlay on programs, administrative tasks, and support services. For better or worse, it carries the identity that our programs use in their interaction with the outside world. It is also the basis of accountability and the reconciler of conflicting demands on resources.

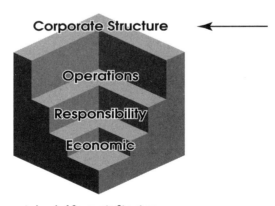

Exhibit 11.1   Corporate Level of Corporate Structure

Up to this point, the levels and examples of collaboration we have discussed had this one thing in common: *No one other than the participants cared.* This may sound odd, but it is rooted in the inward-facing nature of most of the C.O.R.E. Continuum. Of the lower three levels, only Operations has an element that might be visible to consumers (or funders) of a nonprofit's services. Consumers typically are unaware of the amount of work that goes into most collaborations because they occur out of the consumers' sight. When one is dealing with purchasing decisions and back-room operations, this is easy to manage. But combining corporate structures also means operating in the same space that the brand occupies, and this means it is vulnerable territory for most nonprofits. Touch the brand, and the consumer may notice.

Collaboration at the Corporate level means moving from an alliance to a merger. Several characteristics of mergers distinguish them from alliances, and many are firmly grounded in the fact that the corporate entities of the participating organizations experience some kind of change (usually either an abrupt increase in size or dissolution). One differentiating characteristic of mergers is that they have a cascading effect on the lower levels that is not replicated in an alliance. An alliance on the Economics level, for example, does not lead to changes on the Responsibility level. However, mergers inevitably change things on the three lower levels in addition to the Corporate Structure changes they create. A merger will eventually lead to changes in Operations, although not usually right away. Mergers will also consolidate back-room operations, and they will produce changes in economics, if for no other reason than that they greatly increase the volume of transactions and therefore produce the potential for savings.

Authority Is Concentrated

Another difference between mergers and alliances is that the authority in an alliance is diffuse whereas in a merger it is concentrated at the executive level. This creates greater power in a merger and more focus on alignment. Increased power for top-down decision making tends to offend egalitarian-minded nonprofit advocates, but it increases the impact of executive decisions. In a newly enlarged organization, there is usually greater distance between those at the top and those at the bottom, which only reinforces the Mount Olympus–like quality of the chief executive officer's (CEO's) new perch.

This change in scale can lead to a change in atmosphere, especially in the months of a newly merged administration as decisions are being made and implemented at a rapid clip and everyone feels as if they do not have time to absorb the full scope of the changes, let alone to oppose them. Eventually, the culture may return to a more collegial style (or not), but in the beginning, it may seem decidedly more corporate.

Along with the changes in culture come other changes, large and small. For non-direct-service people, such as executives, managers, and administrators, the totality of the small changes can be quite large. Many will be going to work in a different physical location doing different things than they did before, with different systems and different procedures to absorb. Even if one set of managers stays in its original physical location, the managers will have to get used to new colleagues and altered reporting relationships.

The relative abruptness of a merger becoming official—the legal system will affix the official time of the merger to a single day—underscores the magnitude of the change. But to put this fact in a larger context, consider that the speeded-up pace of change in the early twenty-first century is already so well accepted as to be almost a cliché. In addition, as mergers become more widely accepted as a legitimate strategic tool, some organizations will go through so many that they will in effect be in a period of constant change. That three-year tail of a nonprofit merger means that over any five-year period, a given organization could be at the beginning of one merger, in the middle of another, and at the tail end of a third. Serial integration will be the norm for some entities as we enter the second decade of the new century.

Official Start Dates May Be Anticlimactic

Paradoxically, for those involved in a merger, the official date probably means nothing. This fact only seems to contradict the message of the last section. Postmerger integration takes place in calendar time, but its milestones are measured as part of a chronology: Next week we move, the week after that the new e-mail system goes into effect, and so on.

This raises an intriguing question: When, exactly, does a merger occur? Attorneys will say that the date of a merger is when the articles of merger were filed and accepted by the authorities. But in human terms, that date is nothing more significant than a coffee stirrer planted in beach sand. We once consulted with a pair of nonprofits that had worked on a merger for several months. One of them was on its second interim CEO and for this and other reasons accepted a merger as desirable. The official date of the merger was July 1, a Saturday, and the organizations had planned a public announcement for noon on the day before. Eight days beforehand, for reasons unrelated to the merger, a major government funding source that they both shared raised significant concerns about the way one organization had been delivering those services. One very plausible impact of this glitch was that both corporations would have to be kept intact, and one would have had to become the parent of the other. At the last minute, the funding source was satisfied with some operational changes, the original plan to dissolve one of the corporations was reinstituted, and the announcement went on as planned.

But the back story was that on March 15, the two organizations had signed a contract for the leaderless one to purchase management services from the other one. As negotiations progressed, it was decided that on March 15, the two board memberships would intertwine in such a way that they would essentially become the same board for the two corporations. At the same time, concerned that further discussions might produce a deal-breaker surprise, the entities had embedded in the management contract a provision that, if triggered, would have unwound the entire arrangement.

So on what day did this merger occur? A casual observer would say that it was June 30, the day of the announcement. The legal papers said it was July 1. But for all purposes, March 15 was the day that the two boards became one—except that the unwind provision still could have ended the merger shortly after it started.

A more relevant question is: What difference does it make? The real effects of the merger had begun to be felt months beforehand as the two organizations discussed how they would combine, and the continuing CEO had begun providing valuable (and uncompensated!) services weeks before the signing of the management contract. The actual dates on the management contract and the official corporation filings were largely irrelevant to everyone. A tolerance for ambiguity can be a useful asset in dealing with mergers.

Mergers, as noted, change the corporate structures of the participating organizations. So do collaborations involving a management company model, in which one entity is the parent and multiple other entities are subsidiaries. Other choices could also cause changes on the corporate level of the participating organizations without necessarily requiring them to carry out a full merger. Two of the most common choices in this regard are partnerships and limited liability companies, and any arrangement with a for-profit organization. We take up each of these choices and show how they can be used in collaborations at the corporate level of the C.O.R.E. Continuum of Nonprofit Collaboration. For each, we explore the basic structure, typical governance and management control devices, advantages and disadvantages, and special considerations for the model's use.

What It Means to Merge

In order to make sense of the options available for structuring nonprofit mergers, it would be helpful to step outside the field and look first at for-profit mergers. The headlines of the average newspaper in any given year carry regular stories about two companies merging with each other. They talk at length about the personalities of the CEOs, the expected strategic benefits of the merger, the profits to be made by parties to the decisions, and many other things, but they rarely talk about how the merger is actually carried out.

Here is the nuts-and-bolts part that they do not cover. In the for-profit world, the choices for merger structure come down to two. One is for the acquiring company to acquire the target company's outstanding stock. This method gives the new owner control of the ownership of the organization, which in turn usually gives control of the board of directors. Under current accounting rules, the acquiring company must figure out new values for the purchased assets and liabilities based on the price it paid. It used to be possible to do what is called a "pooling of interests," which is just about what it sounds like, but that ended in 2001 with the new rules. The new method is called "purchase price allocation," and it provides for the new assets to be boosted to their fair market value up from book value and for the remainder of the difference between the purchase price and fair market value to be carried as the acquirer's "goodwill," an intangible asset.

The problem with stock-oriented acquisitions is that, while they bring ownership and control, they also bring potential troubles. If stock ownership simply means that someone else gets to sit in the owner's chair, then any bullets and arrows aimed at the former occupant of the chair will be aimed at the new one too. Any liabilities (such as lawsuits or obligations to pay money to someone) incurred in the name of the corporation by the previous owner will be binding on the new one. The way to solve this dilemma is to acquire only the assets of the corporation. If the company is a widget manufacturer, then the acquirer purchases the widget factory, the widget distribution system, and the good widget name. As soon as the transaction is completed, the new asset owner can start operating out of his or her own corporation. The name of the company on the door does not even have to change since that is usually one of the assets purchased.

Of course, in practice, it is rarely that simple. Most owners will always want to sell stock, since that is what enables them to walk away most cleanly, while most buyers will want to purchase only the assets, since it is less likely they will drag in liabilities that way. There are other considerations on both sides, but this represents the essence of the conflict and is why for-profit mergers and acquisitions are tricky things.

Mergers of publicly traded companies also offer the option of the famous hostile takeover. Cultural and other pragmatic considerations aside, if an acquiring company wants to own another company, it need only buy the right amount of stock. Usually this means either buying a controlling block of shares or winning a majority of shareholder votes in order to install management more favorable to the idea. There are many daunting implications associated with a hostile takeover, not the least of which is that the acquiring company usually cannot conduct adequate due diligence, so it cannot be sure of what it is buying until the transaction is done.

The deadly accuracy of the term "hostile takeover" has made it part of pop culture, and it often surfaces as a fear of nonprofit leaders. We began one merger feasibility process involving two large nonprofits with both organizations stating that they wanted to avoid a "hostile takeover" by a local competitor. The irony is that, since nonprofits are not allowed to issue stock, there is no vehicle by which to execute a hostile takeover.

If there is no legal vehicle that one nonprofit can use to take over another, a very practical rule of thumb emerges about nonprofit mergers: In the absence of a device permitting hostile takeovers, all nonprofit mergers must be voluntary. And if all nonprofit mergers are voluntary, it follows that each merging organization must genuinely see some kind of benefit from a merger, or else they will not agree to this voluntary process. Both the spirit and the letter of that two-part conclusion is why nonprofit mergers, done correctly, start out with a better chance of success than their more laissez-faire for-profit equivalents.

The Essence of a Nonprofit Merger

Now fast-forward to nonprofit mergers. Stock questions become irrelevant because nonprofits do not have owners. Structuring a nonprofit merger really comes down to a question of how one gains control of another nonprofit entity. Note that we are talking about control only in a legal sense. A nonprofit organization—or any other entity, for that matter—can be controlled for all practical purposes by people who derive their strength from sources such as personal charisma, long-standing relationships, or simply seniority.

If a nonprofit requires a substantial asset base to operate—museums and colleges demand buildings and significant other assets, for instance—then taking control of the assets gives functional control over the programs as well. However, many kinds of nonprofits need only office space and some routine business equipment. Taking control of the assets in that situation does not mean much. Control of the organization, therefore, has to reside elsewhere. Ultimately, legal authority is given only to those officials who are regarded as official representatives of the community, better known as the board of directors. This is the reason that merging control of the boards of directors is the only reliable way of merging nonprofits.

The notion of change at the board level as the signal of a true merger ties neatly into the idea of corporate level change from our C.O.R.E. framework. Many activities, such as marketing, get carried on at the corporate level, but the one common element of all nonprofits is that responsibility for the overall organization rests with the board. In a merger, the two formerly separate boards become a single board of directors. Responsibility for governance remains at this level, but the size and scope of the entity changes.

Structure

Merged organizations usually can be structured simply. There were two boards and two corporations before the merger, but afterward there will be only one.

In most cases, one of the existing corporate vehicles will be the "surviving" corporation. The decision as to which will survive and which will dissolve should be almost purely techno-legal in nature. On occasion there may need to be an entirely different, third corporation created into which the previously separate corporations are merged. Ultimately, this is a legal nuance of little interest to managers and boards. The point is that the structure of a true merger is simple and straightforward.

Tip: Keep the Old Corporation

Digging in your closet you find that old raincoat hanging limply in the back, exactly where you left it when you bought the new one a few months ago. Seized by a sudden desire to streamline, you bring the thing to Goodwill. What happens a week later? Right. The new one gets ripped at the start of a record-setting five-day rainstorm.

In a merger, one of the two corporations typically is stripped of all its assets and eventually dissolved. But are you sure you will not need it? Sometimes, even in a full merger, there can be a need for a second nonprofit corporation to hold property, conduct training, offer services to certain types of payers, or do any one of several other legitimate management chores. The moral: Until you can be sure you will not need it, consider keeping the old corporation around as a shell for a year or two. Maintaining it will not cost much, and it may come in handy for currently unforeseeable reasons.

As for the metaphor, it is not perfect; donate the raincoat and get an umbrella as a backup.

Control and Governance

As with structure, there is little mystery about how the new entity's board and managers achieve control. The board has a fiduciary responsibility just as each of the two predecessor boards had with the previously separate organizations, and they delegate management responsibility to staff members.

Governance is the area of real uncertainty because there are no recipe cards to follow in merging two boards of directors. Often, in fact, governance of the newly merged entity becomes one of the early sticking points between two organizations considering a merger. Part of the reason for this is because in the early stages, the groups do not fully trust each other. If the merger is handled properly, governance provisions eventually become less of an issue. But the other part of the reason is because governance and control really do matter to the future mission and effectiveness of the nonprofit—and so they really should be debated and resolved to everyone's satisfaction.

Questions about governance normally break down into three distinct areas:

1. Size of the board
2. Composition of the new board, specifically how many members come from one board versus how many from the other
3. Selecting officers

We take each matter in turn and suggest tactics for resolving its inherent conflicts.

Size of the Board

Tools for Determining Size   If boards of directors were cars, the best ones would look like midsize four-door sedans. Small, high-powered groups are too quick for their own good, and the lumbering 18-wheelers take a long time to get up to speed and even longer to turn. Research—and practical experience—suggests that the best size for a nonprofit board is in the 9- to 13-member range. This number gives the group enough members to compensate for temporary absences while remaining small enough to encourage widespread participation.

Opposing this commonsense approach is that the natural tendency when faced with, say, two 15-person boards is to head off possible conflicts by creating a 30-person board for the new entity. The primary means of reducing such size pressure is for each board's leadership to take an active role in surveying its own premerger membership. At any one time, there are likely to be several members who are quietly seeking a graceful exit from the board, and the changes that a merger will bring can offer that exit. Having a heart-to-heart talk with each board member is a good way to gauge his or her interest in remaining with the postmerger board. This tactic alone may solve the problem by reducing the boards' membership to a manageable level. This is a good area of focus for a joint committee composed of representatives from each organization—we will call this a collaboration committee throughout the book. If the collaboration committee feels, as many do, that the best solution is simply to create a new board that is the sum of the old ones, there are a few other techniques to consider.

Pitfall: Missing Organizational Culture's Influence on Governance

A seven-month-long effort to merge two hospitals and their medical schools fell apart because participants could not agree on who would control the newly created medical school. Mount Sinai Medical Center and New York University (NYU) entered talks aimed at merging their two systems. They found that combining the two hospitals would be eased by the comfortable geographic distance between the two locations, which permitted some duplication in the marketplace.

The medical school merger was different. NYU felt that the merged school would operate just like any of its other schools, while the medical center envisioned a more independent, equal partnership. "The issue of governance was always fuzzy and nobody really focused on the differences," one insider told *The New York Times*. "There was always an ambivalent understanding of how the medical school piece would work . . . when we finally got down to . . . this piece we couldn't move anywhere with it."

Reading between the lines of this failed merger is not difficult. As a relatively young (29 years) medical school, Mount Sinai had grown in prestige and amount of federal research funding, a useful barometer of respect in the medical world, while NYU had lost money. Compounding the problem, Mount Sinai negotiators apparently felt they were not being treated as equals. A profound difference in cultures played itself out in the arena of governance.

Cap Total Size and Reduce Membership through Attrition   Capping total board membership at the sum of the two component boards will help prevent the problem from getting worse. Preventing any new members from joining the board for a period of time will set in motion a self-reducing mechanism. The risk is that the board will stagnate as a leadership vehicle and that the original, or charter, members will become a closed circle. In a subtle way, it also encourages continuation of any us versus them feelings ("They're not

making any more of Us so we'd better hold fast against Them").
Still, it may be preferable to gridlock if the board cannot agree on
total size. Odd numbers are best for governance, of course; even
numbers allow for even splits.

Staggered Terms   It may help to assign staggered terms to
different board members. Although this technique alone does
not resolve the question of board size, it may help because board
composition is associated with control. Stretching the transition
period over a longer time may ease the stresses associated with a
change in control. In addition, individual board members' actions
or perceived interests may be an obstacle to effective collaboration but may have to be included in the final entity for separate
reasons. Staggering terms gives members reason to hope that the
newly discovered problematic board members eventually may
move on. It may also help by symbolizing the transitional nature
of the newly constructed board, not to mention that the whole
concept of term limits is an accepted best practice of nonprofit
boards as well as elective bodies. Staggered terms as a strategy for
limiting board size work best when linked with a cap on charter
membership.

Ancillary Boards   Ancillary groups, such as advisory committees
or honorary trustees, can relieve pressure on the collaboration
committee to create a large board for the new entity. Anything
that begins "Friends of . . ." probably will not be an effective
substitute for full board membership, but for some members, the
idea of a less involved form of participation may be appealing. It
can also be good for narrowcasting fundraising appeals to special
interests, geographic subsets, or small-volume services. Often, high-
visibility groups, such as symphony orchestras and art museums, have
oversized boards of trustees (or overseers, etc.). Either their function is largely ceremonial and is separate and apart from that of
the board of directors, or the smaller executive committee of the
board of trustees is the real governing board. For the board member
seeking visibility with little time commitment (but probably a significant commitment of money), this role could be ideal. If a good
ancillary board does not exist and the merged organization would
be large enough to support one, this is a good time to think about
creating one.

Tip: Offset CEOs and Board Presidents

The positions of CEO and board president are highly symbolic. In a two-way merger with two continuing CEOs, the greatest harmony comes from naming as board president the person formerly holding that role in the organization whose CEO does not continue as CEO in the new organization.

Board Composition   Next to board size, the stickiest governance matter to be resolved in a merger is likely to be the board's membership. This is one of the areas in a merger where it is very tempting to take a formulaic approach: "If we have 60 percent of the assets, we should get 60 percent of the board seats," or "We own four buildings and you only own two, so we should get twice as many seats as you get."

Using simple formulas is clear, understandable, and very pragmatic. What is so attractive about formulas is that they *seem* to be fair. The problem is that they are not effective. Done properly, mergers are about looking to the future. Formulas for board composition look backward. Worse, there is no reliable connection between what any individual board member can offer and from which organization he or she came.

Our solution to these twin problems is simple, effective, and all but certain to be ignored. To counteract the regressive tendency of formulas, think of board members as strategic assets that need to be carefully matched with the newly merged organization's future needs. All things being equal, if a museum is moving more toward contemporary art exhibits and away from sixteenth-century Italian art, the board member with a specialty in that area will be more strategic than the board member who is an expert in Titian. Of course, the idea is to avoid losing any valuable resource, but sometimes choices must be made, and it is always better to make them strategically than to expect them to make themselves.

The second part of the solution is to sever the implied connection between individuals and their nonprofit of origin. There is a great temptation to choose between one president and the other, between one treasurer and the other, and so on. Often participants feel pressure to start making these choices early in the process. We suggest waiting. In any task-oriented group, such as a collaboration committee and its various subcommittees, people tend to take on roles with which they feel comfortable. People become leaders in response to a unique set of circumstances. Just because someone was a vice president of a predecessor organization does not mean that he or she could or should hold the same office in the new entity.

Selecting Officers   Selecting officers of the new board is the third task in creating the new governance function. During the merger process, individual board members will tend to assume distinct planning roles. If the collaboration committee can put aside for a few months its understandable desire to finalize officers while it concentrates on other tasks of the merger, there is a good chance that the appropriate people for those roles will emerge naturally.

Of course, this is not always going to happen automatically, nor will all parties allow it to proceed unhindered. No matter how well intentioned the participants—and, make no mistake, when economics are at stake, good intentions can be overwhelmed— the integrity of the process must be protected. This is a good role for a facilitator. In fact, we would argue that the seeds of a failed merger are sown when one side or the other acts exclusively as the agent for its own interests and regards the merger planning process as a contest to be won. It is difficult for many board members, especially those with personal experience, to get out of the win-lose mentality that characterizes so many for-profit mergers. The thinking and action that flows from this model can scuttle the whole process.

Pitfall: "Winning" at Governance

In governance matters, one of the advantages that nonprofit mergers have over for-profit mergers is that no one organization can be said to have "won" since financial gains to individuals are not at stake. Consequently, "winning" occurs largely on the ego battlefield, where the dynamics can be subtle.

For example, board members usually know that they have a fiduciary responsibility to the public at large, so very few will explicitly and visibly advocate for their own organization's selfish interests; to do so would be indiscreet. Nevertheless, sometimes board members are wedded to their own organization's way of doing things. To feel vindicated in this faith, it is not enough merely to "win"; one must be perceived by others as having "won."

To determine whether board members are in the I-win-you-lose mode, look at the way symbols are handled. Organizations intent on being a dominant partner will tend to reduce or eliminate, at all costs, areas where the other nonprofit might have influence in the future. The new CEO will be "theirs," the new logo "theirs," the surviving information system "theirs," the board "theirs," and so on.

In a true merger, even a dominant nonprofit will be able to signal its interest in partnership by sensitively handling decisions with deep symbolic content.

Advantages and Disadvantages of a Merger

There are numerous advantages to the straight merger choice, and a few disadvantages. The primary advantage is that it is simple to understand and implement. One need not worry about creating a new corporation or putting in place a structure that no one understands, as is sometimes true of other choices. Because of its simplicity, a straight merger takes less time to arrange. It is definitive: There is a single focal point of leadership, governance is straightforward, and the organizational boundaries are simply the sum of the formerly separate corporations. Mergers also have the advantage of being the tightest and most formal means of collaboration. They consolidate a lot of power in the service of a mission.

Mergers tend to be horizontal by nature, meaning that they occur between similar organizations. They are excellent for creating more of the same. Consequently, they are the preferred tool for achieving economic size. The work of bringing two organizations together is so complex and taxing that fundamental differences in operations can make a merger nearly impossible.

Predictably, the disadvantages of mergers are often the same as the advantages. Their simplicity, unity of leadership, and tightly knit nature sometimes are precisely the points of greatest worry for ambivalent board and staff members. It is not uncommon for groups approaching a merger to seriously pursue the idea of building in a "demerger" provision. (To be fair, it is smart to have an exit strategy.) Since in most cases demerging is like unscrambling an omelet, this provision offers reassurance that is more emotional than realistic. Perhaps the greatest disadvantage of a merger is that it is somewhat limited in flexibility and sophistication. Mergers also are time consuming, as noted earlier. A merger can take years to gel.

CEO veterans of their first merger routinely report that the postmerger integration process took far longer than they expected. Should an organization's management feel a need to be on a fast track, it may very well be disappointed at the amount of time that needs to be devoted to making a merger work.

Although it does not technically relate to structural considerations, the issue of the size of the merging parties can also be a factor in making a merger complex. There are two ways this problem typically arises: Either, one of the nonprofits is much larger than the other (takeover merger), or they are arguably comparable in size (merger of equals). Different considerations apply in each case.

Takeover Merger

When one partner is significantly larger than the other, often the merger is seen as more of a takeover. It does not necessarily have to be this way, but perceptions are hard to shake. In the takeover style of merger, the dominant organization by definition becomes the template for the new entity. The administrative infrastructure of the smaller nonprofit either gets dismantled or its people and systems are absorbed into the larger organization's administrative system. The real suspense comes around questions of programming. The partners must choose how to organize the smaller nonprofit's services. Usually the decision is between operating the previously stand-alone nonprofit corporation as a new and self-contained program or parceling out its various services to different parts of the larger group's existing service system.

This is a question of no small consequence. There are no automatically right or wrong approaches, but whichever route is taken will have a significant effect on the success or failure of the merger. Operating the old corporation as a self-contained program is the quickest and clearest option, but doing so risks missing an opportunity to rethink the entire system of services and make it more integrated. Personnel in the old nonprofit-turned-program may also grow more ingrained and isolated, feeling that they have outlasted one management structure and will be able to do it again.

Yet reorganizing an existing operation is always a challenge. If program service people draw a distinction between what they do and the management of the old organization, there may be a kind of programmatic arrogance. Rightly or wrongly, they may view the merger as a sign that prior management failed. This can increase their resolve to demonstrate their own competence. They may also fear for their jobs. These impulses of self-confidence and fear may seem contradictory, but they can easily coexist and make for a potentially volatile mix for the entity taking over.

Merger of Equals

The other distinct merger model is between equals. Obviously there can be differences of opinion about what constitutes equality. Should it be based on total revenue? Asset base? Management team size? Public identity? For purposes of clarity, we simply say that two non-profits are equal if a reasonably educated outside observer would consider them equal.

There is another way for nonprofits to be viewed—and to view themselves—as equals, and that is if they share a common mission carried out in a franchise-like way. These national entities sometimes are known as federations, although there is no universally accepted terminology for them. Many local chapters of national federations are beginning to rethink their histories of operating as hundreds of small, autonomous units in favor of efforts to consolidate and strengthen their regional presence. Girl Scouts USA carried out a series of top-down mandated mergers starting in the middle of the last decade. As of this writing, there are indications that this general trend could continue for many other similar groups as well.

The structural implications of mergers between equals can be more challenging than takeover mergers because they can catapult both organizations onto a different level of management from where either had been before. This change means systems of all kinds must be overhauled. To take a concrete example, a nonprofit with 75 employees may be able to keep track of all the human resource management information, such as vacation time and sick time tracking, personnel records, and regulatory compliance, with part-time administrators and a largely manual system. But if it were to merge with another 75-employee nonprofit, the new entity would almost have to invest in automated human resource systems and at least one full-time human resources professional.

More important, a merger of equals may also force organizational and structural changes that will affect leadership. "Structural" here refers largely to programmatic and administrative activities. Doubling in size over two or three years is a daunting management task for any nonprofit. Merging equal-size organizations produces the same result overnight. Managers at all levels must grow with the new organization; this includes keeping pace with its changing structure.

For these reasons, it is critical to resolve certain service delivery questions at the front end of any merger between equals. For thoughtful collaboration committee members, there will be an inherent tension. On one hand, they need to make sure that the operational needs of the new entity can handle the suddenly increased size. (Will the cash flow hold up? Do we need to get another payroll service right away? Can we still handle that huge Monet exhibit next year?) On the other hand, this is an excellent time to throw out the old ways of doing things and bring in fresh perspectives and new ideas.

How to decide which direction to choose? For practical reasons, the answer is likely to be a blend of maintaining the old and creating the new. What matters is how committee members get there, because this issue is a miniature of the entire merger. It is especially critical in a merger of two equal nonprofits because there is no natural position of authority. Any one person's ideas seem no better or worse than another's. How they come to terms with a direction implicitly defines the new entity's values and sets a precedent for the process they will use for governance in the future. This type of merger is particularly well suited for an outside consultant to manage.

In a merger of equals, the service delivery system needs to be focused on early and rigorously because rejuvenating and strengthening the system of service delivery is what mergers and alliances should do. It is necessary to get this planning done early, not just because it is central to so much else but because resource-related areas, such as finances and space allocation, are inherently limiting. If programming needs do not quickly dominate the way resources are distributed, they will be dominated by it quickly.

12

Models of Collaboration:
Merger by Management Company

A second option in the merger choice is the management company model. This choice is also known as a holding company. It sometimes is known as a management services organization, although this is not a completely accurate term, as will be discussed. In essence, in this type of merger, a formerly freestanding nonprofit corporation is managed by another party, and both are under some form of common control. The circumstances leading to this somewhat complex structure are themselves complex. Often the forces behind the organizational and legal structures described earlier do not line up neatly. Many times they are blatantly contradictory, and equally desirable objectives simply cannot be accomplished within a single organization. For example, there may be two or more strong brands involved in a merger, or the primary funding sources demand that their funds be isolated even while the services they support be integrated. Community development corporations often have this tension throughout their organizations.

These are not rare situations. The inherently different elements of theater production are another good example. Theater ownership requires responsibilities and property management expertise. One also needs to be able to mount successful productions on a regular basis. This artistic effort has to be properly supported, with an artistic director, a casting function, and so on. This person-oriented function requires skills very different from property management— and do not forget the necessity of raising donated funds, which is a very different task from any of the previous ones. The demands of designing or purchasing, maintaining, and storing costumes, props, and scenery are different from property management too. Finally, one needs to advertise and market the shows.

All of these functions require very different skill sets and tangible assets as well as different ways of managing the people engaged in each function. The funding sources, spending models, and business risk profiles are all very different. This diversity of needs and resources adds up to a natural recipe for a multicorporate structure. In this case, the parent would probably be the theater company itself, with subsidiary nonprofit corporations for property ownership and management, production management, and marketing and advertising. This is not to say that all organizations with complex multiservice models should adopt this kind of corporate structure. Rather, this kind of decision should be made one organization at a time. Form should follow function.

Structure

A management company model looks very much like the traditional organizational chart, except that the boxes on an organizational chart representing programs and services in a management company setting signify corporations. Exhibit 12.1 shows a hypothetical management company structure for the theater company. It represents four separate corporations, all of them nonprofit public charities.

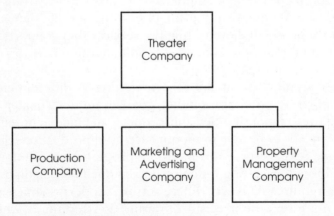

Exhibit 12.1   Sample Management Company Organization

The most significant thing about this chart is the public's perception of it: It does not care. Chances are that the theater company was the first entity of the four to come into existence. Its evolution into a four-corporation management company structure could have evolved gradually, or it could have occurred almost literally overnight. How someone outside the organization perceives it at this point depends on the nature of his or her relationship to it. Subscription ticketholders might be dimly aware that the organization putting on the production is somehow different from the organization that owns the theater, but perhaps not. And virtually no one will understand—or care—that different companies handle production duties and marketing and advertising. As long as the four groups work together to present a seamless theater experience, why should any consumer or aficionado care?

For the outsider with a commercial interest, the copy paper vendor would look at the management company as a large account, and the fact that it was providing management services for three other groups would probably be nice but immaterial. Or one of the subsidiary companies might handle paper purchasing for all four groups. In a multicorporate structure, you see what you're closest to.

All of these perspectives are "right," but the size and complexity of the organization causes different observers to see the same picture in different ways. No one other than those involved with the management company is likely to have an overall vision of the organization. This is both good and bad, depending on one's starting point.

Control and Governance

It is in matters of governance and control that some really interesting things distinguish this merger-by-management-company model from all others. Start with the board of directors. The theory is that, in a nonprofit organization, the board members have a fiduciary responsibility for it. That is, they do not own the entity but must manage it as if they did. They also have control. Legal theory has it that a nonprofit corporation is composed of a membership that has some interest in its mission. From that membership, and possibly other sources, comes a board of directors, which becomes the oversight body. Therefore, to control the corporation, one needs to control the membership.

How does one go about controlling the membership? If the entire membership happens to be composed of a single entity, and if that entity happens to be another corporation, then that other corporation effectively controls the board. Consequently, the easiest way to control a subsidiary corporation is to make the parent corporation the sole member of the subsidiary corporation. Doing this allows the parent board to retain control of the subsidiary's board by appointing from 51 to 100 percent of the members. (Other measures, such as the parent holding ownership rights to major assets, reinforce the board interlock.)

This bit of legal legerdemain is at the base of the most common control mechanism in a management company structure. It offers the great benefit of single board control over multiple corporate structures. The parent company board needs only to become the sole member of another corporation to be able to exert control over it. This can happen either through a vote of a freestanding nonprofit or by the creation of a completely new nonprofit corporation to be the subsidiary. However it is done, the management company, or "parent" corporation, has complete control of the subsidiary.

There are other ways to ensure control. A slight variation on the sole corporate member model is to simply appoint the same board to both corporations. Once this is done it is practically impossible to reverse, since the board would have to vote itself out of the subsidiary. In practice, this model may be little more than a theoretical variation on the sole-corporate-member model, since it does not offer any special advantages that the other model cannot also offer.

It is also possible to link two corporations through the same management structure. Appointing the same chief executive officer and/or management team to two different agencies gives de facto control. This structure might be used if an outsider, such as a funding source, insists on granting funds to a single asset corporation. Federal programs, such as some Housing and Urban Development grants, require that the money go to such single-asset corporations, and there could be other compliance-related effects as well.

For example, one organization wanted to offer services in a different community. The political and regulatory climate in that community was such that it strongly favored "hometown" groups, so the solution agreed on with local leaders was that a second corporation would be formed with all the same leadership as the nonlocal parent corporation.

This model could also be flipped around: A local, formerly freestanding group could seek to merge with a larger parent by accepting that parent nonprofit's leadership team without changing the existing corporate structure. Although helpful in dealing with things like regulatory dysfunction, this model has several pitfalls. One is that sharing management without changing board governance to match it is confusing and wasteful for professional staff. Another and perhaps more significant problem is that it shifts the true locus of control from the board to the staff level. Sharing management in this way is also a golden invitation for double billing, such as when the CEO is effectively paid twice for doing one job. Finally, it makes function follow form, instead of the reverse. Management has to act as if it handles two different organizations when in fact it really is trying to operate a single one under an appropriate legal umbrella. In short, this model may work as a temporary solution, or as an accommodation to quirky circumstances, but it could be messy in the long run.

An approach that does not change board control or corporate structure is for the parent company to sign management contracts with its subsidiaries. These management contracts could be as narrow or as expansive as desired. They may supply only a single executive, or they could provide a turnkey package with everything from human resources and financial services to purchasing and marketing provided by the parent. Most nonprofits budget some amount of money for general and administrative costs, so some or all of these funds would go to the parent for goods and services that would otherwise have been acquired as an independent. The economic rationale is that a larger entity could provide the same services less expensively.

A final option for control involves special assets needed to do a job. If an asset, such as a particular building, is needed to deliver a service, controlling the building may amount to controlling the service. Although far less complicated than any of the previous models, this approach may be impractical in many circumstances. The exception would be if a nonprofit has an endowment so sizable that it dwarfs even the operating budget. In this case, managing and conserving the principal of the endowment becomes such a massive undertaking that the demands of the operating unit pale in comparison. Some major universities are in this situation.

Advantages of a Management Company

As an organizational model, the management company model is more robust than a simple merger. Among its greatest advantages is its flexibility. It offers single-source management to corporations that could use it but that for a wide variety of reasons may not be practical to meld into a single legal entity. Within the system, one can use a variety of control mechanisms: single corporate membership for three subs, turnkey management contracts for two others, an individualized menu of administrative services with two others, a single paid executive for another, an agreement just to manage the research laboratory for yet another.

Because these arrangements are usually invisible to program services, they can also feed off each other and lead to more (or less) collaboration in the future. The single paid executive may realize through management company meetings that two of the other subsidiaries need her, or the research laboratory management contract might lead to joint grant seeking. To some extent these are exactly the kinds of interdependencies that system planners may have envisioned initially, but it is the creation of a more integrated management environment that actually makes it possible.

The management company model can be expanded almost indefinitely. It will take some time to set up the management capacities needed to run a truly integrated management company/subsidiary relationship—longer in fact than it would take to do an

Note: Toward Truly Integrated Services

Those familiar with corporate America may recognize in these descriptions of the management company model some parallels with the business conglomerates of the 1950s and 1960s. These are the groups for which "The business of business is business," so it did not matter to these owners and managers what business their subsidiaries pursued as long as they were profitable.

The shortsightedness of this strategy later became clear as many of these conglomerates fell apart or spun off some of their companies to be managed closer to home. Nonetheless, twenty-first-century nonprofit entrepreneurs risk duplicating the same mentality on a smaller scale, with equally unsatisfactory results.

The solution is to keep in mind the objective of all this restructuring in the first place: integrated services and better value for society and the immediate consumer. There is no other good reason for creating all these corporate structures, devising suitable control mechanisms, and persuading skeptical boards of directors and anxious staff members to give them a try.

ordinary merger. But once the setup phase is completed, bringing in a new sub should take less time than a merger. The hardest part in that case is likely to be how—or whether—to incorporate the new entity's board of directors into the management company's governance.

A final advantage of a management company is the possibility for preserving local identity. Although there is no reason for changing a successful local identity even in a merger—why change something that is working?—it is easier and less emotionally charged for managers to keep local identities intact with a management company structure.

Disadvantages of a Management Company

There are potentially significant disadvantages in using a management company, starting with the model's complexity. There really has to be enough at stake to justify the high-level restructuring that must be done, with all its accompanying costs and time demands. Most of the time it does not make sense to create a management company–subsidiary relationship for just a few million dollars' worth of programming. Legal and accounting costs alone to set up and manage the relationship may make it cost prohibitive.

The flexibility can also be elusive. Capital may not flow easily from the parent to subsidiaries, as planners may have hoped. (Lenders do not always agree that it should.) Even though it may appear to be a good idea to put all these programs together in a management company merger, it does not mean that the integration will actually happen, especially when the system is created by putting formerly independent entities together. Without good information technology (IT) to support the whole system, it will be hard to realize any gains, and good IT is hard enough to put in place for a single entity, let alone an entire system.

Other, less concrete factors can influence the success of a management company model. Most notably, it may not help integrate programs and services. This is largely a failure of frontline managers to grasp the benefits of moving out of their silos, but it could also come from top executives' singular focus on structure ("form") rather than programs ("function"). And it could actually be an easy way to avoid the hard work of a merger of corporations. Of all the forms of collaboration, the management company structure is the easiest to create by top-down planning: Record a few board votes, design a governance structure, and file the necessary forms.

This tempting prospect can be a short-term victory at the expense of true collaboration in the long term because it violates the principle that nonprofit mergers are planned top down but implemented bottom up. Usually some deterioration begins with the departure of veteran managers for whom the promise of the system gives way to the realities of no support and inadequate strategic management.

How to Recognize a Parent/Subsidiary Corporation Relationship

For those of us interested in this sort of thing, the Internal Revenue Service (IRS) provides a handy way of learning whether a nonprofit is related to any other entity, tax exempt or not. In the old Form 990 (which stopped being used in calendar year 2009 in favor of a new version), the key question can be found on line 80a. (In the new form, the same question is on line 34, with additional disclosures required if there is a related party relationship.) This is where most parent/subsidiary relationships will be disclosed by all of the related entities that file the Form 990, which is the nonprofit world's rough equivalent of the 10-K annual report that publicly-held companies must file.

Faulty Integration in a Management Company Model

Postmerger, integration on just the C level in a management company structure is not enough. The participating corporations should also concentrate on integrating at the O, R, and E levels or much of the promise of collaboration could be lost. In fact, failing to integrate beyond the C level can be a prelude to disaster. Exhibit 12.2 shows an actual multicorporate structure that was hardly integrated below the C level. The shading and pattern combination illustrates which entity performed the functions listed on each line for which corporations. Corporation A was the parent. Corporations B and C were the oldest of the five entities, and they used a large number of the parent's services, but not all. Corporation B insisted on doing its own financial functions; C handled key IT functions on its own; and for a long time Corporation D was actually located in a different physical location altogether. Needless to say, the waste, duplication, and fragmentation in this system was excessive. And Corporation E was not only unintegrated with any of the others; it was actually located in another country.

Function	A	B	C	D	E
SHADING CODE					
Application support					
Technical support					
IT project management					
Call center				NA	
System architecture					
Payroll				NA	
Accounting					
Cash flow					
Reporting					
Asset management					
Facilities management					
Security				NA	

Exhibit 12.2   Multicorporate Integration, Sample of Faulty Integration

This situation came about incrementally over time, as many do. For a variety of reasons, no one caught the severe operational fragmentation, and it caused multiple problems, including rendering the CEO functionally unable to exert her authority over most of what should have been true subsidiary organizations. With weak integration on the C level and insufficient integration on the O, R, and E levels, the CEO had few tools with which to carry out policy. As a result, the organization was far less effective than it could have been. Ultimately, a new CEO followed a policy of integration and improved the multiple corporate entity's effectiveness, but by that time many years and resources had been lost.

Special Considerations

Management company structures seem to work best to vertically integrate organizations or to knit together entities that otherwise might be too different to merge easily into a single entity.

The management company model was made for vertically integrated systems. Its virtues are the reason why most large hospitals-turned-integrated-health-systems are now organized as management companies ("holding companies") with subsidiaries in diverse other lines of service, such as nursing and rehabilitation, home care, and mental health. Their flexible and open-ended nature makes them ideal structures to take on the task of integrating an array of service providers under a single umbrella.

In the nonprofit field, "vertically integrated system" is virtually synonymous with health care. However, in the future, there is every reason for it to include social services, community development, arts organizations, and other types of services. In fact, as of this writing, many such organizations exist all over the country, and there are indications that the recession of 2008 will bring the structure to other parts of the sector. This will expand the model itself. For example, while health care is diversified by services (hospitals, nursing homes, etc.), education is diversified by population (municipalities for public education, nonprofits for special education, universities for adult populations). Integrating services across different types of programs is a different matter from integrating services across populations, and so the management company model itself will expand its definition to accommodate the differences.

13

Models of Collaboration: Alliances

Nonprofits that want the benefits of merger without giving up control should consider alliances. Operating on the three levels of collaboration below Corporate Structure—Operations, Responsibility, and Economics—alliances offer an alternative to a merger. For reasons that will become clear, they are not as well developed conceptually or operationally as are mergers, but there is no doubt that they can offer value in the right circumstances.

Structure

In their early stages, many alliances do not even rise to the level of a defined legal identity; we might more properly call them a state of mind rather than a specific entity. If and when they do take on a recognizable legal shape, it is likely to be determined by legal and financial considerations as much as by anything else. Alliances can take an almost unlimited number of shapes, and for that reason we must use the term "alliances" as a catchall applying to highly formalized structures as well as informal ones. A fully developed alliance may even look like a network of nonprofits, each with its own corporate structure but each participating collectively in one or more common tasks. To more fully describe the options, it might help to categorize alliances as either task oriented or process oriented. The difference is largely one of degree. To the extent that an alliance develops for the purpose of accomplishing a single defined job or series of jobs—for example, to mount a joint orchestra/ chorus performance series—it could be considered a task-oriented alliance. Conversely, if it is put together to have an impact on an ongoing area of management, we would consider it more of a process alliance.

Note: How Much Should an Alliance Cost?

Financially gun-shy nonprofits often want to know the exact cost of a new venture, and an alliance will be no exception. Unfortunately, no widely reliable cost estimates are available because different alliances will try to accomplish different things. However, we can suggest a framework for evaluating the possible costs.

Start with the two types of cash outlays an alliance typically requires: operational costs (consulting fees, studies, legal advice, etc.) and investments. Since an alliance, by definition, is an effort to gain economic or other advantages from bringing together large numbers of organizations, operational costs should generally be modest for all but the largest nonprofits, measured in the thousands and tens of thousands of dollars. This is getting-started money and should be viewed as an expense without any identifiable payback likely.

Sizable cash outlays are the true investments that membership in an alliance may require. The nature of these investments will vary but may range from equipment purchase to leasehold improvements to up-front money for staff or contributed capital in a mutual insurance alliance. These costs ought to be treated just as one would treat costs for any new venture, evaluating the cost versus the anticipated benefit. Keep in mind that some of these outlays will hold their value: Rented space may be able to sublet if the venture does not work out or the special software might be resold to another group. Other outlays could mean wasted funds.

Many groups will also want to hold down certain costs, especially staffing-related ones, by contributing sweat equity—the labor of one's own staff. This works best if there is really no other alternative, or if staff members are asked to operate only within their own comfort zone.

The difference between task alliances and process alliances has to do with future expectations. In the former, there is little expectation that the alliance's life will extend beyond the task at hand. In the process alliance, there is every reason to expect that it will continue as long as it is useful to all parties. Since the orientation is to a process rather than a product or task, there is no telling exactly what path the effort will take.

Confusion over the nature of an alliance is one reason why many of them are so poorly defined and poorly understood. A merger has a distinct beginning, middle, and end. In a task-oriented alliance, one can at least step back at some point and say that the task was accomplished or that it was not. For instance, a four-organization program alliance consisting of funders, technical assistance providers, and intermediary organizations created a task-oriented alliance for the purpose of bringing national collaboration experts together to begin giving greater shape and structure to nonprofit collaborations. Although the work was expected to continue, the explicit goal of the alliance was accomplished when the experts convened.

By contrast, in a process-oriented alliance, it is never truly possible to say that one is past the beginning stages—or that one is at the end. There will always be questions of whether to grow by adding new members, how to adapt to changing external conditions, and the general tasks of maintaining the internal operations of the collaboration. The process, in short, will always continue.

Like mergers, alliances can be either horizontal or vertical. Horizontal alliances are likely to occur among organizations that already know about each other and have something in common, such as a service model. One can even argue that a trade association is a form of alliance, except that a good trade association is usually much more complex, involves more groups, and has broader goals. One of the key characteristics of these types of alliances that may distinguish them from vertical alliances is that they have a more inclusive, almost egalitarian flavor. Based on the premise that more is better, they will rely on economics and signals from the outside world to know when to stop.

Tip: Associations as Hotbeds of Alliances

Attention, associations of nonprofits: There is a role for you as originators of horizontal alliances. Associations have all the advantages needed to encourage the development of what we are calling horizontal alliances: knowledge of participants, access to them, mutual trust, keen awareness of members' operating environments, and public credibility. It may even be possible to make a dollar or two through carefully crafted economic programs, in addition to the fact that it is just the right thing to do.

Vertical alliances tend to grow out of a specific market. They get put together for specific strategic reasons, so they attempt to incorporate participating organizations that support that strategy. They may be large, but they will be far from open-ended. Rather, they will close to new entrants once they have achieved sufficient mass.

What is the difference between a vertical alliance and a vertically integrated merger? To the outsider, probably very little. Whatever the origins and initial intent of collaboration, a vertically integrated merger using a management company model will look very much like a large-scale vertical alliance. To say that participants in an alliance retain corporate control may be functionally irrelevant if half or more of the total referrals are coming from participation in the alliance. Separate governing boards in this instance grant independent authority, but reality suggests otherwise. It is for this reason that some large integrated health care delivery systems can be seen as vertical alliances even though they are in fact the product of mergers.

Control and Governance

Alliances are a good example of the way that management is evolving away from traditional command and control toward a more sophisticated tendency to shape and influence events through collaboration, communication, and consensus. A different way of putting this is that controlling an alliance is like herding cats . . . by cell phone. To the extent that "control" applies to an alliance at all, the term typically refers to things like the structure of the various committees and subcommittees, their composition and size, group agendas, overall pacing, and strategic goals.

Without a specific legal entity in place, controlling an alliance is a political and negotiation-based process. Virtually everything that alliance members do has to be voluntary; to pretend otherwise would be fruitless. The easiest things to agree on tend to be governance matters: Each participant gets one vote, new members must get a certain number of votes to join, and so on. This early-stage formlessness is natural for a new organization, but eventually the alliance may need to choose a more definitive governance process, and it is at this stage that members must make hard choices.

Advantages and Disadvantages

As noted previously, alliances offer many advantages to the nonprofit seeking the benefits of collaboration without giving up control. They offer enormous flexibility plus the power to bring to bear the combined weight of many similar organizations in the service of finding a solution to everyday problems, such as purchasing commodities more cheaply. They also offer a means of involving staff at all levels in productive, nonthreatening collaboration.

Alliances can be a good way to explore formal collaboration as a strategy for the future. There is something reassuring about their strength-through-unity message, and they are quite compatible with the theme of social sharing that many nonprofit managers bring to their work. For managers and boards that are skittish about entering into mergers, alliances can be a good alternative. It is even possible to participate seriously in more than one alliance, as long as one can spare the staff time necessary. It is not hard to imagine a time when the work of some CEOs largely revolves around alliance partners in one way or another.

There are also disadvantages. Done properly, alliances take more time than mergers. Particularly without a formalized, operating legal structure, it is very hard to identify savings and other direct benefits of the collaboration. They can be highly unsatisfying for those who desire a clear-cut beginning, middle, and end to projects (who doesn't?). And the lessons of one alliance are not necessarily easily transferred to another.

14

Models of Collaboration:
Partnerships with and between Nonprofits

Unlike many terms in this chapter, the word "partnership" has a very specific legal meaning. In legal terminology, a partnership is simply an arrangement in which two or more people or entities agree to cooperate in order to achieve some common business goal, in the course of which they agree to share profits and losses.

Tax laws treat partnerships as if they were porous; profit, loss, deduction, credits, and the like simply flow right through the partnership to the partners just as if the partnership did not exist. From that simple formulation comes a wealth of possibilities—and complications.

Two elements of the definition of a partnership are worth noting:

1. *A partnership is not a corporation.* This may seem a trivial distinction, but for legal purposes it is huge. Corporations—nonprofit or for-profit—are treated very differently under the law from partnerships. Everything from tax status to liability law to operations management is different in a true partnership as compared with a corporation.

2. A point that is implicit in the previous definition but is worth highlighting, *partnerships are created for profit, not for charitable purposes.* After a change in the law many years ago, a nonprofit has just as much right to be a partner in a partnership as any other person or legal entity, but the act of forming a

partnership for any purpose is so definitive that there is no point in making it simply an extension of one's preexisting tax exemption. Partnerships are intended to be vehicles for profit.

As legal entities, partnerships are rather curious affairs. To form a partnership, one need do little more than declare the existence of a partnership on paper, then go through the appropriate legal requirements, if any, for starting up a business. Most of the subsequent paperwork produced in the course of a partnership is little more than the formal effort to solve mundane albeit critical operational questions, such as how the partners get paid, what services the partnership will offer, and who can belong to the partnership.

Part of the problem that nonprofits will have in even thinking about partnerships in the context of a collaborative structure is that the word itself already means certain things. There probably is not a state in the nation where the government purchases services from nonprofit corporations and the two entities do not refer to each other as partners at least some of the time. And even the most casual exchange of value between two nonprofits tends to be called a partnership. To complicate matters, partnerships may also be called joint ventures, split operations, alliances, and similar terms.

Note: Partnerships versus Joint Ventures

The difference between a partnership and a joint venture is that a partnership is presumed to be an ongoing relationship, whereas a joint venture is a one-time affair. Tax laws treat joint ventures as partnerships. In practice, joint ventures usually involve blending things such as services or resources, not property. Partnerships are more likely to entail property ownership and maintenance. They can also incur debt, but because of the stickiness of dividing up which partner owns what part of which debt if the partnership were to dissolve, debt is not always a good option for partnerships or joint ventures.

To acknowledge the obvious, we are using the word "partnership" in a very different way from its typical casual application. We do so deliberately. Partnerships in this context are definable legal forms that employ people, pay taxes, take on debt, and do myriad other things characteristic of other types of businesses. They are a bona fide choice for structuring certain collaborations and a sophisticated way of fulfilling complex financial, economic, and legal needs of collaborating nonprofits.

Structure

If the fundamental collaborative nature of partnerships is clear, the permutations of the way partnerships can be structured are almost endless. Provisions for governance, profit sharing, and management can be so different that they effectively create a whole other set of variables in structuring partnerships.

Note: Partnerships 101

Partners may be people, corporations, or other partnerships. Each partner owns at least one interest in the partnership, which is called a unit. There are two types of partners: general and limited. (The terms have to do with the extent and nature of liability for what the partnership does.) Every partnership has to have at least one general partner. There can be more than one general partner, and, if so, one of them is usually designated as the managing general partner. Limited partners get their name from the fact that their liability is limited to the amount of their contribution to the partnership. (Typically the contribution is the same for all limited partners.)

One of the virtues of partnerships is that they can be designed so flexibly. This flexibility can also be a liability if it is not handled properly. The best approach is the form-follows-function philosophy described earlier: Decide what it is that the partnership needs to accomplish, and then figure out how to design it to achieve that result. And be sure to get qualified legal advice along the way.

Control and Governance

Partnerships are notoriously difficult to control, which is why they tend to be better as vehicles for holding property or distributing wealth than as active platforms for operations. If everyone has a piece but no one is in control, there will be no clear line of authority.

If there is no line of authority, then participants in a partnership—even employees—are free agents, able to operate independently. The partnership as an entity has to rely on something economic to unite and shape collective action. That something will have to be gains, such as increased referrals, shared possession of some otherwise unattainable asset, and so forth. The more sharply that goal is defined, the easier it will be to manage the partnership.

Ongoing governance of the partnership will be a challenge. The smartest thing that the nonprofit partners can do is to spell out ahead of time exactly how they will govern themselves. The specific provisions of routine governance can be just about anything as long as everyone agrees to them, they are in writing, and they are reasonably comprehensive.

An often overlooked point is that someday the partnership will end. It may turn into a corporation or some other legal form, or it may just dissolve. It is a good idea to plan for that eventuality from the beginning. Organizational planners call this an exit strategy, and although it may seem unnecessarily pessimistic, it makes a great deal of sense to spell out ahead of time under what conditions and in what way the partnership will end. It makes for smoother transitions, and it forces today's planners to think through the possible implications of today's decisions.

Special Considerations

The preceding material discussed partnerships as if they were always entities created to accommodate the intentions of two or more nonprofits to accomplish a specific collaborative purpose. The reverse is also possible if an existing entity puts together a partnership of nonprofits. Most often this kind of thing happens at the Economic level of the C.O.R.E. model, and it frequently involves a trade association or similar organization. Two examples illustrate the application.

An association of nonprofits realized that the office supply business was highly fragmented, with the bulk of distribution carried out by a lot of very small corner stationery stores supplied by a much smaller number of wholesalers. By uniting its members, the association was able to put together enough business to deal directly with the wholesaler, thereby cutting out that small but expensive last stop. Best of all, the association could receive the same commission that the wholesaler already was accustomed to paying whoever won the accounts of those corner stores. In the eyes of the wholesaler, the association became just another salesperson; in the eyes of its members, it was the source of significant savings.

Does this arrangement sound very similar to Staples, Office Depot, and other mega-stationery supplies distributors? It should, because it is virtually the same model. But this arrangement began in 1982, well before most of today's superstores even grew large enough to sell shares in the company. In a historic context, it is not much of a stretch to see these superstores as today's "partnerships" with the consumer.

Another partnership was put together by a quasi-public authority that had previously concentrated on issuing state government–backed bonds on behalf of hospitals, clinics, and schools. Reading the trend toward deregulation in the electric power industry correctly, the authority set about to take advantage of the trend before it occurred. A year before electric power deregulation was to go into effect in its state, it assembled an impressive group of nonprofits, including but not limited to the organizations for which it had issued bonds, and then issued a request for proposals on the group's behalf to purchase electric power supply contracts.

Again, we note that these models are not partnerships in the precise legal sense of the term. However, they are good illustrations of partnership-like structures that are increasingly intriguing to many nonprofit managers.

Partnerships with For-Profit Companies

Some collaborations will involve for-profit companies. Unburdened by owners and investors demanding yearly dividends and robust stock appreciation, nonprofit organizations have enjoyed a long-standing presumption of moral purity in the marketplace. Although this may be eroding slightly due to well-publicized scandals, the fact is that nonprofits have a reputation in the average citizen's mind for taking action unskewed by narrow profit motives. To suggest that a nonprofit and a for-profit may enter into a true business relationship from which each can profit in ways important to them is still well beyond the comfort zones of most people and many nonprofit managers.

Yet this is exactly what is going to happen in nonprofits' new strategic collaborations. After all, the designation "nonprofit" is a tax status, not a moral state. Even the most rabid ideologues would grant that it is possible for a nonprofit to engage in morally reprehensible behavior just as much as it is possible for a for-profit to hold to the highest ethical standards. And as businesspeople of all kinds begin to understand the flexibility and partnering that will be necessary in the new century's economy, they will start to appreciate the role that a well-managed community nonprofit occasionally can play in their business plans. The result will be an increase in the number of nonprofit/for-profit collaborations and an increase in the numbers of nonprofits and nonprofit alliances that establish at least one for-profit subsidiary.

A side note here: We are not talking about head-to-head competition of the kind that sometimes leads for-profit companies to charge nonprofits with unfair competition. This happens when a nonprofit and a for-profit do the same thing and compete for the same customers, as when a YMCA operates a high-end health club or a research institute develops commercial software. The kind of nonprofit/for-profit collaboration that will occur in the future is the kind that grows from the mutual awareness that each can easily do something the other cannot.

Irony in Partnerships

There is a subtle irony in the whole subject of partnerships. For-profit organizations desiring to enter into some form of partnership are often well advised to create a nonprofit entity, especially if many companies are involved. This is because no one company is likely to fully trust another to act impartially and because each company would prefer not to give the joint organization any incentive to compete with any of them.

Nonprofits, however, would be well advised to create a for-profit entity for three reasons:

1. For-profit structural choices offer true ownership and explicit control options.
2. Ownership shares make the venture easier to shape.
3. Any profit returned to the nonprofit owners typically will be unrestricted since there is no donor or government entity involved.

Of course, nonprofits are unlikely to use for-profit collaboration vehicles extensively because there are multiple social, political, and cultural barriers against the profit motive in nonprofits. Moreover a well-meaning board or senior team could impose various prohibitions or limitations on a partnership. That does not lessen the validity of the idea; it just means that it will not happen as often as it could in a different context.

Mostly, the way nonprofits will get involved with for-profits is through partnerships. We have already seen many partnerships designed as cause-related marketing. (There are moments when Susan G. Komen for the Cure seems destined to turn every major commercial product pink as part of its cause-related marketing efforts.) Doubtless we will see many more, especially with the advent of corporate social responsibility and corporate America's growing comfort with approval by association. How those partnerships will be structured is likely to be determined by the income tax implications for for-profits and unrelated business income tax (UBIT) for nonprofits. Sometimes the nonprofit will want to be the general partner. Here, the acid test is whether a partnership advances its charitable purpose, since the IRS has stated that such partnerships require "close scrutiny" as the first step in its approval process. If the IRS decides that the partnership does advance the charity's tax-exempt mission, it must then decide whether the partnership agreement allows the charity to operate in exclusive furtherance of the mission. Although this may sound like a slight variation on the first test, it is different because certain provisions in a partnership agreement that otherwise advance a charitable purpose may turn out to be in conflict.

Any time an entity becomes a general partner in a partnership, it assumes certain liabilities as well as the responsibility for helping the partnership make a profit. Either one of these demands can lead to conflicts with a nonprofit's tax-exempt mission, so planners must be careful to structure the partnership carefully. As an alternative, the nonprofit can be a limited partner, typically a passive investor. If a college, for example, contributed money to a partnership with a housing developer for off-campus dorms but had no responsibility for day-to-day management, it would get a share of profits but be considered a limited partner.

Partnerships with for-profit companies can take other forms. For instance, nonprofits might lend funds to a for-profit. They can also lease the rights to develop land they own. And because the tax implications of nonprofit/for-profit partnerships can be so complex, they may find the need to create a whole new for-profit subsidiary that will work with the for-profit partner. This strategy can protect the tax status of the nonprofit and make UBIT matters clearer.

Limited Liability Companies

Nonprofits can also use limited liability company (LLC; note the use of the word "company" rather than "corporation") structures. These have become more widespread in the last 15 or so years as federal laws have allowed their formation and state governments have steadily adopted supporting legislation. With limited liability, an investor usually is held to be liable only for the amount of his or her investment. Any lawsuit targets the company, not its shareholders, so the worst that can happen is that a member of an LLC could lose his or her investment in the company, but no more. By contrast, a sole proprietor or a general partner in a partnership is said to have unlimited liability.

LLCs are often more flexible than a traditional corporation. LLC members own the entity in the same way that shareholders own their corporation. Usually the members get to control the entity in the same proportion as their ownership (or "interest") bears to the whole. This provision has a pleasing clarity to it, especially in contrast to other organizational types that permit unlimited liability. LLCs normally have an operating agreement that spells out the exact nature of members' rights. Their attractiveness to nonprofits under certain circumstances is obvious.

In recent years, there has been more innovation with the basic LLC format. One of the most intriguing is the limited liability low-income company, also known as the L3C. This structural choice was explicitly designed to support social enterprise—thus the "low-income" provision. As of this writing, the L3C had been approved in a handful of states, although approval in one state is tantamount to approval in all states since the structure can then be domiciled in one state while operating in another. In truth, the L3C does what a good team of attorneys and accountants can do by carefully writing the terms of an LLC operating agreement, but the check-the-box aspect that state approval gives the vehicle is expected to make it a popular choice for certain types of social enterprises. Doubtless more such experiments will arise in the coming years as our economy keeps at its never-ending task of revising, replacing, and rejuvenating existing business structures.

15

Merger Myths

Mythology permeates most discussions of merger, and now that the reader has covered the merger process in depth, it is time to puncture some myths about it. Of course, the topic of merger gets portrayed in reliably myth-building ways in the media, and few of these myths are reassuring. In the nonprofit sector, the stigma carries over. Considering some of the legendary train wrecks that for-profit mergers have turned out to be, this is understandable. On that basis alone, many people reject them. Yet when myths dominate thinking in place of clear-eyed analysis, decision making gets skewed.

We Will Save Administrative Costs

The most persistent myth about nonprofit mergers is that they will save administrative costs.

Maybe.

Or maybe not.

Many well-meaning outsiders looking in on the nonprofit sector conclude that there are "too many nonprofits" and that there should be a lot of mergers in order to save money. Mostly this myth taps into everyone's shared distaste for spending more money on administrative costs than is absolutely necessary. There is no constituency for wasteful overhead spending, so it is a risk-free proposition.

Let us look at the economic realities of nonprofits' mergers and alliances. The vast majority of nonprofit public charities have revenues barely into six figures, and the majority rarely clear even

$2 million per year. Many pressures keep administrative spending low already, so trimming even a small slice of that amount is a nearly heroic accomplishment. Those entertaining a merger with the primary idea of achieving major administrative savings will almost certainly be disappointed.

More important, any merger whose chief goal is to achieve, say, $20,000 in administrative savings is quickly going to seem like cruel and unusual punishment to those trying to make it happen. At some point they will likely stop, look around, and ask each other, "We're doing all this just to save $20,000?" Better to have a lofty strategic goal and be realistic about administrative savings. What is more likely is that any savings will show up as more bang for the same buck. Only when one of the entities is much larger than the other and has far more established and efficient administrative systems will there likely be significant administrative savings.

There Will Be Massive Job Cuts

The second most pervasive myth about nonprofit mergers is that they lead to massive job losses. This one is largely a carryover from mergers in the for-profit sector and the simplistic media coverage they usually get. Investors generally like mergers, but they dislike the dip in stock prices they can bring. Chief executive officers (CEOs) need to produce a quick offset to the additional cost of the merger, and the fastest way to do that is to lay off staff. The real heart of a merger is pretty unglamorous stuff, but local television news reporters get a ready-made, instantly understandable story, and that becomes the lead. Interestingly, it may be the announcement itself that they are counting on to achieve the effect. One study tracked a year's worth of merger-related job cut announcements from the *Wall Street Journal* and calculated that if all of the announced job cuts had actually happened, the unemployment rate in America during that year would have reached 50 percent.

In the nonprofit sector, there is nothing comparable to investor pressure so there is no inherent pressure to cut jobs. There may be incidental job losses, but any major level of job loss that occurs during a nonprofit merger was probably going to happen anyway. In fact, a merger may actually reduce some of those losses if it promotes more efficient service delivery models.

We Will Lose Our Identity

Of all the merger myths in this sector, this is one of the most persuasive. We have dealt with this question already so we will only touch on it here. For practical purposes, "identity" means "brand," and managing brands is one thing that the nonprofit sector is just beginning to master. In the days when the prevailing nonprofit model was one-corporation-one-site-one-brand, this may have been a legitimate fear. But many nonprofits are learning that it is possible and sometimes even desirable to have multiple brands under the same roof. The decision to merge corporate structures is not the same thing as the decision to merge brands. It just seems that way.

Let Us Figure Out the Structure First

Once the initial exploratory discussions are over, many board members and some CEOs want to jump right into a discussion about a desirable corporate structure. Big mistake. Again, form should follow function. Decide what you want the merger to accomplish and be clear about your shared assessments and desires. Only then is it worth having a discussion about structure.

Shhhh

For-profit mergers are done in secrecy because they have to be. Large amounts of money are often made or lost on swings in stock prices, and there are laws and regulations governing what merger planners can say. Premature disclosures can sink a deal, and unauthorized outsiders (and insiders) are sometimes willing to try to cash in on a tip.

Nonprofit mergers may well have to start out in secrecy for vaguely similar reasons. No nonprofit wants potentially damaging rumors to scare off donors or unnecessarily alarm government funders. And the wrong kind of disclosure can create staff anxiety and even worry consumers.

But if the best nonprofit mergers are decided from the top down, they must be implemented from the bottom up. Owning the company in a for-profit context confers now-hear-this authority, but in the nonprofit sector, authority is diffuse and employee buy-in and goodwill are essential for implementation. Nonprofits can often manage the message effectively to external stakeholders such as donors and even the media. Without the lost-jobs theme, nonprofit

Myth of the Hostile Takeover

Hollywood script writers, novelists, and even local media types love the term "hostile takeover" because it neatly captures the juiciest images of lost autonomy and soul-sapping tension in a merger. Given its enduring place in our collective gallery of awful experiences, it may be a welcome relief to know that there is no such thing as a hostile takeover in the nonprofit world. To execute a hostile takeover of a public company, one has to buy enough of the right kind of stock to ensure control of the company. Since nonprofit organizations cannot issue stock, there is no vehicle to accomplish the same thing.

But it is the logic beyond the impossibility that reveals the important message. If there can be no hostile takeover, it follows that participation in a merger is voluntary. If participation in a nonprofit merger is voluntary, it also follows that each participating organization must see something in the proposed merger that benefits them. And if both participating organizations see benefits to be gained in a merger into which they enter voluntarily, that combination will be stronger than one in which one of the parties is an unwilling participant. Very appropriate for the voluntary sector.

mergers take on less urgency for most media outlets. Even today, when the mainstream media pick up on stories about nonprofit mergers, the treatment tends to paint nonprofits as a monolithic industry, with specific mergers used as illustrations of broad trends rather than as the story itself.

Only Failing Organizations Merge

Ironically, the idea that only failing organizations merge tends to be a self-fulfilling myth. If they do not clearly understand and accept the implications of their financial condition, many struggling nonprofits tend to hold on longer than they should. By the time they are finally ready to consider the idea, it may be too late to salvage the programs. Again, the most constructive use of mergers is not to rescue organizations in trouble—which might be able to be done in other ways—but to strengthen community capacity by building nonprofit organizational strength.

Increase in Mergers Is a Product of an Economic Downturn

Although it is logical to associate the increase in merger activity with the economic downturn, the fact is that many nonprofit resources are currently locked in outdated corporate structures and aging program models. Economic downturns such as those that occured in 2001 and 2008 make mergers seem like a logical choice, but in truth it is only a catalyzing agent for trends that were already under way. In the end, mergers are simply another leadership tool. Reflexive loyalty to unneeded corporate structures or to program models in need of innovation is not a virtue.

It is time to lighten the baggage of mythology.

CHAPTER 16

First Steps

Several distinct characteristics can suggest a compatible collaboration partner. They do not all need to be present for a merger or alliance to work, nor does the absence of all of them predict trouble. However, they can help paint a reliable portrait of a good partner in a successful collaboration. Keep in mind that these charactcristics are described from the perspective of an outsider. If there is a different reality from that first perceived, it will become clear during the due diligence phase of the process.

Geographic Proximity

To appropriate an old saying, "All nonprofits are local." Most nonprofits have a defined geographic focus, and it is often local or perhaps regional. Large national nonprofits usually have local chapters. Fundraising efforts and locally identified services reinforce local identity regardless of where the corporation is chartered. Many boards of directors maintain a fierce commitment to their community. In the past, health care and social service organizations even received government funding according to carefully drawn boundaries. Terms like "catchment area" and "health systems area" are relics of those days that have little or no operating significance today but that nonetheless are consistent with the self-identities of many organizations.

This predisposition to local identification can make collaboration both more likely and more difficult. Local organizations often know each other well, but local rivalries can run deep. Still, the shared experience of a local culture usually builds at least some mutual respect. Geographic proximity also tends to mute the fear that funds raised locally will be siphoned off to assist another locality, which is one of the most common fears of all organizations involved in a merger. On the whole, a common local focus is a strong advantage.

Absence of a Permanent CEO

Without question, the single best catalyst to a nonprofit merger is the absence of a permanent CEO or executive director. In a nonprofit organization, the CEO has almost unparalleled power. In fact, with the possible exception of a self-financed sole proprietor, no other managerial position in the American economy carries the potential for power to such a degree as the nonprofit CEO.

The reasons are complex. Board members serve without pay and cannot hold a stake in the organization. Their chief source of industry-related information will almost always be the CEO who, they are fully aware, spends many more hours each week pondering strategic issues than they can. Lenders rarely assert themselves in internal leadership matters, and there are no stockholders to face. Funding sources tend to be more interested in accountability for funds than for performance, and external watchdog agencies are few in number and concentrate mainly on extreme cases. Within these very broad limits, the CEO has virtually unassailable power to set and maintain strategic direction.

Take that person away, and what does the average nonprofit have left? The answer will vary according to each situation, but, owing to the very personal nature of nonprofit leadership, there will at least be a period of transition before the next leader is comfortably in place. It is during this period that the nonprofit is liable to be most open to new ideas.

With the imminent retirements of baby boomers, there is a precedent in most areas for nonprofit boards to consider merging instead of replacing their CEO, especially when that person is also the founder. This precedent represents a change in just the last few years. Now it is entirely conceivable that an empty CEO's chair will automatically prompt consideration of merger at some point in the future. Note, however, that the situation is reversed for developing an alliance. Since these types of collaboration typically require intact corporate leadership, a CEO transition is the hardest time to initiate an alliance.

Nonoverlapping Markets

A second aspect of a potentially compatible partner is nonoverlapping markets, ideally physically proximate. Although not essential, it is helpful if the partners do not routinely compete with each other. When the competitive hormones have been stimulated regularly over a period of years, it is difficult for misunderstandings and hard feelings not to develop in one or both parties. The obvious way that markets can be nonoverlapping is through geography (see the next paragraph for a detailed discussion of this method), but a more sophisticated segmentation is through services offered.

One three-way merger was actually a kind of 20-year attempt at organizational closure. Three different behavioral health clinics, one each concentrating on children, adults, and the chronically mentally ill, had been part of the same smaller organization many years earlier. Funding source pressure and philosophies of the time had led them to split into three different groups, each operating program sites no more than four miles from each other and in one case actually maintaining headquarters three blocks apart. Although almost none of the original personnel or board members remained, the merger represented a closing of the loop as three distinctly different agencies melded their identities to create a new large service provider.

This is a classic example of how nonoverlapping markets can help the collaboration process. With each clinic focused on a different population, there was little opportunity for the three to collide. In fact, all three groups routinely referred clients to each other in order to achieve a better fit between what the individual needed and what the clinics could provide. Incidentally, this is the same dynamic behind vertical mergers and alliances: Each entity occupies compatible market spaces.

The smaller or more controlled the market, the more likely it is that groups will feel competitive with each other. Government funding often deliberately reinforces an ethic of competitiveness, while a largely foundation-funded sector tends to segment organizations along economic and cultural lines. Long-established services, such as nursing homes or museums, are likely to be quite starkly segmented, while newer services will have more blurred boundaries. These factors can make collaboration easier or more difficult, depending on the individual situation.

Industrializers and Prototypers

The distinction between the two odd words in this section's title gets at a crucial element of commonality or difference. The non-profit sector in the American economy plays an intermediary role. For a variety of reasons, the for-profit sector gets the first chance to respond to a societal need. If it is unable or unwilling to respond, the nonprofit sector is the next choice. For example, when the AIDS crisis first arose in the 1980s, no one knew very much about the scale and intensity of the disease or how to deal with it. The for-profit sector is based on standard buyer/seller relationships, but there was no agreed-on product or service that could be provided (medication had not been developed yet), and no source of money to pay for it anyway. As a result, the nonprofit sector stepped in.

The first step in resolving societal problems is to define the problem; the second step is to come up with solutions. The nonprofit sector excels at devising solutions to local problems (think hospitals, home health care, and credit unions, all of which came out of the nonprofit sector as ways of dealing with local problems). This is the prototype stage of societal response, the virtual social laboratory that grows up around the country as localities struggle to devise workable solutions for shared needs.

Prototyper nonprofits tend to be small, fast-changing, and highly responsive to local expressions of need. This general description also happens to fit the vast majority of nonprofit public charities whose budgets rarely grow far into or beyond the single-digit million-dollar mark. They must constantly figure out how to do the right thing, because that is their job.

As soon as four conditions are met, services can be industrialized, or mass-produced. These four conditions are:

1. An acknowledged social need or problem
2. An accepted response to that need or problem
3. A response that can be replicated and is not dependent on a single heroic founder/CEO or a highly unusual organization
4. Scalability of the response proportionate to the need

This is where it gets interesting. Industrializer nonprofits are a relatively rare phenomenon in the voluntary sector. These organizations have figured out how to deliver large numbers of services at a consistent level of quality. Hospitals and visiting nurse associations are classic nonprofit industrializers. Organizations like these must constantly try to figure out how to do the thing right. But where those four initial conditions have been met, for-profit firms often see an attractive business opportunity and they begin to move in on formerly nonprofit turf. This is why about 15 percent of hospital care today is delivered by a for-profit organization and why most home care is delivered by publicly held companies.

The implications for nonprofit mergers are significant. Combining two organizations is always easier when they resemble each other. Economies of scale are easier to achieve and market share usually improves. Industrializer nonprofits tend to fit both criteria, but prototyper nonprofits do not. The latter tend to be small and unique, so their common points of contact and pathways to understanding are minimal and irregular. Moreover, in prototyper nonprofits, cultural differences seem magnified, and the rewards of a merger are neither clear nor large in scope.

This is one key reason why small nonprofits find it difficult to merge their operations. In addition, small nonprofits—like all small businesses—get treated brutally by the laws of economics. Even if the will to create a merger is present, very often the CEOs are already stretched dangerously thin and cannot afford enough time to devote to the process.

Consequently, industrializer nonprofits typically find it easier to speak the language of merger. The economic rewards in absolute

Tip: Use Zips

One of the quickest ways of determining market and geographic compatibility is to get a list of the zip codes of all current service users from all partners as of the same point in time. Plot the numbers of users from each zip code on a map. (There are inexpensive computer mapping programs for this purpose, though a plain old map from under the driver's seat will work too.) As a rule of thumb, consider the primary market to be the area encompassing approximately 65 to 70 percent of all the zip codes. Put the two primary markets together on the same map. Is there overlap? Is it substantial? Does it represent direct competition or just different ways of serving the same population? The answers to these questions will help determine how compatible the partners will be in these two categories.

terms are higher, and there are more management resources to devote to making the merger a success. This does not mean that prototyper nonprofits should not consider mergers as a legitimate strategic tool. If anything, they may need it more than their larger cousins. But the mountainside tends to be steeper and the challenges more forbidding without the scale that comes with an industrial nonprofit model.

Compatibility of Services

A sensible first step in evaluating a potential partner is to determine how compatible the two sets of services seem. Nonprofits are organized around the delivery of services. Staff members are hired and trained in a certain way, sites are acquired and managed according to particular needs, and the whole administrative and programmatic infrastructure is organized to support those services. None of these things changes easily, and sometimes they do not mix well with another version of the same elements. If you are considering a merger, it is particularly helpful to know ahead of time whether the parties' services are compatible or not.

One useful way of analyzing service compatibility is the idea of core competencies. First articulated by management theorists Gary Hamel and C. K. Prahalad, the notion of core competence is a powerful management tool. Briefly, a core competence is a blend of institutional knowledge and structure that accomplishes a generic task for a market in a unique way. For example, a core competence of a foster care program is the ability to broker relationships. The fundamental core competence of a residential school is hospitality services: food, room, and safety. One of the core competencies of a trade association is information management, and so on.

Pitfall: Premature Disclosure

Though it may seem unnecessarily cloak-and-daggerish, it is usually better to conduct the type of research described here with discretion. Why? One reason is that publicity would be premature: There will be plenty of time for complete disclosure later if collaborating seems to make sense. Another is that it can easily be misinterpreted. Once two parties are identified in the context of seeking a partner, both are likely to be stamped with that perception, no matter how accurate or inaccurate. Premature full disclosure loses more than it gains.

The difficult part about core competencies is that certain major ones can exist in the same entity only with a great deal of effort and managerial self-awareness. The core competence of hospices is palliative care as part of a social model that accepts death as a part of living; home care providers operate in a medical model in which death is a failure. The competencies required for care versus those required for cure are difficult to reconcile on many levels. In the end, there is no substitute for getting inside an organization and seeing its various competencies from the inside out. Until you get a chance to do that, everything else is just informed speculation.

Tip: Beyond Web Sites

As publicly approved and monitored entities, nonprofits must make key types of information readily available, and many do so on their Web sites. Most mandated information is financially based, but it still can be useful for general research, especially by someone who knows how to read and interpret it. Nonprofits must give copies of their IRS Form 990, the nonprofit tax return, to anyone who asks for one, but the Web site Guidestar.org publishes three years of tax returns on each organization for free. In recent years, public charity regulators in some states have been putting audits online. And do not overlook the organization's own marketing material for some insight into how a nonprofit partner presents itself.

Another way to assess a possible partner's services is by the degree to which a merger or alliance would create a fuller continuum of services. Although the notion of a continuum of care started in the health and human services field, where it was initially hastened by the coming of managed care organizations, the principle of a continuum of services is so economically sound and programmatically attractive that it is applicable in fields such as corrections and housing. Payers and users alike are going to insist on seamless integration and a full range of services. When they do so, the only strategic response is to begin putting together groupings of services with natural pathways in between them.

Special Assets

Sometimes the characteristics of a good partner do not fit neatly into one of the listed categories. Sometimes the attractiveness of another nonprofit is not easy to quantify or even to describe. We put these situations into the general category of special assets. These can range from things as common as real estate ownership and endowments to features as abstract as good political connections or a strong entrepreneurial culture. One merger we know of occurred in part because one CEO tired of the day-to-day management demands of the organization he had created and wanted instead to concentrate on his first love, making political connections and doing neighborhood development as the respected president of an organization. For his part, the other CEO was more than happy to slide sideways into a different chief executive officer role since he had long cherished the notion of taking a service delivery system to a higher volume of quality services.

Making the Approach

Not surprisingly, the simple act of suggesting that another nonprofit consider collaboration can be a difficult proposition. Since in many areas of the nonprofit sector, the idea of merger is still synonymous with failure (old ideas die hard), it is possible that the comment might be seen as insulting. The bearer of the suggestion has a lot to do with how it is taken. For this reason, it is usually best to use an intermediary. Finding the right intermediary is the challenge.

The board is a good place to start. One of the bits of homework that often can be done through publicly available sources such as the 990 form is to obtain the list of the board of directors of a potential partner. Particularly in towns, suburbs, and small urban areas, there is a good possibility that one of your board members will know someone on the other board. In that case, initiating a

---

Tip: Your Next Boss Could Be an Alliance

Alliances, once they get formed, often need staff. One of the most intriguing boomlets in the nonprofit field is—and will continue to be—the jobs created by alliances themselves. Obviously there is a great temptation simply to slip excess staff from one of the alliance partners into newly created alliance jobs, but the need for people who can facilitate and get groups working together is so different from the operations-oriented jobs that most employees currently have that this may not work. Future job seekers should keep an eye on alliances.

discussion about aligning in some way might be done over a casual cup of coffee between old friends.

If board-to-board contact does not work, there are always built-in intermediaries, such as auditors and attorneys. Professional advisors often specialize in industries, so there is a good chance that these individuals will know people in the potential partner. One of these professionals might be willing to help out. Funding source representatives may also be able to initiate a contact, although there are enough inherent tensions in the funding source's relationship with its recipients that this can be risky.

Paid intermediaries can serve a useful purpose. These are individuals who act as agents on behalf of one or more nonprofits seeking collaboration partners. Chances are that they will be management consultants of one sort or another. Like all consultant populations, they will probably fit one of two descriptions. The first will be professional, permanent management consultants, either employed by firms or in a sole practice. The second category of consultant will be professionals in between jobs who are simply filling the time until the next full-time permanent role comes along. In the case of alliances, some of these people may even go on to become alliance staff people.

Role of Culture

Culture is stronger than strategy, so it is crucial to understand and be comfortable with a potential partner's organizational culture. Nonprofit organizations start with ideas. Whether the idea is as simple and universally accepted as the notion of educating children or as complex as preserving the artistic heritage of an entire community, the founding idea is the starting point. Eventually that starting idea gets developed into what is more commonly called a mission, and this is what gets communicated formally and informally to leaders, staff, and funding sources.

What carries a mission is values. These are largely implicit statements about what matters to the people associated with the leadership of a nonprofit. Values underlie behavior. If I regard something as important enough to be done, I will organize my behavior in order to get it done. I may not always be successful, but I will try. Similarly, over time, the leadership of a nonprofit will organize it and direct it such that, generally speaking, it will be true to those underlying values. Values are embodied in actions, not spoken words or even written policies. The true values of an organization are the ones that find expression in hundreds of specific actions (or inaction) by many different people every day.

Since many people in a nonprofit must take action reflecting its underlying values every day with little notice or advance preparation, they need some guidance as to the appropriate actions to be taken. The glue that links actions to values is what we call the "organizational culture," and it is here that we see the greatest divergence among nonprofit organizations. It is entirely possible, and in fact it is likely, for groups of people all around the country to recognize the same general need for a specific nonprofit service at about the same time. It is equally probable that their true values will look a lot alike. Where they will diverge is in the ways they make those values work—that is, in the culture that they develop to link values to action.

The culture of a nonprofit invariably begins with the founder and his or her board of directors. Thereafter, the CEO (and other senior executives in a large nonprofit) is the starting point for culture. Everything the CEO does sets the tone for the organization. What this means is that nonprofit culture is normally the one thing on which there is greatest alignment throughout the organization, although it is usually not explicit.

We once worked with two different behavioral health centers that had every reason to merge their organizations. They were located in the same (relatively small) college town within blocks of each other. They each had similar and in some cases identical funding sources. Discussions with board leaders on both sides revealed remarkably similar values; their service area was rooted in Vietnam War–era political philosophy, and a good many of the board members themselves were just entering their personally and professionally productive middle age.

Where these two organizations differed was in their cultures. One was highly focused on what it saw as its public responsibility and related accountability, with former clinicians occupying the top managerial spots. This organization favored traditional means of organizing itself and was noted for the slowness of its strategic reactions. The other was highly entrepreneurial and willing to take risks. Its fiscal performance tended to fluctuate dramatically over the years, and it seemed that management was always consumed with one or another grand plan, such as rescuing a third local entity from bankruptcy and bidding to take over the management of an inpatient psychiatric unit in the local hospital even though no one had asked it to do so.

The differences in management style were reflected in differences at the board level. There were explicit concerns about being able to "trust" the entrepreneurial chief executive officer who, thanks to the other CEO's retirement, was slated to become the CEO of the merged entity. These frictions were compounded by the fact that the entrepreneurial nonprofit clearly had the better management talent in place. The merger occurred, but blending the two cultures was not easy. Years later, the more traditional nonprofit's core board members still expressed tensions and dissatisfactions.

Cultural differences between organizations considering collaboration need explicit and sustained attention. Some researchers suggest that as many as 75 percent of hospital mergers fail if cultural issues are not taken into consideration. One of the most reliable rules of thumb for postmerger implementation is that *the tighter culture always prevails*. The culture of the larger organization will not automatically dominate, and the loudest or flashiest culture will not always carry forward. Rather, it is the stronger culture with the most viable ways of transmitting it that will eventually color the newly merged organization.

Role of Class

A major subcategory of cultural considerations are the differences rooted in socioeconomic class. In many ways, economic class issues are woven into the very mission of nonprofit organizations. Civic symphonies require large numbers of people schooled in western classical music, and they therefore tend to attract the middle- and upper-class participants who are most likely to have been exposed to it. Conversely, grassroots organizations inevitably take on the socioeconomic character of the geographic locale they seek to serve.

In view of nonprofits' role as carriers of values, this dynamic should be no surprise. It becomes problematic mainly when it is not recognized and incorporated into planning the collaboration. Often, unrecognized class and unacknowledged ethnic differences are the real driver behind a lingering feeling of us versus them.

Most observers of the evolution of nonprofits in the past few decades seem to agree that the character of boards has changed from small clusters of social elites united by common culture and values to larger and more diverse groups of people who have more ideas than relationships in common. This trend derives from the general tendency of the current American elite to be created not so much from social position as from cognitive accomplishment.

An enduring if subtle dynamic in mergers—less so in alliances—is that people in every position, from board to staff, who most readily identify with the class-related aspects of the service will have the hardest time accepting a potential partner who does not share the same characteristics. One nurse who worked in a medical-surgical unit of a hospital about to be merged with another put it bluntly: "We get a lot of our referrals from suburban doctors and clinics. They [the other hospital] get most of their referrals from the city. There's no way that any of our patients is going to be willing to wake up from surgery next to a crack cocaine addict." While this theoretical possibility could not be discounted, the real message of this statement was the speaker's own personal discomfort.

Another dynamic in mergers that can complicate the process is that board members may very well have a different class perspective from employees. In large nonprofits, board members probably will have more in common socioeconomically with management than with the majority of people who work for the organization. For this reason, they are liable to see major issues—including the need for a merger itself—very differently. Again, the solution is to recognize these differences from the beginning and to incorporate them into planning. One of the advantages of the Collaboration Committee/subcommittee structure described in Chapter 18 is that it helps mitigate the effects of cultural differences.

Pitfall: Do Not Confuse Culture with Governance

Culture is not the same thing as governance. Cultural issues typically are resolved long before governance matters arise. In fact, the tendency of a nonprofit to homogenize its value set is what frequently reduces matters of governance to a series of lopsided votes. In a merger of two strong and healthy agencies, questions of governance will be far less contentious if the organizational values are compatible.

Quick Culture Check

Superficially, it is relatively easy to find out about a nonprofit partner's corporate culture: Just ask around. Rarely does informed
public opinion completely misread an organization's culture. It may
be a bit dated because there has not been time for it to catch up to
the effects of a major change, such as the departure of the CEO,
but in general it will be reliable. Skilled analysts will also find evidence of culture in the large amounts of information on the public
record about most nonprofits. Tax returns are available for the asking,
and some states keep copies on file for public inspection. Bond
prospectus documents, when available, make for tedious but enormously useful reading. Even marketing material, when read carefully, can provide strong clues as to what an organization's culture is
all about.

Tip: Where to See Organizational Culture at Work

There are many good places to look for evidence of a nonprofit's culture. The
key is to look in as many as possible and to assemble what you find into a coher-
ent portrait of the organization. Not every one of these places will yield insight,
and some will contradict others, but overall the list represents a usable road
map to the nature of the culture. In alphabetical order, here they are:

Composition of board and management team
Degree of centralization versus decentralization
Demographics of clients
Demographics of staff
Financial investment policies
Financial performance
Geographic location
Management compensation policies
Marketing materials
Number and type of management meetings
Number of board meetings per year
Philosophy regarding staff turnover
Process for recruiting and selecting new board members
Requirements of major funding sources
Size of board
Size of management team (especially versus comparable nonprofits)
Unwritten/unspoken hiring preferences

Once a discussion is under way, valuable bits of information can be picked up from a review of the areas described earlier. For a fast gauge of the potential partner's culture, try another approach. Engage the chief executive officer and a few key board members in a discussion, explicit or not, of the organization's last three major decisions. How were the issues framed? By whom? At what point in the decision-making process? How was the decision finally made, or was it never made at all? Once made, how was the decision communicated?

All of these questions will help get at the nature of the decision-making process in the organization and will reveal a great deal about its values. For example, the issues that various respondents choose as the three most important ones and the degree of consistency among them will say something about the organization's culture. In the end, however, a judgment about organizational culture is just that: a judgment. All participants in a collaboration must make their own assessment of a potential partner's organizational culture and use it as the basis for future action.

Building Trust

Trust is easily the most underrated economic force in our society. Acts as simple as hiring a nonfamily member—someone who until recently was probably a complete stranger—and giving him or her control of assets and paying the person money in return for future results are things we take for granted, but they are at the heart of developed countries' industrial and postindustrial economies. Nonprofits, of course, hold it as a virtue to operate outside of the family business mode. To do otherwise would invite mistrust and perhaps risk violating the law.

Nonprofits are hothouses for trust. The Internal Revenue Service grants them nonprofit status and rarely attempts to second-guess the exemption unless prompted to do so. Funding sources give public charities money without the protection of a contract. Community leaders trust that nonprofits are doing something for the larger good. Boards of directors trust management to execute decisions in line with a larger vision. And so on. It is no exaggeration to say that the entire fabric of nonprofit organizations, more so than any other private entities, is based largely on an intricate web of trusting relationships.

Seeds of Trust: Disclosure, Consultation, and Collaboration

When two or more nonprofit organizations decide to form some kind of strategic alliance, creating an atmosphere of trust is absolutely essential. As described earlier, carefully selecting a potential partner can lay the groundwork for trust to grow, but organizations interested in forming any kind of collaboration can do things to accelerate the process.

Tip: It Is Not Just a Matter of Being Nice

Saying that trust is all-important is not just a knee-jerk vote for motherhood, apple pie, and playful puppies. It is also easier. When the parties share a high degree of trust, their process will be free of much of the time-wasting digressions, requests for clarification, and misunderstanding that thrive on mistrust. Think of trust as a cheap productivity tool.

Disclosure

The first step in building trust is disclosure. Nonprofit corporations operate in an environment of public accountability, a big part of which is the routine disclosure of information that in a privately held for-profit company environment would be unthinkable. Shrewd leaders make this high level of built-in scrutiny work for them, but some try to act as if they have no responsibility to the public. Needless to say, they are not good candidates for collaboration.

Disclosure is necessary throughout the process of collaborating but is pivotal at two distinct times. The first is early on in the process, when both parties are first contemplating a merger or alliance. The second point is when the parties conduct what is known as a due diligence investigation after they have decided to pursue a collaboration but before it has taken serious shape. We elaborate on the due diligence process in Chapter 18. Now we focus on early disclosure.

Disclosure early in a merger—disclosure has greater legal weight in a merger than in an alliance—is largely an informal matter. Board members who meet to talk in broad terms about "getting together" should engage in it, as well as CEOs who play the same role. All parties need a reliable thumbnail sketch of the other to use in future discussions, and it should amount to a balanced portrait of the organization.

What should be disclosed? How detailed does one have to get? What things should be disclosed early in the process? Use what in other contexts is called a "materiality standard": If a reasonable person would make a different decision had he or she known a particular fact, then it should be considered a material fact and should be disclosed. In this stage, it helps to get agreement on a set of common operating principles—for example, "We will disclose to the other organization any intention to hire a new executive no less than four weeks before we select a candidate."

Consultation

Once two or more organizations have decided to form some sort of merger or alliance, they need to know that they will always have the most up-to-date information about their partner or partners. The simplest way to know this is to agree ahead of time—verbally *and* in writing—that no major decisions will be made without the other party's knowledge.

This is a proposition best agreed on early in the process. In many areas where nonprofits are involved, the pace of change is unusually fast, and it may not take long for a major change to occur in one of the partners. Being so close to the issue, managers do not always recognize the implications of a decision or an external development. We were once working on an alliance between several elder care organizations. Unknown to most of us, one of the participants was also in discussions with a new and rapidly integrating health care network. When the participating organization made a long-term commitment to the larger network and announced it in a meeting, the confusion was palpable and took a while to resolve.

Collaboration

Unlike the previous two principles, collaboration is less a functional necessity and more a symbolic one. In some ways, it does not matter exactly how the parties collaborate as long as they do. Note that we are using the word "collaboration" here on a somewhat less grand scale than usual, meaning cooperation around the daily demands

Tip: When to Consult

It is a good idea to spell out exactly what the parties agree to consult each other about during the process of a merger. Here are some possibilities (not an exhaustive list):

- Board of directors' role or composition changes
- Changes in accreditation status
- Changes in major leases
- Changes in office or program site space
- Collective bargaining status
- Insurance coverage lapses
- Major asset acquisition or disposal plans
- Major media attention planned or anticipated
- Major new positions being added
- Management changes of any material kind
- New programs or services
- Planned borrowing activity
- Plans to submit proposals/new revenues received
- Possible or actual litigation
- Public processes anticipated (e.g., license renewals)
- Significant budget variances
- Unmet tax liabilities

of management. Everybody likes a little help to get the job done, and a prospective merger or alliance partner is nicely positioned to offer uniquely valuable help.

Two of the easiest and quickest ways to get into the collaboration frame of mind involve human resource management. One is to share job postings. Simply being sure to send notices of open jobs to the other organization is a good way to build goodwill, signal that the prospective alliance is real, and possibly gain a good staff member or two in the process. Even "losing" a staff member this way can be a win if it places a friend in the ranks of the other group.

Another way to collaborate on a person-to-person level is to seek joint opportunities for staff development. This can be as simple as arranging cross-organization carpools to conferences or as complex as mounting a joint training program.

Premerger Agreements

Put all of the preceding into a premerger agreement. Not to be confused with the final merger agreement, a premerger agreement acts as a formal kick-off to the merger or alliance-building process. (It tends to be more useful for mergers than for alliances, since most alliances do not change corporate structure.) Other terms for this kind of document include memorandum of understanding (MOU) or a memorandum of agreement (MOA). Although such a document is not always essential, it will spell out a framework for mutual learning and collaboration. Generally, the larger and more complex the organization, in alliances involving some type of nonprofit/for-profit combination, the more a premerger agreement will be necessary. The premerger agreement will acknowledge that the signatories plan some form of collaboration, and it will describe the responsibilities and roles each will have. If confidentiality is a concern, the premerger agreement will detail what is expected of the parties, especially if the process does not result in any formal collaboration.

Use a Nondisclosure Agreement

Although it may seem contradictory to speak about trust and then suggest that parties sign agreements not to disclose sensitive information about the other, nondisclosure agreements (NDAs) have the advantage of being tools tailored for collaboration. NDAs spell out the circumstances under which the information gained can be used. Signed on an individual level, the NDA is most effective when it is sought before sensitive information is disclosed. The legal strength of any one NDA may be debatable, but when used in the context of some the previously discussed tools, it helps make the point that the two organizations are engaged in a sensitive undertaking that needs to be treated accordingly.

CHAPTER

17

Merger or Alliance? How to Decide

In structuring nonprofit mergers and alliances, form should follow function. In practice, participants almost always know going in
whether they are more likely to attempt a merger or an alliance,
even if they did not work through the logic in a formalized way. In
part, this is because most planners either intuitively understand
that a merger has the broad power to change so many things in
the participating organizations or they were specifically interested
in achieving only the kind of focused goals an alliance can provide.
The reasons for choosing a merger or an alliance need not be
expressed in complicated language or legal terminology. They may
not ever be explicitly summarized in a sentence or two, but instead
may exist as a collection of shared understandings and objectives
that most participants would cite independently if asked to list their
joint goals. Either way, there are several elements that go into deciding whether to attempt a merger or an alliance, and it is worth taking
up each in turn.

But before considering these elements, it is important to acknowledge the confusion that many may feel when trying to analyze
the difference in "connectedness" of a large multicorporate structure compared to an alliance. These large systems knit together
diverse types of programs and services in a sometimes dizzying array
of corporate structures that seem to have little in common other
than a shared name, if that. Casual observers may well ask what is
the true difference between a merger and an alliance.

The answer lies in the nature of authority in the multistructure
merger versus the alliance. A line of authority will stretch throughout a

properly constructed multicorporate structure, whereas authority in an alliance will always be diffuse. What seems to the casual observer to be diffuse authority in a large multiple corporate structure entity is really more of a reflection of its larger scale and greater complexity. Inevitably, as an entity grows in size and complexity, the bonds between identifiable parts of the whole tend to weaken. Microsoft as an international corporation cannot be as tightly controlled as it undoubtedly was when it was a ten-person start-up. But that does not mean that the component parts are not connected as tightly as the law allows.

The topics in this chapter suggest some of the common influences on choice of structure. The list is not intended to be comprehensive. Generic factors quickly give way to very specific circumstances that will not always fit neatly into one of the listed categories. Nevertheless, these elements should cover a large number of the key factors nonprofits will consider when deciding how to organize their collaboration. When they fall short of describing a specific situation, they may be of some use by stimulating thinking about the factors that do matter.

Corporate Control

Without a doubt, the pivotal factor shaping the choice of structure in a nonprofit collaboration is the nature of corporate control desired. The term "control" here refers to actions taken at the corporate level in the C.O.R.E. model. In our framework, whoever has responsibility for corporate actions in an organization has corporate control. In freestanding nonprofits, this means that control is shared by the board of directors, the chief executive officer (CEO), and a management team, if one exists. In our model, *if the focal point of Corporate Structure changes as the result of a collaboration, a merger can be said to have occurred.* If change occurs only at the Economic, Responsibility, or Operations levels, it is an alliance (or affiliation). Mergers are about the transfer of the locus of control.

This question of what happens at the corporate level is behind most discussions about structure in a nonprofit collaboration. We are talking only about the legal and systemic levers of control here, the provisions in the by-laws and similar documents that set out who is responsible for what and how they exercise their control. A strong CEO or board of directors can effectively exert more control than they are given on paper, but that is more of an interpersonal quirk not supported by the underlying legal structure.

For-profit mergers tend to focus a great deal on the structural aspects of management control, such as stock ownership, voting rights, and board composition. Management control comes from these things almost automatically. In nonprofits, by contrast, there are fewer structural sources of control, and they function more to facilitate the emergence of leadership than to define it.

What all of this means in plain English is that leadership positions in a nonprofit are not transferable. If I own a big block of stock in a for-profit company that has merged with a comparable-size firm, I will still have a significant economic interest in the merged entity, though it will be diluted; if I were the single largest stockholder in the original firm, I may even be the single largest stockholder in the merged one. Not so with nonprofits, because there is no universally recognized means for transferring interests. Depending on how things go, I may not even have a role in the new organization.

This is why corporate control is so critical to nonprofits considering a collaboration, and why they are reluctant to give it up. It is not so much that boards and management cling to specific corporate vehicles—if asked, for technical legal reasons, to close down a corporation that had run a respected museum for 50 years and immediately replace it with another new corporation with the same name, most would not hesitate—but rather that they recognize intuitively that their interests are wrapped up in the existing set of relationships and legal structure.

This dynamic also explains why the idea of an alliance rather than a merger can be so attractive to many nonprofit managers and their boards. For this reason, this next wave of mergers in many parts of the nonprofit sector will undoubtedly include a significant number of alliances. The impulse to retain control of the corporate vehicle is strong enough that some creative energy may be devoted to devising brand-new ways of knitting organizations closer together without transferring corporate control. We explore some models of alliances in Chapter 21, as well as some of the techniques for ensuring control.

A final note on management control in nonprofit organizations. We have stated that the essential difference between a merger and an alliance is whether the locus of corporate control shifts to another entity. But at some point, the distinction grows murky. For example, do we call a collaboration whose members are integrated at the Economic, Responsibility, and Operations level and who share a minor number of key board members a merger or an alliance? Technically, this is still just an alliance no matter how much functional control those common board members really possess. Sharing only a board member or two should make it an alliance, albeit a tight one. But if the common board members are a majority in both entities, it is a merger.

Certain faith-based health care facilities in many parts of the country are already in this murky zone. Any two of their nonprofit provider organizations may share only a single board member and may feel and act as if they were independent of the religion's authority. But when that single board member is a major figure in the faith, the control issue gets muddied. Moreover, there are nuances and gradations in corporate control. Casting a board of directors' tasks as subservient ("advisory") to another group is a clear message that will probably be heeded, even if the actual structure does not support it. Conversely, the regular physical presence of a senior religious leader as a board member of a subsidiary corporation may be enough to tip the balance of power regularly in that direction.

Speed

Without doubt, mergers are faster to design and implement than alliances. In purely legal terms, a merger can be done by filling out a few forms and filing them with the appropriate authorities. With the correct signatures from board members and other responsible parties, the merger can be done in a matter of days or weeks—on paper. Securing the practical advantages of a merger takes a lot longer. Of course, in the absence of a valid and compelling push from the outside—and it is hard to imagine what that would look like—speed should not be a major consideration in entering a collaboration anyway. Mergers and alliances are really nothing more than operations planning exercises, and haste rarely improves planning.

Corporate Independence

If corporate independence is strongly valued by participants, they have little choice but to try to create an alliance. As noted previously, carefully designed and managed alliances can give participants some of the benefits below the Corporate Structure level in the C.O.R.E. model that mergers can offer. They can save money, do administrative chores more efficiently, and work closely on programs. What alliances will not do is break down the insularity of the corporate vehicles. Participants still will be individually governed, legal and fiduciary responsibility for operational results will remain with each entity, and alliance members still will have a separate identity.

Is this desirable? The simple answer is that it is desirable if participants feel it is. From a systems perspective, there are too many nonprofit agencies in fields such as health and human services. There are valid historical and legal reasons for this situation, but nonetheless it is increasingly an accepted fact in many parts of the country. There are also many reasons to believe that reducing the numbers of nonprofits will make the field as a whole stronger.

Still, people and organizations show a strong attachment to the modern fiction known as a corporation, especially when it is *theirs*. And mergers as a strategic choice are still not well enough known or understood in the nonprofit field. Worse, the process itself has been thoroughly discredited by excesses and shortsighted blunders in the for-profit world. The result is that merging is not often considered a desirable or healthy option for most nonprofits.

In this conceptual vacuum, alliances can play a major role. Ultimately, some alliances will prove to be the warm-up phase to a multi-party merger. Others will help restructure everyday ways of delivering services while still others will serve to increase trust and a sense of bondedness among participants. And, yes, some will be fleeting. But whatever their accomplishments or lack thereof, the form of collaboration we are calling an alliance will have provided an important and irreplaceable bridge to the new generation of service delivery systems.

Management Flexibility

The manager thinks: "Funding source regulations. State laws. Federal oversight. Labor laws. Employment taxes. Inspectors. With all the requirements I have to watch out for, I can barely move. Give me flexibility."

The various funding sources and inspectors think: "We are giving these nonprofits a lot of money and responsibility. We have to make sure they do a good job."

Where you stand is where you sit, as the old saying goes. Flexibility is the deepest operations wish of most nonprofit managers, and when they look at a potential merger, they see the possibility of bigger operations and less flexibility. This is understandable, but while we know that there is such a thing as being too small to carry out a mission, we really do not know if there is such a thing as being too large.

Some managers always will look at a potential merger and see the danger of creating an encrusted bureaucracy that is twice as large and three times as hard to move as either of the previous partners was separately. This may be more an emotional statement than a supportable fear. The rugged individualism that characterizes so many managers of small nonprofits—often cloaked in more acceptable terms, such as grassroots activism or lack of money—frequently comes with an abhorrence of (others') bureaucracy. With more than 95 percent of all nonprofits tallying less than $25 million in revenue, the truth is that very few nonprofits have even a vague chance of developing truly bloated bureaucracies. Most of the time what this fear expresses is both a worry that the organization will grow disconnected from its founding community's needs and the more subtle fear that current managers will not know how to manage the newly enlarged organization. In particular, the fear is that supervisors will gravitate to the distrusted "corporate" characteristics of a large entity that attracted many employees to a small organization in the first place.

The kind of flexibility that managers initially desire in a collaboration is not really to help them do things proactively and respond to new opportunities so much as it is to help them avoid entanglements. Some of those possible entanglements will be described later. It is usually only after a while that management (and then their boards) begin to see the proactive benefits of the collaboration if it is designed with maximum flexibility.

For example, at first the management services company model may seem to offer mainly a solution to tricky questions involving a merger between two organizations. Only if managers look beyond the terms of the immediate collaboration will they see that the model could also incorporate a third, fourth, or even tenth organization and that there are no logical reasons for stopping at managing just two.

Antitrust

Sophisticated managers and board members may have concerns about violating antitrust laws when considering either a merger or an alliance. In most cases, this concern will dissipate when the facts are analyzed. Antitrust regulation is intended to prevent suppliers from gaining unfair advantage over buyers. If otherwise independent businesses representing a significant portion of a market could agree on the amount of services to be delivered, their cost, and the means of marketing them to the public, those businesses would hold virtually all important means of control and thus an unfair advantage.

Most antitrust action in areas where nonprofits are active has occurred in the health care field, particularly hospitals. The federal Department of Justice and the Federal Trade Commission each have responsibility for antitrust enforcement, but large service providers or those who have reason to believe that their collaboration may involve possible antitrust violations will want to conduct their own preliminary analysis.

Significantly, federal authorities have challenged only a small fraction of all hospital mergers. The rate at which they object to proposed mergers fluctuates with the political convictions of those holding federal office, so there can be fairly dramatic deviations from administration to administration.

Tip: What Regulators Want

Antitrust regulators showed what they expect in nonprofit mergers in a case in Florida. Three hospitals in the Tampa-Clearwater area, two of which had already created a single health care system, engaged a consulting team to analyze potential savings from a merger. The results suggested possible savings of $80 million over five years, and the institutions decided to go ahead with a merger.

Antitrust officials saw it differently. Noting that the three hospitals were among the 4 or 5 largest in the 17-hospital market, they argued that the collaboration would unwisely diminish competition. An intense legal battle ensued, and its resolution created a strange three-headed creature.

Accepting the economies-of-scale argument, the legal solution was to allow the hospitals to collaborate fully on joint purchasing and other economic strategies. However, in order to preserve competition, the three institutions were forbidden to market jointly or share information about contracting and pricing strategies with managed care organizations. This Solomon-like compromise was by no means ideal, but it at least allowed the collaboration to proceed. It also created a living, operating monument to antitrust theory.

Collective Bargaining

Collective bargaining matters, the most volatile topic in any merger other than those concerning who will lead the new entity, can threaten to derail the entire process. Even in situations where union issues are not unusually intense, the whole subject of labor unions is so emotionally laden and operationally complex that it can be a constant source of anxiety.

Let us wade directly into these dangerously swirling waters. The reason labor unions pose such a problem for many nonprofit administrators is rarely discussed directly, but it goes like this. Labor unions have historically drawn most of their political support from the left. Many nonprofit administrators, especially those who began their careers in the 1960s and 1970s, have distinctly leftward political leanings themselves.

Superficially, there would seem to be a fair amount of common ground here. However, on the whole, nonprofit administrators are a resolutely individualist lot. One of the reasons they may have gotten into the field was for the opportunity to make a large difference on the strength of their own ideals and hard work. Unions, however, must draw their power from collective action. So the 1960s advocate-turned-nonprofit-administrator who is thwarted by the twenty-first-century labor union not only loses on a management question but may easily feel like he or she is betraying the values that brought him or her into the field in the first place. The fact that labor negotiations take place on the dual levels of operations and ideology accounts for the ambivalence and unpredictability of some nonprofit managers in dealing with their unions. By contrast, for-profit managers are not likely to feel the same conflicts and so will tend to be more straightforward and "businesslike."

Wading deeper, we turn to another delicate subject. Ask any nonprofit manager to assess the effects of a union on their organization, and at least two themes will probably emerge. The first is that the existence of the union limits organizational creativity and flexibility and that this fact alone is frustrating even if relations with the union itself are positive. The second theme may not be explicitly stated but rather embedded in anecdotes and casual remarks. It is that the existence of the union, in some curious ways, actually makes the managers' jobs easier. That is, because it so precisely defines so many aspects of the employer-employee relationship, the union environment removes a great deal of the usual messy guesswork associated with managing people. Needless to say, this is another source of ambivalence for managers, since it offers the short-term gain of reduced aggravation in return for the probable long-term loss of creativity and flexibility.

Now at the deepest point of this dangerous water, we take up the immunization that many nonprofits have against union actions. Just like the nonprofits they sometimes seek to organize, unions are businesses, and they have to operate by the same laws of economics as any other business. To organize a bargaining unit, a union must incur what is effectively a series of fixed costs. It needs some level of union staff to handle day-to-day matters, and it must fund its own administrative functions. Elections, when they occur, also cost money. So does organizing the unit to get it into the union in the first place. Legal advice in tricky situations represents another type of fixed cost. The result is that unions have little economic incentive to organize undersize bargaining units. That fact suggests that the vast majority of nonprofits are not likely to be desirable targets for union organizing.

At the same time, these are not absolute barriers to organizing a small nonprofit. Any union may decide for a variety of reasons to serve a small nonprofit employer, and in recent years unions generally have begun to recognize the organizing potential of the nonprofit sector. Also, there are often union-friendly legislative proposals on a state or federal basis, depending on the prevailing direction of the political winds.

Nonprofit mergers will often turn on questions of collective bargaining. Predictably, when a unionized entity and a nonunionized entity are discussing a merger, the latter will feel uneasy. It will perceive the union shop as almost tainted, worry that the union will "take over" management in the new entity, and privately wonder about the unionized entity's competence if it allowed a union to organize its employees.

For boards and management harboring these feelings about a unionized organization, we offer this advice: *Get over it.* Unions are a fact of life in many areas of nonprofit management, especially since traditional areas of union organizing, such as manufacturing, are shrinking and being replaced by public and nonprofit targets. Unions cannot be wished away, they are not entirely bad things, and most bargaining units are amenable to open, honest, and firm management negotiations.

The most important thing that nonunion personnel can do is to begin discussions with a clear set of expectations. Boards of directors and management personnel with no union experience tend to enter into merger negotiations with a unionized counterpart secretly hoping that the union will somehow go away. This is highly unlikely. Even under the most peaceful and stable of circumstances, labor unions do not typically decertify (dissolve) themselves. Once a merger discussion is announced, the resultant uncertainty and ambivalence is, if anything, likely to drive employees closer to their union.

Part of the reality that a nonunionized organization has to accept is that as soon as the merger talks are public knowledge, there will likely be a union organizing drive among its own employees. Representatives of the organized entity's union will interpret the merger discussions as an open door to the other organization. Even if there is no formal drive, it would be wise to assume that informal organizing will begin as early as a few hours after the merger is public knowledge.

Collective bargaining considerations can shape structure in subtle and not so subtle ways. The principal way this happens is through what might be called compartmentalization. In most cases, employers are organized by work site. Simply because one program in one city is organized by a specific union does not mean that a different program run by the same organization in a different city will be organized too. This puts up a substantial barrier to easy organization, but it also means that there can be no smooth exchange of unionized and nonunionized employees such as may be desired between different campuses of the same nonprofit testing lab.

The impulse to compartmentalize union employees in a certain site or sites may also lead managers to consider some form of alliance rather than a merger. Although the informal channels of communication and therefore potential union organizing are still open in an alliance, the lack of corporate unity will impede full-scale organizing. Since ultimate corporate control remains in different hands in an alliance, unionization of the nonunion shop is not a foregone conclusion.

If managers need to be free to move employees from site to site, however, they may be well advised—at least theoretically—to choose a full merger under a single board and CEO. The reason is that one generally cannot mix union and nonunion employees in the same job classification at the same site. When all employees are unionized, they are subject to the control of the single employer. However, union contracts often include provisions prohibiting management from reassigning employees to different sites, so in practical terms, this advantage may be neutralized.

Nonunionized management and boards would be well advised to seek out an experienced labor attorney if for no other reason than simply to act as a sounding board and resource. Not only is there a large body of laws, regulations, and policies in this field, there are numerous practices and policies that only a specialist knows. For example, the National Labor Relations Board (NLRB) is frequently called on to arbitrate disputes or advise on areas of employer-employee relations. Like any large organization, in some types of disputes the NLRB tends to behave predictably; in others it does not. Even the knowledge of whether one's case is on a well-worn path or if it could be precedent setting is useful and can come only from a specialist. Their advice can be worth many times their fee.

Liability

Nonprofits often enjoy an unusual degree of protection from liability laws, and preserving that advantage can shape the structure of a collaboration. Often the protection goes away if the tax-exempt entity engages in commercial activity within its own corporate structure or as part of a related entity's structure. This is one of the reasons why substantial amounts of for-profit activity are almost always carried on via a separate corporate entity.

Geography

Related to both liability and reimbursement, geographic considerations greatly shape collaborative structure. Many nonprofits doing business in another state—and sometimes even in another city—will find it advantageous to form a separate corporation. Two nonprofits from different states contemplating a merger may actually find it preferable to keep the two companies intact and use other ways of linking them.

Reimbursement

It will come as no surprise to veteran nonprofit managers that reimbursement considerations play a major role in just about everything that some nonprofits do. Reimbursement regulations from government sources for health and human services are particularly detailed and actually can play a role in determining corporate structure. For example, Medicare pays for home care services on a fairly strict cost-of-service basis. The only way to financially justify expanding services into Medicare populations, therefore, is to charge a share of overhead costs currently being paid by other sources to the new Medicare services. The effect of this move is to free up monies that otherwise would have been spent elsewhere. The cleanest and most acceptable way of shifting overhead costs in this way may be to establish a separate Medicare-only corporation.

Foundation grant makers in the arts and education may be reluctant to support for-profit activity, such as a museum gift shop. Government sources, especially state governments, can be especially swift about scooping dollars generated through other sources in order to reduce their own costs. Both of these practices are frustrating for nonprofits that compete for private revenue sources and may lead to the creation of separate corporations.

Management Clarity

One of the secondary benefits of different corporate structures is that often it makes keeping track of things easier. If the symphony orchestra is run out of the symphony orchestra corporation and the newly merged youth symphony is run from an entirely separate corporate structure, the job of keeping separate operations is much easier. Of course, it is possible to overdo this notion and to erect undesirable administrative barriers between the entities. Merger participants need to think through the implications of keeping separate corporate structures and decide whether the benefits outweigh the costs.

Bond Covenants

When large nonprofits need to raise capital for a construction project, they typically float a bond. Investors purchase the bonds in return for a steady stream of interest income over the next several years, and they also insist on certain conditions. Those conditions will vary according to each borrower, and they are written into the terms of the borrowing. Consequently, bond-based covenants can have a significant effect on everything from the merger's corporate structure to whether the organization can merge at all. Management staff members involved in the bond issue tend to remember such covenants in detail, but if there has been executive-level turnover since the bond was first issued, it is wise to check for possible restrictions.

Note: How Bond Underwriters Influence Corporate Structure

The senior services organization had built an assisted-living wing and a new independent-living program on its existing campus when it turned its attention to a new assisted-living project in the next town. To finance the project, the growing nonprofit turned to the bond market. Financing specialists were interested but wary of the freestanding nonprofit's increasingly stretched financial position. To allay their concerns, the organization had to create a separate corporation solely for the purpose of holding title to the new development. For the next several years, until some of the debt was paid off and it could refinance, the nonprofit had to hold two separate annual meetings, run two separate boards of directors, and keep a separate set of books for each company.

Local Realities

Nonprofits sometimes can be adopted by a town or city as their own. Museums, for example, have always represented the character of their surroundings in some way and often become community prizes. Years ago, community hospitals were more or less forced to exist because transportation systems were nonexistent, outpatient physician care was almost unheard of, and civic pride was fierce. In these cases, the establishment of a local source of service was a natural and sensible response to the nature of the demand.

One of the things that occasionally accompanies such determinedly local service provision is equally localized control mechanisms. The land used for the museum may be publicly owned, for instance, or a long-ago capital gift may stipulate that the asset is to be returned to the donor if the organization ever stops providing services as described in the bequest. Provisions like these can powerfully shape the choice of corporate structure.

Salary and Benefits

Most nonprofits' single greatest expense is personnel compensation. A salary and fringe benefits package is like an organizational fingerprint, the unique result of the interaction of a huge number of factors. Even in the absence of collective bargaining, managers need to consider the impact of a merger on salaries and benefits. Since it is rarely a wise practice to take benefits away, the typical choice is to bring the less generous package up to the standards of the other. Naturally, this is expensive, so the ideal is when the two organizations coming together will create enough cost savings to offset the normalization of the benefits plans.

Some organizations choose to leave current practices in place, correcting the worst disparities as early as possible and attempting to adjust the remainder gradually. Another potential strategy, especially in rural areas, is to use the management company model from Chapter 11 to reinforce the differences between the two organizations. Sometimes there will be enough differences between the labor forces and compensation practices of two merging agencies that there will be no clear disparities.

Merging compensation plans is more philosophical than regulatory since pay levels are so individualized. The key is to be sure that equally qualified people are paid equally. This can be a hidden cost of merging a unionized employer with a nonunionized one.

Regulatory Policies

Regulatory compliance is a fact of life for most nonprofit organizations, regardless of the service they provide. Regulation is particularly intense in health care, social services, and education, and it can cause planners to make different decisions about corporate structure than they otherwise would have made. Its effect can be magnified when combined with reimbursement policy.

Set-asides are a good example of how regulatory policy can make a difference in organizational structure. For many years, governments have tried to encourage the development of minority-owned or -controlled businesses. Typically they would "set aside" a certain percentage of government contracts to be awarded to minority vendors, including nonprofits, which they would certify after evaluating the minority status of the entity's ownership or board composition. To the degree that the certifications actually gave a competitive advantage, they were valuable designations. The same principle was at work in comparable efforts to slightly favor employers of people with developmental disabilities.

If the government entity favoring a particular kind of employer was shrewd in designing its program—and most were—the key concept was minority *control*. As long as minorities either owned or were in control of a vendor, it would be eligible for special status. (In nonprofits, the equivalent test was the composition of the board.) Consequently, a noncertified group merging with a certified group threatens this preferred-vendor status if it dilutes minority control beyond whatever is deemed the acceptable minimum. It may help to leave government work eligible for minority set-asides in a separate corporation, so this is one way that regulatory incentives strongly influence corporate structure. However, keeping the work in a separate corporation may not help. Ultimately, minority vendor status may be one of the casualties of a merger that is otherwise highly desirable.

There are thousands of ways that regulatory matters can influence the structure of a collaboration, and most of those regulations are a function of state government. Other regulatory demands, such as licenses, inspection authority, and even operations or governance requirements, can be strong enough considerations to force certain corporate structural choices. Clear thinking about what the collaboration is intended to accomplish, a shared understanding of the nonprofits involved, and some good legal advice will be the best way to ensure that form follows function.

First Phase of a Merger: Feasibility Assessment

The work of collaborating falls into three formal phases: feasibility assessment, implementation planning, and postmerger integration. In the first phase of feasibility assessment, the objective is for planners to learn about each other's organization and to conduct some serious analyses of the major aspects of each. The result of this stage should be an agreement to proceed—or not. If the decision is to move forward—we call this a "light green light"— the work moves into the implementation planning phase. During this stage, the participants carry out deeper analyses as necessary and formulate a plan for how to make the collaboration succeed. Once the merger is official or the alliance is considered ready to begin operations, the integration phase begins. This is where the plain old day-to-day management work occurs. Often the bulk of executing the integration plan falls on managers and staff support people who were not as intimately involved in the first two phases.

This shift happens because the leaders' and executives' job is to help their organizations cope with change whereas managers' job is to help their organization cope with complexity. Once the high-level choices have been made, it is up to managers and staff to execute the detailed work necessary to complete the task. More important, these are the people closest to this level of work and so they are best positioned to deal with implementation.

Designing and implementing a nonprofit merger is not a linear process. Many tasks must be accomplished at the same time, and planners should expect false starts and dead ends, especially when participants have never been through the process before. What is even more confusing is that the same experience can look like a straight line or a hopelessly jumbled mess, depending on the stage of the process and one's role in it. Still, a well-organized planning effort following the proven guidelines of this section can help smooth out and streamline the procedure.

Informal Phase of a Collaboration

Before going any further, we need to backtrack a bit. We already noted that there are three formal phases in a collaboration. But the real first step is far more informal, far less predictable—and it may be the most important phase of all. Unofficially, we think of this as the restaurant phase.

Executives who were part of a collaboration planning phase from the beginning may reminisce about how it all started. Sometimes the seed was planted during a chance conversation between two chief executive officers (CEOs) at a conference. Sometimes (often, actually) the two executives had been in constant contact about routine matters, and the conversation just took an interesting turn one day. Occasionally board members were the key participants in an early discussion, especially if one of the organizations was missing a CEO. In federated organizations, a national staff member sometimes plays the key matchmaking role. These conversations between two individuals have the advantages of being quiet, nonthreatening, and easy to forget if things don't seem promising.

However the conversations first started, the next impulse is often to include a small number of additional individuals. Turf immediately becomes at least a subliminal issue because now the conversation has taken on a more deliberate tone, and that raises the awareness of the collaborative being an intentional act. Even if everyone feels perfectly comfortable in the other organization's physical setting, holding the second conversation in one of the lairs seems somehow unseemly and possibly even foolish.

Enter the restaurant. We have lost count of the number of mergers (especially) that got serious for the first time in a pleasant, low-profile restaurant somewhere not close to either organization's main office. And why not? This is a perfectly appropriate way to discuss an important step in both organizations' history, blending business with a naturally social setting. In fact, it is such a natural step that we recommend it. Just be sure to leave a decent tip after tying up that booth for so long.

The first formal phase of collaboration work is feasibility assessment. Although the term is self-explanatory, the details are not. We should say at the outset that the field of nonprofit collaboration is so early in its development that there are no agreed-on frameworks and no generally accepted processes. So although this three-phase method has been battle-tested, it is not the only method out there. It remains to be seen whether it becomes the standard one.

A judgment of feasibility must be inferred from the sum of many different analyses. We suggest a framework for the process as well as some of the more common analyses. Unique facts and circumstances may point to other analyses, and the process may have to be altered for similar reasons. But first, a few words about the role of consultants in nonprofit mergers.

Role of Consultants

One of the biggest differences between nonprofit mergers and traditional for-profit mergers is that the latter use consultants as agents of private interests whereas nonprofits use them as facilitators of the process. The difference is rooted in what is at stake. In Wall Street mergers, great personal and institutional wealth is at risk, so it is only natural that participants want and need to have strong individualized representation. What is missing in these agent-driven transactions is a mediating influence. The stock market itself frequently plays this role, and sometimes the courts, but no other entity has a rightful claim to shaping the process itself as opposed to the interests of the participants. This is why the transactions are tacitly accepted as adversarial affairs.

The situation is different for nonprofits, which are charitable institutions in which great personal wealth is at stake only insofar as it is represented in paychecks. Except for the largest and most generous of nonprofits, a year's pay hardly constitutes true wealth. The other element at risk is institutional and personal ego, but that is not the kind of thing that consultants can reliably preserve anyway. Consequently, consulting in mergers and alliance development at its best tends to be a classic use of outside advisors as facilitators.

Consultants can bring two distinct advantages to a merger: an independent perspective, and specialized knowledge and skills. Trusted consultants can offer unbiased feedback on any major aspect of a merger or alliance. It is also easier for them to adopt any number of roles—coach, planner, cheerleader, dictator, referee, beggar, or schemer, to name just a few—and during the course of the average merger, there's a fair chance that several of these will be needed.

Using their position as outsiders, merger and alliance consultants can facilitate the process and signal participants when there is a problem. Without the same internal agendas as the participants— for one, the consultant already knows he or she is "losing" his or her job when the transaction is complete—a collaboration consultant can be a steadying influence. As more and more nonprofits choose to collaborate in one way or another, there will come into being a steadily expanding pool of highly experienced consultants. Given the future of nonprofit collaborations as the new strategic planning for the twenty-first century, it is highly likely that strategic planning consultants of the late 1990s will gradually become merger and alliance consultants instead. We are already seeing this happen in most parts of the country. In time, there will be a more than adequate consultant supply.

Pitfall: Lack of Agreement about a Consultant's Role

Because the idea of a facilitator dedicated to a *process*—as opposed to a facilitator hired by and accountable to a single organization—can be new to many participants, it is important to be explicit about the expectations. A consultant hired to assess or develop a nonprofit merger works for both organizations, not just one. (Otherwise, he or she is simply an agent.) This means that there are joint obligations between the parties, such as candor, accountability for assignments—and paying the consultant. Without these explicit agreements, there can easily be misunderstanding about who can expect what from whom. It helps for both parties to do everything regarding the consultant jointly, from introducing him or her to evaluating the work product.

This is not to say that nonprofits will never use consultants as agents of their interests. Mergers between very large and complex organizations such as hospitals require specialized assistance for each party. Typically that kind of assistance is rendered by large law firms, but that is chiefly because nonprofit hospital mergers tend to have been defined as legal affairs due to the high asset values and potentially intricate corporate structures involved. What these large groups are really paying for is a temporary addition to their own professional staffs. In the future, that same kind of support is likely to come from a number of potential suppliers, such as accountants and professional merger specialists as well as attorneys.

The absence of a CEO is also a good time for nonprofits to consider using a merger consultant as agent. In this case, a consultant could act in lieu of the CEO for merger-related items. Sometimes the consultant will act as a full-time interim chief executive officer too. We know of a hospital that, seeking to merge with one of many local systems, moved a board member into the vacant CEO chair in an attempt both to lead the organization and to firm up a merger. Often a consultant will be a valuable assistant to a sitting CEO who is simply not able to give the process all the time it requires.

At the moment, relatively few nonprofits have gone through even a single merger, let alone several; a consultant who has been through the process knows where the problem areas lie and may be able to predict how certain issues will evolve. If nothing else, it can be a great comfort for participants to know that what they are facing is normal and to be expected. If desired, the consultant should also be able to go beyond simply providing knowledge and offer private strategic advice.

Tip: The Agnostic Consultant

Unless two or more organizations have already made a commitment to merge or create an alliance, a consultant should be agnostic as to whether they do either one. The only inalienable benefit that an outside consultant brings to collaboration is an independent perspective with no preconceived leanings in one direction or another. Without a preordained result, the consultant can let the facts and circumstances dictate the proper course of action based on what the parties themselves want to achieve. The decision to move ahead belongs solely to the organizations themselves, particularly to their boards of directors.

Form a Collaboration Committee

Emerging from the restaurant phase, participating organizations should compose a collaboration committee (or some other such name) whose job it is to oversee the feasibility and implementation planning phases. Ideally the committee membership will be drawn from about three to four positions from each organization. A workable composition of members would be the CEO, board president, one other board member, and one other executive. Equal numbers are important for obvious symbolic reasons. The fact that this is not a vote-taking body means that the equal numbers are not a parliamentary problem. A larger committee is manageable if it is so desired, but when a group like this grows much beyond a total of 14 members, it becomes more audience than committee.

The role of the collaboration committee is to act as a kind of de facto board of directors for the collaboration planning process. In small nonprofits, a single committee may be able to handle most of the planning tasks itself, but in larger organizations, a system of subcommittees is the only feasible way to incorporate all internal stakeholders in the process. The collaboration committee must then step back to keep its overall role as an ad hoc board while looking to the subcommittees to carry out the more functional tasks.

Determine Hopes and Aspirations

The first step in any feasibility assessment is to identify participants' hopes and aspirations for the collaboration. Those who have consulted to even a handful of nonprofit mergers will almost certainly be able to identify ahead of time a large number of generic aspirations, such as improved or expanded programming, greater efficiencies, staff improvement, and competitive advantage. But whether an outsider can correctly estimate the hopes of the committee or not is irrelevant. The key to this first step is to bring out the committee's collective voice to describe the desired outcomes.

Document Fears and Concerns

The next step is to use the same kind of process to identify the group's fears and concerns. The facilitator asks the participants to name the aspects of the potential collaboration that most concern them. The descriptions do not have to be extensive, and they can be as detailed or as high level as desired. Again, a facilitator can help the group shape its output. The fears and concerns most often cited will be things like these: "The process might not work"; "Management will be distracted for a prolonged period of time"; "Our funders and donors won't approve"; and "We'll lose our identity."

These two steps, which should take less than an hour to complete, accomplish three purposes:

1. They produce a natural set of objectives for which the members of the committee will feel some ownership since it came directly from them. Subtly, it gives the newly formed group its first tangible product as a synthesized entity. These two sets of data should become the measure by which the committee judges its effectiveness: Did they accomplish their objectives while avoiding or at least neutralizing their concerns?

2. It allows committee members to articulate their views and to hear that the opinions of others are very likely comparable to their own.

3. It begins to build at least some small element of trust among the members.

Observers and participants in this process may notice distinct differences between the two lists. Hopes and aspirations will usually be strategic in nature, while fears and concerns will be operational. This is yet another behavioral tendency of groups that planners can use. Strategic hopes are essentially statements of faith in a shared future, and so they tend to bring people together. Concerns and fears related to operations can be handled chiefly by carefully managing the feasibility and implementation process. In effect, committee participants have signaled what they consider to be the most important elements of their joint effort, and this is where most of the collective attention should go.

Exchange Documentation

The next logical step is to exchange documentation. This should be the beginning of a culture of transparency in the collaboration.

Nature of External Merger Support Infrastructure

The greatly varied role of consultants in nonprofit collaborations, especially mergers, is an indicator of a larger fact. Unlike in the for-profit sector, where federal laws and government entities have prescribed oversight and regulatory authority over many areas of day-to-day business as well as one-time transactions such as mergers, the nonprofit sector has no accepted processes, no clear expectations, and no metrics for dealing with the merger process. As a result, every nonprofit going into a merger has to make it up as it goes along. Because of this, every merger process will be unique: When you have seen one process, you have seen one process. With a homegrown process, there will be a higher-than-necessary rate of failures, and there is likely to be no accepted vocabulary, let alone a common framework with which to evaluate the outcomes.

The federal government is not going to remedy this problem, nor should it. The great strength of the nonprofit sector—its voluntary nature—will also be the source of its guidance on mergers and alliances. As of this writing, several national foundations and thought leaders are beginning to communicate about how to build the infrastructure necessary to support the nonprofit restructuring needed in the coming years. Look for this effort to pick up momentum and ultimately to fill this glaring gap in nonprofits' collective ability to rework their service delivery structures.

Most of the documentation exchanged should be standard materials routinely produced and filed in the ordinary course of providing services. In fact, a useful rule of thumb underlying the document exchange is this: If it does not already exist, do not create it. Sometimes it is more important to know that a particular kind of document exists than it is to know the content itself. For instance, if in July one asks for the most recent internally produced financial statements and the most recent statement is for the period ending on February 28, the fact that there is such a large gap in updated financial information is itself highly revealing. Facilitate the documentation exchange with a nondisclosure agreement as described in Chapter 16.

The kind of information to be exchanged deals with routine management material. Here is a good list for starters:

Board member listing

Budgets and forecasts

Detailed description of each program

Detailed profit and loss for last fiscal year

Executive management resumes

Health benefits—rate sheet

Insurance policies

Legal disclosures

Listing of executive team

Mission statement

Most recent strategic plan

One year worth of board meeting minutes

Operating procedures manuals for finance, human resources, operations

Organization by-laws

Organizational charts

Other employee benefits—rate sheet

Profit and loss of each program (if available)

Program metrics

Real estate listing of property owned and leased

Salary by department

Salary by job title

Three years' worth of audits

Some of this material may already be available on a group's Web site, while some of it may be available only on site (such as the board minutes). No matter. Collect it all, and be sure that the key members of the collaboration committee absorb the data.

In any nonprofit merger, there will always be surprises. Count on it. Perhaps the locked room in the basement of the dingy office building you just acquired turns out to be stuffed full of priceless artifacts from the Revolutionary War. Or a big new opportunity pops up in a completely unexpected way. Or your own ten-year controller is unmasked as a convicted felon wanted in two other states . . .

Surprises like these can and do happen at any time, but when they occur during a merger or alliance with another organization, they can delay and possibly even scuttle the process. The momentum that two or more organizations build up when considering a structured collaboration is a very fragile thing, and a single surprise (negative or positive) can easily derail it. And it may not even be the unexpected thing itself that does the damage but rather the fallout, such as broken trust, distraction, and delayed decisions.

The antidote is to deflate the surprise factor. Most "surprises" are really just information that only a small number of people possess. Assuming goodwill on all parts, most surprises can be overcome with a commitment to transparency and good planning. By doing some homework, each party can expand the number of people possessing the information. The name of that homework is a due diligence investigation.

Tip: Know What Is Really Happening in the First Step

The most important thing that is happening during the mutual learning phase is rarely articulated. Most of the substantive knowledge that the collaboration committee and the respective boards and management teams need can be taken from the resource book and due diligence reports. Assuming that the participants actually read the material, the calendar time required for most people to absorb the information would be equivalent to a moderately diligent study weekend before college final exams. What is really going on—and what takes so much calendar time—is a gradual process of familiarization, trust building, and private testing of the merger proposal. This is why initial meetings tend to be scheduled somewhat leisurely. It is as if the participants are saying, "Let's pursue this idea, but let's do it so that we can back out easily if it really doesn't feel right to us."

Why Due Diligence?

The term "due diligence" may be familiar to nonprofit managers as legal terminology that has made its way into broad public usage in recent years. The term often rolls knowingly off many people's tongues in matters like these. Newcomers to mergers often assume that the term refers to a fixed and well-known process. The reality is that "due diligence" is usually shorthand for "doing one's homework." There is nothing fixed or standardized about the process. For that matter, even professionals do not agree on what constitutes due diligence. Accounting firms deal with this lack of standardization by using the far less alliterative yet oddly more descriptive phrase "agreed-upon procedures."

In most uses, the term "due diligence" refers to the systematic investigation of an organization's operations. When Wall Streeters conduct a due diligence investigation, it is usually to verify the presence and ownership of reported assets, to check for the possibility of unrecorded liabilities, and to assess in a deeper way the proposed fit between the two companies. Nonprofits conduct due diligence investigations for similar purposes but different motivations.

For-profit managers must be sure that the takeover target really does have the value in their context that a valuation specialist assigned it. If the transaction eventually occurs, there will be an exchange of money for value. For that reason, these managers concentrate on the more quantifiable aspects of financial health. Matters of strategy and long-term value were factored into the decision earlier in the process; at this stage, they can be considered most easily only if there is some way to build them into the fundamental financial evaluation.

In most cases, nonprofit managers and their board members need not worry about an exchange of money for value. Their fiduciary role requires them to exercise good judgment in the oversight of a quasi-public asset, so the true goal is more of a planning and management challenge than it is a matter of generating or protecting wealth. At best, they are free to ignore questions of private benefit and to act on behalf of the larger good, at least as they see it.

Another way of saying this is that in the case of nonprofits, the issues raised by a due diligence investigation will be almost purely political or even interpersonal. That is, they will involve questions that will be resolved only through discussion and negotiation. Whenever legal ownership of assets is not at stake, values and philosophy tend to take on primary importance. Ideally, this frees directors and managers to contemplate benefits of a merger from the perspective of the true fiduciaries that their roles imply. It can also mean, however, that issues raised may have no common basis for resolution, which can cause the merger to stall and eventually collapse. All participants should understand what is at stake in the due diligence portion of their collaboration.

What Is a Due Diligence Investigation?

Incorporating a nonprofit or any other corporation requires one to follow certain steps in a fairly linear fashion as stipulated in various laws. Audits of financial statements are carried out in a manner proscribed by the auditing profession. Bonds offered for sale to the public by large nonprofits go through predetermined processes with specific standards for the terms of the offering and the means by which it is offered.

Due diligence investigations share none of these characteristics, and for good reason. What the processes have in common is that they are initiated by the principal organization on behalf of some type of external interest group (such as the general public or the bond-buying market) and that they involve a mediating third party of some kind, such as an investment or accounting firm. Over time, those interest groups have figured out exactly what they need to know in order to approve or evaluate or invest in the nonprofit initiating the transaction. Since hundreds of these projects take place each week, the formats have become highly standardized. Interested parties usually can find what they need with a minimum of effort.

In contrast, mergers between nonprofit organizations are inherently private affairs, despite the existence of their public tax subsidies. Third-party interest groups have no legal right to command disclosure beyond the generalized and relatively light responsibilities placed on all managers of quasi-public entities to operate with a certain degree of openness. Due diligence investigations, therefore, start with deciding what it is one needs to know and then figuring out how to learn it.

This is the heart of why due diligence explorations are not codified in the same way as other investigatory or auditing processes. Each potential merger partner will have its own special areas in which it wants more information about its peer. The design of the collaboration itself may suggest particular areas of investigation, and there are almost always unique characteristics about one or both organizations that bear detailed investigation.

The due diligence investigation is most relevant to mergers. When nonprofits collaborate without changing their existing corporate vehicles or the responsibility for overseeing them, as in alliances, there is little justification for doing the kind of formal due diligence exploration we are talking about here.

Typically, due diligence investigations are carried out by outside advisors. Internal staff can be involved if the advisor permits, although one of the advantages of hiring outsiders is that they can be held accountable. Mixing internal staff with outsiders can blur the lines of responsibility.

Most advisors probably will have their own format for due diligence investigations, and it is difficult to make generalizations about one format versus another. However, certain predictable areas need attention no matter what other issues may arise. For convenience, we cluster these into distinct categories. Next, we concentrate mainly on the areas of focus for due diligence. Evaluating the results of the investigation and making plans for implementation will come later.

Governance

Start with the basics. Your potential partner should be legally incorporated, probably as a nonprofit, and it should have appropriate incorporation papers on file. The articles of incorporation detail the goals and purposes of the corporation and will have been filed as part of the original incorporation package. By-laws should also be in place, although, unfortunately, they rarely are up to date. This is such a common condition that it should not cause any particular problem, unless the organization has made some sort of key change in a major process or policy that will affect its ability to collaborate.

All nonprofits should have a functioning board of directors that meets regularly and keeps minutes. A good sign of the level of organization and professionalism of the organization is whether key administrators can easily lay their hands on the last year's board meeting minutes. A three-ring binder full of board minutes is a reassuring sight for a due diligence team.

Here is an example of how a due diligence team should operate. Not only should a complete set of board minutes be readily accessible, but they should support the major decisions actually taken by the organization during that period. For example, the board should have documented its decision to acquire a major asset, such as a building. It should have noted when the entity received notice of a legal action against it, documented the process and rationale for hiring the new CEO, and so forth.

Don't forget: If multiple organizations are involved under the same corporate umbrella, there should be proper corporate documentation for each.

> ### Tip: Check Authority and Approval Process Now
>
> Since you are in the neighborhood anyway, this is a good time to check out each other's provisions and likely timetable for approving a merger. The by-laws should spell out who approves such measures and the notice for voting that management must give. This will save a bit of time and aggravation later in the process.

Finances

Not surprisingly, the greatest amount of work needs to be done in the financial area. The justifiable fear here is that the surviving corporation will take on hidden liabilities. The most worrisome liabilities are the ones a nonprofit partner itself does not know about itself. We once saw a promising merger fall apart because one of the partners' office managers had been not paying payroll taxes in order to cover a cash flow deficit. It was a small organization with a relatively unsophisticated board of directors, and the shortfall was discovered by the other partner during its own investigations.

There is a fair degree of overlap between a due diligence investigation and other disclosure processes already required of a nonprofit organization, particularly its yearly audit. Consequently, the team should obtain at least three years' worth of audited financial statements; five years' worth would be helpful. The team should study the trends exhibited in the financials and benchmark them against other comparable organizations, if possible. At this point, the details are not as important as the overall trends.

Many auditors issue management letters at the same time as their yearly audit statements. The team should obtain these letters as well as any written management responses to them. Management letters can offer important clues about the nonprofit's financial management style and effectiveness. Sometimes nonprofits are audited by funding sources as well, so the team should obtain these audits plus a report on the current status of any audits not yet complete.

The team should request unaudited financial statements to supplement the audited financials. The latter are produced only once each year, so their specifics are quickly out of date. Ideally, unaudited financial information is produced monthly and routed to senior management and the board of directors. Along with that information

Pitfall: No Unaudited Financial Statements

There is a second reason for requesting unaudited financial statements, in addition to the obvious search for knowledge: to see if management can produce them. Good nonprofit management requires constant financial self-awareness. If the organization cannot produce unaudited financials for the purposes of a due diligence, it probably cannot produce them for its own internal monitoring either. Computerized financial accounting packages usually will create financial statements at the touch of a button, but if the data has not been properly entered and maintained, this capability is meaningless. If the statements are available but routinely late—for example, if the March unaudited financial statements are not available until, say, July—it means that management always operates as much in the dark as the due diligence team.

should come reports on aged receivables, cash flow, and utilization of services.

If the nonprofit does fundraising of any kind, the team will want to look at that material. Pure financial information will reveal fundraising effectiveness, but the way that an organization presents its case to the public will be a window into the thinking of the entity that cannot be captured in mere numbers.

Since nonprofits cannot sell shares of ownership to the general public, they have to generate capital through profitable operations or by borrowing it. Due diligence investigations must take into account the level and type of obligations the potential partner has incurred. Smaller nonprofits will have used the financial equivalents of convenience stores and medium-size grocery stores for their borrowing—that is, commercial banks—but larger nonprofits, such as hospitals and universities, will use the financial warehouses of capital finance, the tax-exempt bond markets. These arrangements require professional evaluation.

Unpaid payroll taxes are one of the reliable red flags in any close look at an organization; more on that later. In some instances, nonprofits engage in nonexempt business transactions which produce a taxable profit (unrelated business income tax, or UBIT). In all cases, the ground rules are the same: Taxes must be paid, and if they are not, the new board of directors could be taking over a major headache. Due diligence teams need to check on the status of all taxes payable.

An integral part of the financial reporting system is the financial planning system, more familiarly known as budgeting. The first step is to verify that the organization does have a viable, operating budgeting system, preferably one that operates on a multiyear basis. The second step is to examine its outputs. Small and medium-size nonprofits probably will have the most minimal of budgeting processes, but they ought to have one.

A quiet but critical aspect of operations is insurance coverage. The average nonprofit of even nominal size will have a surprisingly large number of coverages, ranging from workers' compensation and malpractice insurance to business interruption insurance and directors' and officers' coverage. Figuratively speaking, the due diligence team should gather up copies of all the insurance policies in a big box and study them to make sure that adequate coverage is in place and that no policy has lapsed. Practicality is another matter; we try to reconcile the two issues later in this book.

Although it does not affect many nonprofits, a few types of organizations may need to maintain a sizable inventory in order to provide the material needs of clients, such as food and clothing. If so, there may be reason to examine the extent of the inventory and its value in the transaction.

Assets

Part of the financial review, but an important enough area to be treated separately, is the assets of the corporation. In a for-profit merger, the assets' value affects the ultimate profitability of the entire transaction. In nonprofit mergers, the stakes are a bit different, but misreading the value of assets to be acquired could have a lasting effect on long-term financial health. In the case of large assets, such as buildings or art collections, there may even need to be a valuation. This is unequivocally true for for-profit purchases of nonprofit assets, but it may also be necessary in nonprofit to nonprofit transactions.

The team will want to verify ownership of major assets, including real property and any endowments that may exist. For a due diligence investigation, simple copies of lists that probably already exist would be sufficient, along with evidence of ownership, since the asset base does not change dramatically, and confirming assets is usually part of a yearly audit anyway. (Note that the audit validates "book value," not the value the real estate market assigns it.) Sometimes ownership of an asset will bring with it the necessity of making major routine expenditures, such as 24-hour security, or the asset might be on the brink of needing a major capital improvement, such as a new roof or the rebuilding of a wing.

Pitfall: Beware the Money Pit

Beware money pits: the assets that cause unexpected, unavoidable, and un-predictable investments. For instance, environmental laws in many localities sometimes are so strict that simply owning polluted property can require an organization to make a major investment in fixing it. Waste disposal regulations are becoming more complex and restrictive. The Americans with Disabilities Act may require substantial renovations to a program site. Historical preservation laws in some cities, particularly in the Northeast, can have the same effect: The first floor of one association's headquarters was decimated by a runaway car, but preservation laws forced huge delays in rebuilding while obscure crafts-men were located to re-create ironwork, and waivers were sought to permit less expensive replacements. Other less visible laws and regulations unique to a locality can effectively mandate a major capital investment. Due diligence investigators need to be sensitive to these possibilities.

Liabilities and Obligations

There is a whole range of relationships that potentially create obligations or liabilities for the nonprofit corporation. In addition to contracts to deliver services, there usually will be contracts to purchase services. There may be employment contracts and agreements to purchase supplies. Larger and more complex nonprofits will have a variety of management contracts—agreements between universities and food service vendors, for example, or between nursing homes and pharmacy supply companies. Retirement plans, employee benefit options, and investment management agreements are other examples of obligations that can be transferred to another organization. Restrictions on monies raised in the past can also affect current operations. These should be documented and reviewed by appropriate experts on the due diligence team.

Look for large and/or unusual liabilities. One of the significant kinds of liabilities is deferred revenue from advance ticket sales, such as in arts groups, because there is always a temptation to spend the cash associated with those ticket sales today, leaving the organization vulnerable to financial turmoil if it cannot come up with fresh cash at the point in the future when it has to deliver the services for which it has already collected and spent the money. The integration phase of a merger between a major American symphony orchestra and an opera company was almost derailed because an incomplete review of liabilities failed to note that one of the parties routinely spent revenue from advance ticket sales well before delivering the services that that revenue was supposed to support.

Some Financial Red Flags

A due diligence investigation is very likely to turn up one or more items of concern. In fact, if a due diligence team does not discover at least a few unexpected twists, it may not have done its job properly. The important thing is not the item itself but rather how the parties react to it. The same situation in one merger may be a deal breaker, while in another it may be simply a moderate obstacle or perhaps no obstacle at all. Whatever the case, some red flags warrant further investigation. Understand that these are only signs and that they may not amount to anything at all. Here they are, in alphabetical order.

Balloon Loan Payments Coming Due

Look at the back of the audited financial statements where there are a series of numbered footnotes. Find the section that describes future years' long-term debt levels. The dollar amounts should decline as the years increase. If one year shows a higher amount of payback than the years before, it means that, at some point in the future, the organization will have to suddenly start paying back more on its borrowings. Ask the organization's management two questions:

1. Are you aware that you will owe an unusually large debt payment in the future?
2. Do you have a plan for paying it back?

If the answer to the both questions is yes and the plan seems reasonable, move on to the next item on the agenda.

General Records Disarray

If no one can ever seem to find the files you requested, if the records are stacked everywhere in cardboard boxes, if nothing seems to work right in the partner nonprofit, it may indicate a more profound breakdown of systems. Ignorance is not bliss in this case; it is dangerous.

Indispensable Staff

The presence of indispensable staff should serve as another red flag during a due diligence investigation. One can infer the presence of indispensable staff when all questions seem to lead to the same individual. It could be the CEO, a business person, a program manager, or even a board member. Indispensable staff is an inevitable phenomenon in most small nonprofits, and many such individuals truly are gifted. Still, if a partner organization seems to operate mostly through the brilliance and hard work of one or two individuals, it means a potential problem for the collaboration if these people are lost.

Lapsed Insurances

Life is full of risks, and there is an insurance policy available to cover most of them. One of the frequent symptoms of slipshod management is insufficient or lapsed insurance coverage. Considering the complexity of many nonprofit operations, this is perhaps inevitable. Chances are that coverage was canceled to save money, or it was overlooked. Either way, the surviving corporation faces a gap in coverage. If a claim is filed during that period, the assets of the organization may be exposed to settle it. Worse, in some states, it may not even be legal for an employer to operate without certain types of insurance—workers' compensation insurance and unemployment insurance being two prime examples. Lapsed insurance coverages are important not only for the substance of the threat they pose but for the signal of mediocre management they send.

Loss of (Pick One): License, Accreditation, Large Donor, Large Payer

Here is another one red flag that is important as much for what it says about the future as for the substance of the problem itself: Nonprofits usually do not lose major pieces of their operations without reason. If anything, authorities and funding sources may tend to stay with a nonprofit a bit longer than they should, so their departures can be extremely significant. The details of the loss should be thoroughly aired and understood; generally they should be disclosed to the full collaboration committee.

Maxed-Out Line of Credit

Lines of credit are intended to be temporary sources of capital. Any organization that is using all of its line of credit throughout most or all of the year is waving a big red flag. Check the cash flow, revenue and expense estimates, and management controls carefully here.

Tip: Beware the Little Secrets

Some will resist a merger for reasons that they will talk about only reluctantly. For example, the executive director of the small nonprofit may come in late and leave early every day. Or family members may quietly occupy positions throughout the organization, fearing for their jobs if new management comes in. One executive director who has discussed possible mergers with smaller agencies refers to these as the "little secrets" of a potential partner that will be revealed only after trust has been established. More insidiously, they may not be revealed at all, but instead will remain unacknowledged sources of resistance. Keep this in mind when a potential partner resists or delays for apparently inexplicable reasons.

Nonfinancial "Liabilities"

The idea of nonfinancial liabilities encompasses a wide range of things a potential partner should know about before committing to anything. In one merger between a small organization and a larger one, the small nonprofit's office manager was one of the original founders who over the years had become disillusioned with the organization's direction. Her quiet resentment, combined with poor financial skills, helped get the little organization into some serious fiscal difficulties. In other cases, the nonfinancial liability may be something like a negative media story that has yet to be released, or a donor list studded with questionable characters.

Payroll Taxes Unpaid

Most nonprofits have a payroll that amounts to as much as 80 percent of their total expenses. For every payroll dollar spent, the government demands a certain amount of tax payments, and it expects payment on a pretty inflexible schedule. When an organization runs low on cash, one classic response is to not pay payroll taxes. This may work for the short term (the *very* short term), but the government always catches up and the unpaid taxes become a liability. Worse, it is a liability that board members can bear personally. An unpaid payroll tax bill sitting in someone's drawer—or, more forthrightly, carried on the balance sheet—can be a sign of cash flow difficulties serious enough to scuttle a merger.

Qualified Audit Opinion

The quickest way to discern one red flag is by reading the first page in a nonprofit's audited financial report. The page takes the form of a letter to the nonprofit from the auditors. If the auditors have any major question about what they saw, it will be expressed somewhere around the third or fourth paragraph. If they say they cannot express an opinion, or if they qualify their opinion in some way, the smart reader will want to ask many additional probing questions. And if the phrase "going concern" appears in the last part of the opinion letter, it means that the auditors question whether the entity will survive for another 12 months.

Unacknowledged and Serious CEO/Staff Conflict

Bosses are rarely universally beloved, but occasionally there is such conflict between the CEO and the staff that it becomes a handicap. Merger talks can let this particular genie out of the bottle, as staff members become fearful that their organization will be poorly represented (or the reverse). The due diligence team should be aware that it may encounter signs of this conflict. Ordinarily it will not take much to get the full story.

Unexamined Accounts Receivable

For many nonprofits, invoices sent to users of their services (called accounts receivable) and unpaid pledges (pledges receivable) represent a substantial corporate asset. Like any asset, they need constant attention. For accounts receivable, there is always the chance that they will not be paid. If the amount of receivables carried on the books is not constantly adjusted to acknowledge the fact that a certain percentage will never be collected, it could present a misleadingly rosy picture of financial health.

Unreported Litigation

Nonprofits may do good work, but unfortunately that does not protect them from getting sued. Like any business entity, nonprofits are subject to a wide range of potential lawsuits. Sometimes state laws offer a degree of protection, and many juries are sympathetic to nonprofits, but a determined plaintiff who does not care about winning still can make life miserable for an organization. Suits involving wrongful discharge are one of the most common types, and malpractice and breach-of-confidentiality suits are common too. Lawsuits should be disclosed in the footnotes to audited financial statements, but it is a good idea to ask if there is any recent indication of court activity.

Low or Negative Net Assets

On occasion, one or more of the potential partners shows low or negative net assets, which is the nonprofit term for "equity" in a for-profit corporation. Often this situation will be cause for a qualified opinion from the auditor, but even if it is not the indicator should be taken seriously. If the collaboration is to move ahead successfully, both partners will need to be able to plan for how this potentially crippling problem will be fixed.

Valuations

Occasionally transactions involving two different nonprofit organizations call for precise valuation of the assets. This should be necessary only when one partner is buying the assets of the other (as distinct from merging with the entire operation). Since no one owns nonprofits or their assets, transactions between them do not change the fundamental fact that the assets are semipublic in nature. However, if those assets—or the entities that own them—are sold to a for-profit organization, it means that they are taken out of the hands of the public. In return, the nonprofit or its "owners," the general public, must be compensated. This question moved from theoretical to real starting in the 1980s when for-profit corporations began purchasing nonprofit hospitals. The resulting entity was usually known as a conversion foundation.

The question of putting a value on nonprofit entities being sold is just about the same one that buyers and sellers of other corporations have had to answer for years. The process is far closer to an art than to a science, but it is the best way the business community has found to make the benefit of ownership quantifiable. There are a handful of ways to derive an estimated value for a nonprofit that is being sold. One is to calculate the present value of the extra cash (profit) the entity is projected to produce over the next several years, and another is simply to look at comparable transactions. If a valuation has been done, its results should be at least generally in line with the expectations of the acquirer.

Present Value of Cash Flow

Consumers instinctively understand that a dollar is worth more today than it will be worth tomorrow because its purchasing power is inevitably eroded by inflation. Plus, there is some hard-to-quantify value in having the ability to spend it sooner rather than later. However, 90 cents may—or may not—be worth the same amount today as a dollar will be tomorrow. If one assumes the inflation rate for the next 12 months will be about 11 percent, then 90 cents can in fact be said to be the equivalent of a dollar in one year. The 90 cents is called the present value of that dollar in one year.

The only obligation-free way of getting capital into an organization over time is by making a profit. Five years' worth of, say, a 5 percent profit on $1,000 will result in a total profit of $250, a tidy sum. But the $50 profit in every one of those years is worth less than the $50 profit of the year before, because by the time it is produced, each $50 will have been worth less as measured in today's dollars. So the present value of five years' worth of a $50 annual profit might be worth closer to $175 or $200, depending on the rate of inflation over that period.

This concept is at the heart of the discounted present value method of valuing a nonprofit. The approach calculates the amount of cash expected to be generated by the organization over each of the next five years, then figures out what each of those profits is worth in today's dollars and adds them all together for a cumulative net present value. This amount may be taken as a lump sum or modified in some way, such as by adding an estimated value for the entire period beginning with the sixth year forward. (Often this means simply doubling the net present value.)

Comparable Values

A somewhat less promising though equally valid approach to putting a value on a nonprofit is to look for comparable transactions. Since for-profit firms purchasing nonprofits is still infrequent, seeking comparable transactions may be an inherently limited strategy. The process usually involves looking for transactions that have occurred in the last year or so in the same general market area. Valuation specialists look for organizations that were similar in size, profitability, market penetration, and related characteristics. After that, it is a relatively simple matter to put the details of each transaction side by side and make some inferences about the specific transaction under study. This is similar to what real estate agents typically do as part of setting an asking price.

Carrying Out the Valuation

Valuing nonprofit–to–for-profit conversions must be done by skilled outsiders who have no economic stake in whether the deal occurs or not. The whole idea of nonprofit public charity status is loaded with such high-minded overtones that the issue can become extremely sensitive, especially in areas where there have been no previous conversions. Often, public accounting and consulting firms are asked to value transactions like these.

The advantages of an independent valuation expert are multiple. Valuation consultants are accustomed to placing a value on assets poised for sale, including ambiguous situations where there seems to be little hard information available. They should have resources and a span of experience beyond that of any participants in the sale. Their independence will shield them from extraneous pressures, and it should be very difficult for aggrieved parties to question their motives. Finally, as licensed professionals, they can be more easily held accountable for the quality of their work.

Pro Forma Financials, Including Cash Flows

Mergers are about the future. The due diligence team should create projected scenarios of combining these two organizations. The way to do this is by putting together a set of pro forma financial statements, or a kind of financial dress rehearsal for what the new entity would look like. At this stage of the due diligence investigation, it is ordinarily enough just to collect the information that would be necessary to do the pro formas. However, it may be easy to forget to compile the pro formas later on, so it is a good idea to consider doing a set now. That way, the collaboration committee can study the calculations and possibly suggest some variations. Obviously, this is one step that needs to be done only once together and not by each team separately.

Regulatory Filings

Finally, investigate the current state of required regulatory filings. Nonprofits in health care and human services are among the most regulated entities in our economy, so there is a reasonable chance that one or both of the merger partners will have a continuing regulatory obligation. Sometimes these arise from the tax-exempt designation itself. There should be a copy of the Internal Revenue Service's confirmation of tax-exempt status in the files, and there may need to be continuous updating for state authorities too. The top state official with nonprofit oversight responsibilities, typically the attorney general or the secretary of state, may have a filing requirement, and local property tax assessment officials may also require some sort of filing to keep current. The due diligence team needs to identify all of these requirements and verify that the potential partner has met them.

Contracts, Licenses, Accreditation

Many times government officials require nonprofits that provide education, social services, or health care to be licensed or accredited or both. Government funding agents also often set up long-term contracts under which they agree to purchase certain services at predetermined rates. For due diligence purposes, all three of these kinds of arrangements are critical to maintaining an organization's future viability.

Contracting for the purchase of services from nonprofits became extremely popular with state and local governments in the last 30 years, to the point that many organizations in the social services and some in the health care fields are largely dependent on such agreements for survival. Typically, a contract is put out for bid to a wide variety of possible providers and then signed by the winner and the government agency for a defined period of time. Renewals may be automatic or contested, but it is possible to amass enough contracts and get them routinely renewed to run a reasonably well-funded organization.

However, the funding source always has the ultimate power to withdraw a contract. Without contracts, an organization lacks a stable base of funding and could face bankruptcy. Further, it often takes only one or two lost contracts to create a public sense of failing confidence in an organization. The due diligence team should pay careful attention to the status of all present and recent contracts, with particular attention to any that have been terminated for any reason during the previous three years.

The status of licensing and accreditation can offer the same kind of insight into an organization, although loss of either is a much more serious situation than the loss of a single contract because it often leads to loss of the ability to generate certain types of revenue at all. This is an area that cries out for special expertise on the due diligence team to help interpret potential weak points.

Human Resources Information

No matter how large and complex the merger partners may be, human resource issues will play a major role. Quantitative information to be gathered here includes complete anonymous lists of all employees, including positions, titles, compensation rates, benefit eligibility, collective bargaining status if any, date of employment, and so on. If desired, employer-wide histories of workers' compensation and unemployment claims can give unusually good insight into both organizational systems and cultural norms. (Never mind the poster in the waiting room; how do they really treat employees?) Obtaining a copy of all personnel policies and related material should go without saying. Employment contracts, if any, are definitely in this category as well. The nature of the gap between executive compensation and line staff can be instructive too.

Some nonprofits will have a collective bargaining unit representing employees. In practice, it can be very difficult to merge a nonunion organization with one that has collective bargaining agreements. We covered the implications of this earlier, but at the due diligence stage, team members need to be especially thorough about collecting information.

One of the most useful things the team can do is to talk to the managers and bargaining unit representatives. It can be very helpful to talk with former managers and longtime or retired union members in order to get a history of union/management relations. Not only will the investigators collect valuable information, but they will also send a signal that they are striving for objectivity and fairness. It is essential that team members behave with utmost professionalism in this highly sensitive area. Collective bargaining matters can be volatile, and there will be plenty of opportunity for debating the substance of labor-related decisions later in the process.

Assess the Feasibility

Assembling the findings from each organization, planners must make an assessment: Is this merger feasible? Will a significant number of the joint hopes and aspirations be achieved? Can the concerns be mitigated or even eliminated? Are there sufficient financial, organizational, and cultural strengths in both organizations to carry out a formal merger? While nonprofit mergers should not be undertaken primarily to achieve cost savings, there will be increased transactional costs as well as longer-term costs, such as increased benefit levels (to bring the lower-paying organization up to the level of the higher-paying one). It is hoped that savings offset costs. Assessing feasibility is a judgment call, of course, but it must be made jointly based on all the available facts.

What is important at this stage is that planners get a tentative go or a clear no-go from both boards. No commitment should be asked or given beyond a willingness to explore and plan in greater detail. As important, the decision on both sides should be based on facts and shared goals, not short-term economic or ego-driven goals. A no-go decision should not be regarded as a failure if it was made after full consideration of the evidence.

This process is more art than science, which implies a very important circumstance. While the costs of a merger, including its failure, might be easily determined, the benefits are almost certain to be impossible to calculate. This is true because the desired benefits are usually strategic and in the future. It is an enduring limitation of our system of business that we know how to calculate costs but we do not know how to value success. In the end, the feasibility decision has to be based on the known facts and rooted in the expectation of successful integration management. In short, it is an act of leadership.

19

Second Phase of a Merger: Implementation Planning

Assuming a positive and shared decision to move ahead, the next formal phase of collaboration is implementation planning. Not to be confused with postmerger integration, implementation planning is a process that helps determine exactly how the two organizations will join up. Again, the details of each implementation planning phase will vary according to the participating organizations' needs, so we lay out a process that should work for the vast majority of organizations irrespective of their circumstances.

Form Subcommittees of the Collaboration Committee

In this phase, the collaboration committee assumes its role as a de facto leadership group in earnest as it expands the number of people involved in planning. Nonprofit mergers are decided on from the top down, but they must be implemented from the bottom up. This is what drives the need for subcommittees. In small nonprofits, there may never be a need for more than the collaboration committee but if the participants are large or complex, subcommittees will be a necessity. One major health system, the giant product of a merger between two large hospitals, took almost two years to complete and involved 14 separate subcommittees. With subcommittees, the collaboration committee delegates most of its functional roles and becomes a kind of legislative body. Collaboration committee members should understand from the beginning which model they have chosen.

Although the presence or absence of subcommittees is clear enough, members need to understand that the two models imply very different things for their day-to-day role.

Pitfall: Home Turf Is Overrated

Perhaps it is because of the lack of serious economic incentives, but in our experience, nonprofit boards and their staffs rarely worry about neutral meeting sites for the collaboration committee and just pick the most comfortable and convenient meeting room. This is probably because there is usually a basic trust between the two parties or they would not have started merger talks anyway. The fact that neutral sites usually cost money may have something to do with it too.

The best way to structure subcommittees is to identify the work that needs to be done and then delegate logical groupings of tasks to subcommittees formed for the purpose. Subcommittee membership will usually be drawn largely from the staff ranks, if only because board members rarely have enough time to contribute to the effort. Board members should be a welcome addition to the subcommittees, though the time demands for many potential committee members from the board will be untenable. Also, since subcommittees focus on implementation issues, it is not necessarily appropriate to have a substantial board of directors' presence anyway. The chief benefit of a board member's presence, other than as a tacit endorsement of the activity, is if he or she has a unique specialty or skill set.

Certain issues arise predictably during a merger. (Alliances also require subcommittees, but their collaboration committees tend to act more as coordinators than as planners.) Each of these matters can easily be important enough to be considered in depth during the implementation stage. Collaboration committees need to decide early whether to concentrate on these issues and, if so, how to group them. Here, in alphabetical order, are some of the areas most likely to need in-depth attention at the subcommittee level. Note that this is nothing more than a list of common areas of planning, not a list of committees. An individual collaboration committee may or may not find them worth assigning to a separate subcommittee, or it may find that it is worth assigning two or three subjects to a single subcommittee.

Administrative Systems

One of the longest and most complex challenges in virtually all mergers is how the parties go about integrating their various administrative systems. These back-room functions (the "R" in the C.O.R.E. model) include such things as accounting, payroll, human resources, and purchasing, and integrating these services can literally take years. This is one of the more complex areas of a merger, and it should be approached with the expectation that true integration will take time and resources. At the same time, success here can mean a payoff for the new entity in savings and efficiencies.

Chief Executive Selection

When there was no agreed-on chief executive officer (CEO) arrangement as part of the feasibility assessment process, the collaboration committee may need to select a new CEO. Rarely will a nonprofit merger go beyond the implementation stage without a clear leadership choice. With two or more existing CEO's possibly competing for a single new position, this will not happen often. When it does, there may need to have a subcommittee dedicated to the task. Needless to say, this subcommittee is likely to be closely watched.

Tip: Benefit of Selecting One of the Incumbents

Note to the collaboration committee: Take the easy way out, if possible. Selecting one of the existing CEOs is always easier than doing the famous nationwide search. A merger is unsettling enough to a nonprofit's employees; to have both sets of employees disconcerted complicates the integration process enormously. This is one of the reasons why we urge organizations without a CEO to consider a merger as a legitimate strategic option.

Of course, selecting one of the incumbents may not be either practical or wise for any number of reasons. In that case, the collaboration committee—and the respective boards—must hold firm in its chosen course of action. This is never easy, for obvious reasons. See why we suggest the easy way out?

Collective Bargaining Agreements

Collective bargaining agreements are important enough to demand their own carved-out focus within the larger area of human resources and staff development. Often there will be different unions involved, different contract cycles, different organizing styles, and so on. The complexity here can easily become enormous and should be monitored closely by a subcommittee.

Communications

Communication is essential in any merger, and it will need to be done both internally and externally. The collaboration committee can be instrumental in establishing constant communication as a condition of the collaboration project, but the best way to achieve it is through a subcommittee assembled for the purpose.

When stockholder-owned companies decide to explore a merger, it is generally a hush-hush affair. Premature disclosure of the proposal can have a major impact—good and bad—on stock prices and on myriad other direct and indirect aspects of their businesses. In addition, top executives who hold significant blocks of stock must observe strict regulations governing nondisclosure, including under what circumstances they are allowed to sell the stock or buy more. In short, the economic stakes are unequivocally high, and there is every reason to keep a lid on the process until the appropriate time.

Not so for nonprofit organizations. For these groups, there is a noticeable lack of financial incentives to keep quiet about their plans. Which is not to say that groups considering a merger should broadcast their initial discussions, just that there is no compelling reason to go into high-secrecy mode.

There are a few reasons for proceeding cautiously when widening the circle of those who know about a potential nonprofit merger. The first is that it is simply more workable that way. If smaller groups need not be concerned about external reaction too soon, they usually can get more done. Another reason is that stakeholders may react negatively to the news unless they are approached privately first. Finally, there may be unique reasons in any given merger for initial secrecy.

Since nonprofit mergers are best planned from the top down and implemented from the bottom up, the communication strategies that best serve them involve a constantly widening array of people. Communication throughout the course of a merger or an alliance development process not only eases fears and makes things go smoother, it also increases the chance of lasting success. For analytical purposes, it is best to separate communication strategies into internal and external communication campaigns.

Tip: Manage Your Message

Be prepared from the beginning to manage the collaboration message for both outside and inside audiences. Different messages will be required at different stages, and the unique facts and circumstances of each collaboration, especially mergers, will change both the details and the nuances of the message. For the next several years the novelty of nonprofit mergers may be irresistible for local media outlets. In those instances the underlying message could be something like this: "These conversations happen all the time, and we talk with anyone about collaborating to serve our clients better."

Occasionally the local media will be keenly interested in a nonprofit merger and will approach management before it is ready to make a public statement. When this happens, deflate the conflict angle. The media outlet—it will almost always be a newspaper or perhaps a radio station because nonprofit mergers are not visual events—may be interested in the story because it believes that the event will lead to massive job loss or some other bad thing. If the merger is really just an extended planning effort, which it probably is, the media hook disappears. No reader of a general newspaper wants to read about endless subcommittees where the worst conflict is over bagels versus doughnuts for the 7:30 A.M. collaboration committee meeting.

If the reporter is still interested anyway, play for time. By gauging how far along the outlet is in developing the story, you can estimate how much time you have in which to take charge of the coverage with all the local media. Alternatively, if you are willing to play a cute media game, you can offer to work closely with the reporter to develop the story as an exclusive—but only according to your timetable. A word of caution on the latter strategy: It will work only in media markets where there is a clear dominant outlet. Even then, you risk incurring the wrath of all those other media folks who were left out. Professional public relations assistance is invaluable here.

Internal Communication

As noted earlier, in most cases, initial discussions about a potential merger will take place between only a handful of people, such as the CEO and two or three key board members. Ordinarily there should be an explicit understanding among these people that the idea is confidential unless and until it is mutually agreed otherwise. Again, the intent is to keep the early planning manageable, not to exclude. Early on in this process, the full board should consider the idea; if confidentiality is a concern, it may be wise to adjourn a board meeting and convene in informal session.

Communication with senior staff tends to be personal and in groups. Note that because nonprofit mergers are initiated by staff so frequently, this type of communication may well occur before communication with the full board of directors. The idea is to get senior staff focused on the feasibility and implementation level of thinking. Note that the term "senior staff" is a loose one. In small nonprofits, it may mean simply anyone in a position of responsibility besides the executive director. Or there may be no true senior staff at all. In larger organizations, it can mean a whole layer of managers.

Pitfall: Getting Too Far Out in Front of the Board

It is not uncommon for CEOs to take the merger initiative too far too fast. The danger here is the possibility that, for whatever combination of reasons, the board of directors of one of the organizations will feel left behind. If that occurs, the CEO has to call a time-out and make sure that the board quickly comes up to speed with the entire thought process. For tactical reasons, it is better that the chief executive calls for the pause. If the board feels this way, it will slow down and very possibly squelch the whole process out of pique.

Internal communication with the full staff about the merger should be formal and should come from the CEOs (or officer, if she or he has been selected at this point). Board officers might be copied as a courtesy, but the staff is the CEO's responsibility. The first official announcement of the collaboration in medium to internal audiences of large-size entities almost certainly will be electronic, and it needs to do three things:

1. It needs to lay out the case for the merger, explaining what changes in the larger environment have created the conditions leading to the collaboration effort.
2. It should explain how the project will position the organization to cope with those changes, including examples of what might be accomplished with the merger that could not happen without it.
3. It should explain what can be expected to happen to staff in general. The message here is reassurance, if appropriate, or straightforward explanation of any bad news that is already known.

Well-designed meetings are another valuable internal communication tool. Given the proper atmosphere, a successful meeting can explain far more than any written document, and it will do much to reassure hesitant staff. Ideally, a series of departmental or small meetings should be held on the same day in the two collaborating organizations to announce the exploration conversations.

Who should speak at the meetings will depend on the style and politics of the organization, but whoever it is (there should be more than one speaker in most organizations), they should lay out the rationale for considering a merger. The answers to the questions "Why?" and "Why now?" will be numbers one and two on the agenda in most instances. The speakers need to be scrupulously honest about where the process stands and about any specific plans for the future, which means they will be saying "I don't know" a lot. Above all, they need to avoid making any commitments unless they are absolutely sure that they can be kept. At the same time, they need to be as reassuring and positive as possible, especially about possible lost jobs. The best way to do this without making unrealistic commitments is to talk in terms of intentions and desires. For example, instead of saying, "No one will lose their job," the preferable way to say it would be, "We do not intend to lay off any direct program service employees unless it is absolutely necessary."

Note: The Power of Vision in Communication

When the executive director announced the merger at the mental health center's program staff meeting, one of the staff members turned to her friend and in a stage whisper said, "Maybe it's time to get a job at that inn in Maine."

Later that afternoon, the same staff member was overheard in a hallway conversation discussing the information presented at the morning session. "They say after the merger we'd cover three-quarters of the county's population and service 85 percent of the Medicaid population. Imagine how we could put some of these programs together."

The moral: There is no substitute for a positive vision in internal communications, especially in the first face-to-face meetings about the merger. Which is not to say that there is anything wrong with inns in Maine.

For most entities, e-mail or a blog or both will be the cornerstone of ongoing internal communication. It need not be fancy—in fact, sending out a slickly crafted message probably would give the wrong message anyway ("Now that we're growing into a larger organization, we can afford expensive cosmetics"). A simple message from one or both CEOs should do it. Interestingly, some nonprofits going through a merger find that the merger newsletter eventually results in a regular in-house publication if none existed before.

Compensation

Compensation planning will attract a lot of attention because compensation patterns are likely to be very different between two prospective merger partners, and these differences can cause conflicts. At the very least, compensation is a highly sensitive area for the new entity. At worst, it will take large amounts of money to even out differing compensation schedules (although that may not always be necessary) and benefit schedules. The role of the collaboration committee and any compensation subcommittee is to handle these differences as skillfully as possible.

Note: Nonprofit–to–For-Profit Is Different

All of this information is keyed to nonprofits merging with other nonprofits. In some cases, there will be a for-profit entity involved, and that opens up a whole other complicated area for consideration. Nonprofit-to-profit conversions are an entirely separate type of transaction and will be treated in a separate section. From a communications perspective, the major difference is that they usually require legal approval from the governmental official in charge of the state's nonprofits (such as the attorney general or secretary of state). Predictably, that process is highly public and ultimately political in nature. Depending on how many a particular state's nonprofit community has undergone, the process may be more or less predetermined.

Development

Fundraising professionals may get spooked at the prospect of a merger, worrying that it will be interpreted the wrong way. Interestingly, their donors do not always share that reaction. A good education campaign can help prevent defections. In large organizations or in those with a high percentage of revenue from fundraising, the donor education campaign will need to be overseen by a separate subcommittee.

Financial Planning and Budget Development

In financial terms, a merger is equivalent to explosive growth. Ironically, explosive growth can be one of the most dangerous things to happen to any organization. The idea is to use the growth positively, of course, but the only way to do that is through careful financial planning. A financial subcommittee can oversee (though not carry out) such critical tasks as budgeting and cash flow planning. Part of financial management involves relationships with outsiders, such as bankers and auditors, and carefully selected financial subcommittee members can be helpful here as well.

Information Technology

Today, nonprofits of all kinds must have sophisticated information-processing capabilities. Under the best of circumstances, getting two different systems to exchange information freely can be a chore, yet that is exactly what they have to do in the postmerger integration process. Whether one is collapsed into the other or whether they continue to coexist in some way, information technology systems need careful planning. Given its highly technical nature, this subcommittee can rarely expect to see more than a token member or two from the boards of directors.

Organizational and Corporate Structure

Somehow, management must capture all of those promises of more effective operations. While organizational structure is largely a management responsibility, often with the help of outside advisors, designing the corporate structure is an appropriate focus for the boards' energies. In large and sophisticated merger partners, or in alliances, this is where a lot of time may be spent.

Professional Development

As used here, "professional development" is a bit of a catchall phrase for a large range of possible activities. In a merger of theaters, the actors' professional interests and desires must be considered, not to mention any potential collective bargaining differences. Hospitals and health systems are looking for ways to include their physicians in marketing plans and are always seeking new ways of relating to physician practice groups. These questions are usually best handled as a delegated task of the collaboration committee.

Tip: What to Do about the December Sag

Planning a merger starting in the fall? Expect a slowdown beginning around mid-November. Board members tend to be hard to schedule for meetings, and staff members take vacation time. By the second week in December, it is virtually impossible to have committee meetings of any kind. The pace will pick up again just after the New Year's holiday, but since people were not around to schedule anything in December, the meetings take a while to get organized. The result is that the two-month period beginning in mid-November is a washout.

One way to make this period work for you is to plan a social event for the two agencies using the holiday season as the rationale. This works well if it is cast as a purely social holiday gathering—perhaps designed to replace a traditional holiday party or open house that one or both groups might have been having anyway—and there is no explicit pressure to accomplish anything. It is a good way to facilitate the kind of social interaction that is necessary to begin building trust during the mutual learning phase. Which, when you think about it, is actually accomplishing quite a lot.

Program Integration

One frequent reason for a merger is the possibility of integrating previously disjointed programs. Programs can be linked in any number of ways, from using common management, to shared marketing, to outright merger. A program integration subcommittee is a good way to plan those linkages, usually in coordination with a group working on organizational structure. This is another subcommittee likely to have little or no board representation on it.

Tip: Program Integration Takes Time

Program integration takes time, lots of it. In addition to the likely pride in programming that the staff of most nonprofits feel, there is little standardized programming in the sector. As a result, there is often no common ground for a dialog, let alone for deciding what is effective and what is not. The program integration subcommittee could take years to complete its task. Be firm but be patient.

Purchasing Committee

For larger organizations examining a merger, a purchasing committee may make sense. This committee's job is to examine the best practices in each organization's operations and then to apply those best practices to a projection for the new organization. The key here is to ensure that committee members see their task as finding the best way to spend the newly expanded resources, not as deciding whose purchasing practices should apply in the new organization. An added incentive: The purchasing committee is the chief source of savings that can be applied to such things as better health care benefits and compensation levels for employees.

Space Usage

Almost inevitably a merger raises issues of office and program space planning. The merger may create vacant space, force offices to be rearranged, or cause leases to be renegotiated. Reducing costs through more efficient use of space often can help justify the merger in the first place. Because the inescapable element of psychological attachment to certain places also must be considered, this committee must cover a complicated and sensitive area.

Tip: How to Find the Leaders

Having staff and board leaders on the collaboration committee is a desirable goal, but how does one go about identifying them? Use McLaughlin's First Law of Task Force Dynamics:

> The leadership of any committee or task force is never greater than the square root of its membership.

If a committee has 25 members, it will have no more than 5 leaders; if it has 15 members, there will be a maximum of 4 leaders. It may also have 3. Or 2. Or none at all. But the total number of leaders will never exceed the square root of the total membership. Why? Because there is not room for any more.

Sounds glib, yes? But it works. Try it in any situation you can think of. (Let's see, if the United States Senate has 100 members . . .)

External Communication

For a nonprofit organization, there are two audiences for external communications: funding sources and the public at large. Each audience is composed of smaller interest groups that may need an individualized communication strategy. Funding source types typically include donors, service users, and purchasers of service. The public at large is generally represented only by the media and one or more regulatory bodies.

External communications should be both proactive and defensive, and a small group from both organizations should think through the components and goals of each type early in the implementation process. In many situations, proactive communication with the media is not necessary because the organizations are not highly visible or do not have local champions or funding sources. Still, merging organizations always need an external message for general use. The external proactive message should parallel the internal one and probably will not change considerably throughout a successful implementation process. The most important proactive communication with outsiders will be with donors and funders. (More on that later.)

Merger planners need two types of defensive communication plans. The first is needed if there is no proactive communication effort. This one should be prepared to handle media discussion of the merger, downplaying its significance and framing it as the strategic, client-oriented business proposition that it is. The second type of defensive communication is needed any time that unexpected negative external attention arises. This can happen even—or especially—if there was a proactive announcement of the merger discussions. This communication is particularly important because reporters will have a predetermined hook for the story—"It's the bad economy's fault" or "This is only the latest screw-up by this management team"—so staying on message will help counter any negative effects of media attention.

Some Sample Collaboration Committee Structures

The needs of the merging organizations should determine the proper mix of subcommittees. No group of subcommittee structures is right for all situations, although we believe that there is a direct correlation between the amount of time invested in subcommittee work and the ultimate effectiveness of the collaboration. Exhibit 19.1 shows a sample of three actual collaboration committee and subcommittee structures.

The first merger was between two medium-sized organizations ($3 to $5 million) that had had a long history of serving noncompeting

Exhibit 19.1   Three Actual Collaboration Committee Structures

Merger	Function	Composition	Nonprofit Partners	Observation
1. Merger committee	Overall monitoring	Board, staff	Two medium-size	Committee was stretched thin
2. Merger committee	Overall monitoring	Board, staff	One large, one small	Used consultants appropriately
3. Merger committee	Overall monitoring, corporate restructuring	Senior management	Two medium-size	No board presence on committees
Personnel	Compensation equity; benefits planning; policy rewriting	Senior management, middle managers		Highly technical issues
Management systems	Integration of existing systems	Senior management, middle managers		A long-term focus
Communication	Internal and external communication campaigns	Senior management		Especially important at front end—generated excellent publicity for the merger
Program services	Integrating programs; development of new initiatives	Senior management		A long-term effort
Real estate development	New initiative development	CEOs		A long-range plan

markets in the same geographic area. They chose to use only the single collaboration committee and to do various administrative tasks in ad hoc groups of senior managers. Consequently, the collaboration committee was taxed to its limit; the positive side is that the new board began as an unusually cohesive group thanks to all the time they spent together.

The second merger also involved only a single collaboration committee, but in this case one party was considerably larger than the other, and the entire collaboration was explicitly understood as a takeover. The larger entity heavily staffed the collaboration committee, and the smaller organization, which had far fewer staff members to handle administrative tasks, had to play a minor role in the process.

The third merger was easily the most thoroughly planned and ultimately most effective of the three. Two nonprofits, each with program services totaling about $9 million plus contracts for processing $19 million of transfer payments (such as weatherization and job training), allowed all members of their senior management teams to spend at least two days per month on a relatively fast-track merger. As a consequence, the merger proceeded quite smoothly and created a major new service entity for its area.

What is most important about subcommittees is not how many there are or what their area is but rather the degree to which they can support the work of the collaboration committee. To do so, they need clear direction from that committee, resources as appropriate, and support from the members' respective agencies.

Tip: Ambiguity Can Be Your Friend

Two of the best things that any participant at any level can bring to the process of merging or creating an alliance is a high tolerance for ambiguity and a sense of humor—and the sense of humor is optional. The process is intrinsically confusing and often misleading, and its complex, nonlinear nature makes it hard for anyone to grasp it all. Is it actually going to happen? When? What is going on now? Who is in charge? These are all excellent, rational questions. The problem is that they rarely have clear-cut answers. Learning to recognize this fact and still operate is one of the most important things that participants can do.

Who Will Be the Boss?

Somebody has to be the boss. In the western world, we have yet to figure out how to make an organization work well over time without designating someone to be the boss. There is a strong collegial strain in much of the nonprofit world, and in some cases there is outright resistance to naming a single person as the leader, but we know of no other way. Someone has to be the CEO of the new organization, and the sooner the respective boards confront the question of who it will be, the more likely it is that the merger will work.

Put another way, leadership of the new entity is such a critical question that if it is not resolved early, chances of a successful merger are cut by half. Moreover, the way that the parties confront the question and answer it says a great deal about how they will work together in the future.

A merger can go forward without agreement on the new CEO, but one of the rarest commodities in the nonprofit sector will be required: high-powered, well-functioning board leadership. In one three-way merger, one of the CEOs resigned to take a new position before the feasibility assessment had even begun. The second CEO was talented but was generally acknowledged to need more seasoning. The third CEO was the logical choice, but she was quietly regarded as temperamentally unsuited for the job. Although this set of circumstances had the "disaster" watermark all over it, an effective combination of board members from all three entities took the initiative to do a CEO search. The merger went forward, and when the new CEO joined the newly enlarged organization, he immediately appointed the two other CEOs to high-ranking leadership roles. Within a year, one of the CEOs left the organization while the other one had become a highly respected lieutenant in the new administration.

For obvious reasons, decisions about who will lead the new entity can take a long time. We define "leadership" here as including senior-most managers as well as the chief executive; regardless of the size of the nonprofits merging, this group should easily fit inside a small conference room.

Once the CEO choice is resolved, the choice of other managers is usually easier and faster. Still, often gaps are left open and managers are left hanging without clear communication about their status, and this situation can add extra calendar time. It is not out of the question that some senior positions will be undefined right up until and through the official merger date. Sometimes this is the result of ordinary bureaucratic or organizational snafus, but it may also be the deliberate decision of the new CEO to study a few incumbent managers in the merged entity before finalizing a role for them.

Leadership selection is one of those areas where the boundary between merger planning and implementation is hard to define. Once most of the senior managers are chosen, the process can move quickly. In the best mergers, the staff members who meet most regularly with the collaboration committee become the nucleus of the implementation management team. Sometimes the collaboration committee meetings end up transforming into the new management team meetings as soon as board members stop attending. A sign that the merger is going smoothly is when meeting attendees realize that the sessions gradually have turned from merger planning to operations management.

The very best way to handle a conflict over the CEO position is to prevent it from occurring. This means that there has to be a clear-cut choice for the top position. There are many ways to get to this state. The preferred one is to time the merger talks so that one of the organizations has a vacant CEO position. The CEO of a nonprofit organization is the closest thing to an owner that this field can offer. Even if the incumbent has no strong will to lead, the very fact that someone is in the position is a potential stumbling block. This is why many merger discussions are triggered by the departure of the CEO.

If one of the positions is not open, the next best alternative is for one of the incumbents to have a clear and desirable pathway out of the organization. Retirement often provides that option for an executive, especially since many of the current leaders of community-based nonprofit organizations founded in the 1960s and 1970s assumed the CEO role when they were in their forties and may be ready to retire. Hospital CEOs, by contrast, tend to be less rooted in a particular community, so their options may lead them to a different geographic area altogether.

Often the leadership question is resolved before the respective boards or management teams get involved; the two executives, sensing the desirability of a merger, work out their own arrangement. Many times the leadership arrangement is part of the initial merger package proposal presented to the boards. For this to happen, the executives usually need a history of trust, mutual respect, and compatible skills and interests. When these arrangements occur, they are often the strongest possible outcomes, since the principals designed them and are more likely to be committed to making them work.

One trio of executives representing three merging nonprofits agreed ahead of time that one of their number would become the new CEO, the second would concentrate on program services, and the third would retire. Another pair decided to split duties by their long-term interest areas. One would concentrate on daily management and strategic direction, while the other would focus on developing his growing political contacts and network that had historically been responsible for much of the success of his organization.

Pitfall: Co-CEOs

Two steering wheels are effective only on big fire trucks.

Key to all of these kinds of arrangements is a frank discussion and shared understanding of the respective individuals' strengths and interests. In fact, sometimes the best course of action to follow in resolving leadership conflicts is to give the parties a bit of time and space to work out their own plans.

If both executives are viable candidates who want to stay on, the collaboration committee will get its first personnel challenge. Again, this is a relatively unusual situation. Few active, in-place CEOs will pursue a merger if it appears that doing so will lead them into a competitive situation that they have little chance of surviving. Of course, outside forces, such as a farsighted board of directors or an aggressive funding source, may force consideration of a merger in spite of executives' self-interests. It is reasonable to anticipate that more CEOs will face this scenario in the future as mergers become more commonplace.

Resolving a leadership impasse is an ideal job for an outside party. Merger consultants often fill this role nicely and spend a fair amount of time working through the intricacies of the leadership choice. Under special circumstances, this function might be performed by a board member or someone connected to one or both of the organizations, but explicit neutrality is very important and is easiest for outsiders to offer.

Some Tools to Accomplish a Leadership Transition

Whoever actually facilitates a resolution of a leadership conflict needs to have some tools at their disposal. Here are five of the classics.

1. Mediation
2. Employment contracts
3. Consulting contracts
4. New corporation
5. Farewell parties

Mediation

No matter who does it or what it's called when it happens, merging two chief executive positions requires effective mediation skills.

The job of chief executive is so complex even in a small organization that rarely do the heads of two collaborating nonprofits have identical skills and interests. Often there will be an internal/external split between the incumbents. One director will have strength in external affairs such as fundraising, political networking, or public relations, while another will be strong in programming, financial management, or operations. Personalities and management styles will also differ markedly, as will personal needs. All of this provides fertile ground for negotiation and mediation.

Usually there is a clear choice for the new CEO position and the effort goes into convincing the candidate not chosen (and his or her supporters) of the wisdom of the decision. A useful approach with the latter candidate is to ask him or her to describe in some detail how they like to spend their working time. Do they enjoy running meetings, speaking to groups, working on a computer, marketing programs, networking? Chances are that their preference will be a valid way to perform a management position. If so, the collaboration committee should give some thought to structuring a position that will enable that individual to contribute in exactly the way that best suits their talents and needs. If a face-saving way can be found to describe the importance of such a position, it will go a long way toward easing the transition.

Alternatively, each candidate might be strong in complementary areas and the effort must go toward deciding collectively which strength set will be needed for the corporation for the next few years. This is where the collaboration committee must show some leadership, because there is no right or wrong decision. Assuming intangibles such as personal style and character are not issues, the primary job is identifying the best match between the tasks needed to be accomplished and the candidate best suited to accomplish them.

Employment Contracts

Only a minority of small to medium-size nonprofit executive directors have employment contracts, but they may be a way to ease the transition to a single CEO. Such contracts express the serious intent of the new board and are a means of demonstrating sincerity when a former CEO is asked to stay on in a different role. Candidly, they also remove a major reason for a nonselected CEO to sabotage the process.

Tip: Dealing with Disappointed Supporters

There are bound to be some hurt feelings when a group of supporters' candidate is passed over for another. Sometimes support for a particular CEO candidate is really support for something else that that person was expected to deliver, such as a strong voice in governance or a symbolic message to program staff. If that is the underlying theme of the vote, it may be able to be handled in other ways. For example, if the issue is representation of a particular program or geographic part of the service area, it may be possible to structure the governance function so as to accommodate the concern.

Consulting Contracts

Consulting contracts are similar to employment contracts except that they are intended to be time limited. They function essentially as a long-term subsidized job-hunting period but have the added advantage of keeping some institutional knowledge in-house temporarily without a lengthy commitment. They also invite abuse and so should be used sparingly.

New Corporation

Some forward-thinking organizations have dealt with the transition challenge by giving one of the CEOs an entirely new corporation to develop. Obviously this tactic will work only if the executive is an entrepreneurial type, but if so, it offers several advantages for all parties:

- It brings proven talent to bear on developing a new service arena, which if successful ultimately will benefit both the manager and the parent nonprofit.
- It allows the individual to continue calling himself or herself a CEO. (Never underestimate the power of saving face, even for those who claim not to be bothered by what seems like a demotion.)
- It creates a focal point for energies apart from the day-to-day operations that the executive is now expected to leave.

Farewell Parties

A good technique for recognizing an executive's contribution while bringing closure to it is a plain old-fashioned party. Especially when a manager has chosen to retire, a grand party planned carefully and publicly in advance is an excellent way of turning the new page in a way that it cannot be easily turned back.

Once the Selection Is Made . . .

Once the selection is made, the chosen executive must begin to take command immediately. Given that the two organizations are still not officially or even functionally merged yet, this requirement is admittedly a difficult one to fulfill. At a minimum, the selection should be announced internally, with all board members and others who played a significant role expressing their support. Next, the executive should meet individually with all key managers to assess their abilities and interest in playing a role in the new entity.

At this point in a merger, there will probably be no formal basis for the executive of one corporation to actively manage the other. In fact, there can be no guarantee that the merger will even go through. Consequently, if a designated individual is to fill a CEO-type role for another organization at the same time, it must be done largely through symbolic actions.

He or she should take the predominant executive role in the collaboration committee. Gradually, the CEO appointee should replace the merger facilitator. The new CEO should take every opportunity to be seen both internally and externally in some connection with the other entity, though taking care to stress that the merger is still in the planning stages. Physical presence means a great deal at this stage. Even if the new executive's presence is peripheral to a meeting, it helps reinforce the notion of an impending change.

Structure of the Merged Entity

The new entity's structure, both corporate and organizational, is the aspect of collaboration most likely to catch an outsider's eye. It is also the subject of much premature internal speculation, perhaps for the same reason that it appeals to outsiders: It is the easiest way to grasp the impact of the change. To skilled outside eyes, the choice of corporate structure is often obvious. To insiders, the choice of organizational structure—that which is represented on the organizational chart—is often almost as obvious. Half the time spent here is frequently the result of each side getting the other to understand its needs.

Choosing an appropriate structure for the merged entity is largely a technical matter shaped by financial, legal, and other considerations. This stage can take several months because it has everything to do with process and little to do with technical issues. Participants need to educate themselves enough about the options to make an informed decision, and then the decision itself needs to be okayed by many different parties. These may range from regulators, to funding sources, to lenders, to outside attorneys. A few of these parties may have to be consulted by law; others need to be consulted only because of internal politics.

We have already covered the question of structure thoroughly, so it is not necessary to repeat it here. What has not been covered is the process by which the structure gets determined. We touch on this subject before moving on to communications strategies.

Computer experts know that the proper way to computerize a business application is to decide what needs to be done, select the software that will do it, and, finally, purchase the hardware that will best run the software. It is much the same with corporate and organizational structures during a merger. Wise managers will concentrate first on what they are trying to accomplish through the merger, as described earlier. Gain market share? Amass clout for use in negotiations with funders? Cut costs? Secure new programming? Only clearly identified goals and objectives to be achieved through the merger will help answer the question about how the new entity or entities should be organized.

This is usually not nearly as easy as it sounds. Often board or staff members feel strongly about one type of structure over another. Frequently, board members will have had some personal or professional experience with a proposed model, and their eagerness to advocate for or against it is hard to contain. Compounding this problem is the fact that matters of corporate structure are like driving a car: It looks easy, and everybody has his or her own opinion about how it should be done.

The best approach is preventive. Try to secure the collaboration committee's agreement to postpone a decision about corporate structure until later in the process. At the very least, it should not happen until the CEO job and most senior management positions have been filled and the due diligence phase has been completed. Shore up that agreement by providing education about the various options available. Dedicate a half hour of one collaboration committee meeting to an invited guest (an outside, neutral expert) who can explain the major possibilities and their advantages and disadvantages. Constantly remind overeager collaboration committee members of the commitment to weigh all the facts before choosing a corporate structure.

In some ways, the most powerful thing that merger planners can do is to make the choice of corporate structure a largely uninteresting technical matter because, well, it *is* pretty uninteresting except to corporate attorneys. In order to do this, the planning dialog has to be kept at a high enough level that participants can consider the implications of various scenarios, exploring each one with confidence. For example, the discussion should be framed as "Will our newly merged entity be strong enough for us to expand into the neighboring state?" rather than "Well, the neighboring state refuses to work with foreign corporations so we better incorporate something right now." Legal and financial advisors need to play a support role in these discussions, which means that they should be primarily technicians. It is easy for boards and management teams to be intimidated by technical knowledge of this sort. To avoid it, one needs an unswerving focus on what is trying to be accomplished, not how it is to be accomplished. This is akin to the difference between strategy and work planning: The latter is useful only in the service of the former.

Naturally, staff and senior managers will be far more interested in the new organizational chart than in the nuances of corporate structure. One of the reasons for resolving the leadership of the new entity as soon as possible is that it permits the new CEO to begin establishing the internal organizational structure. Since mergers tend to occur most readily between similar organizations, the suspense is not likely to center around the boxes on the organizational chart. Chances are they will look like the old boxes, although perhaps more plentiful. The real suspense will be who fills them.

Usually the continuing CEO will create an organization that looks like an enlarged version of his or her old one. Almost as predictably, he or she will be inclined to bring the former complement of managers into the new positions. This is completely understandable, but shrewd CEOs will sense the enormous political implications of their actions and will actively seek to place the other organization's managers in demonstrably important positions.

Often an immediate problem arises because the new CEO wishes to place a former number-two position in a comparable role. The other entity, having given up its "claim" on the CEO's job, feels that one of its people should hold the second position in the new entity. One way to balance off these potentially divisive sentiments is to use the organizational structure to create opportunities for a senior management team that is large enough to accommodate members from both organizations yet small enough and efficient enough to get the job done. Smaller organizations may not have this option, of course. The objective is to create a well-constructed management team, not a bloated one.

Tip: Consider Title Upgrades

One way to take some of the sting out of people not getting the precise roles they had envisioned in the new entity is to upgrade titles all around. This is why many are now beginning to use the vice president title to a greater extent than before. Title upgrades can buffer some of the upset that may go along with a merger. It is an added bonus that some changes in title actually can reflect the employee's role a bit more precisely.

No matter how small the organization or how idealistic the staff, prepare for gamesmanship at this stage. People's jobs, reputations, and self-esteem are on the line. Inescapably, talking about positions and roles in a new structure means talking about real people. Worse, it is hard to hide or be subtle. Some proposals for structure will be blatantly self-serving, and resistance to any proposal is never far away. If it is true, the newly appointed CEO can gain much leeway with the promise that no one will lose a job other than through attrition.

Donors

Development directors often respond to internal news that a merger is being considered with strong fears about what it will do to the donor base. Usually they are wrong to worry. It is a logical and understandable fear, but it reflects the kind of management-centrism that occurs when professionals consider external developments solely from their own viewpoint.

Some people are fond of saying things like "People give money to people." While on a technical level that is correct, it misses the larger reality that donors give money to a nonprofit in the first place because they like its mission; only later on do they develop a fondness for specific individuals. In the end, if they are sincere, it is the mission that they care about. Another way of framing the question is this: Ask yourself if the average donor cares more about the nonprofit's: (a) corporate structure, (b) management team, or (c) mission.

To ask the question is to answer it. In a properly structured merger, (a) and (b) may or may not change, but (c) should stay intact. Professionals' fears about donor losses are a way of saying that donors' major connection is with a particular corporate structure or a certain manager. This is a misreading of most donors' intentions when they develop a relationship with a nonprofit.

At the same time, individual donors may need special attention, particularly at the time the merger is announced. Development staff should be included in announcement planning. For instance, it may be helpful to make personal contact with a handful of major or influential donors on the day the merger is announced—or even the day before, if it can be done discreetly. Unequivocally, within a day or two, all regular donors should receive a written communication about the merger, its rationale, and the explicit wish that they continue as donors after the merger. This is especially necessary if the entity might be perceived as being "taken over" in the merger. A useful appeal might be for special one-time costs of the transaction.

Consumers

Consumers are likely to greet the news of a nonprofit merger first with concern and then with indifference, as long as it does not involve major changes, such as building or program closings. Their greatest interest is usually continuity of the services. A subset of this concern is composed of pragmatic procedural questions: Do I need to renew my membership with the new organization? Will the credit on my bill still be valid? Can I keep my therapist? Communication with them should stress the seamless nature of the transition, if that is true, and provide ample guidance for any changes they may need to make.

Purchasers of Services

We distinguish between service users, who are direct one-at-a-time consumers of the nonprofit's services, and purchasers of services, which are outside institutions, such as governments and businesses.

In the health, education, and human services fields, governments are usually the largest purchasers of service from nonprofit organizations. Naturally, they have a stake in how those services are delivered. The way that they define that stake and their level of sophistication about purchasing services from private nonprofits determines the best communication tactics to use with them.

Although different purchasers will react to the prospect of a merger in different ways, one nearly universal statement about them all is that they should get a courtesy call. Why? Call it business common sense. When a single purchaser is responsible for a significant piece of an organization's revenue, it is wise to engage that entity regularly if for no other reason than to signal respect for its interests. Deciding how and when that call is made in each case is the important part.

Beyond the question of business common sense is the current likelihood that the merger of two of their nonprofit service providers will be a rare event for many governmental purchasers. While this may change in the coming years, in some areas of the country it will be novel and potentially threatening for the purchasers. After all, they probably had just made the decision to use private nonprofits as service providers sometime in the past two or three decades. At first, the purchasers were the ones with all the financial and management know-how. Their service providers were almost certainly loosely structured, informally managed, generally untutored, and maybe even naive. In short, they were dependent on their government funders for more than just funds. Now those same nonprofits are taking the initiative to restructure their own operations and may even be talking about a new way of doing business that could appear to diminish the governmental unit's control over them.

Do not underestimate the importance of this interpretation, or the likelihood of its occurrence. Most governmental units and their managers, especially midlevel bureaucrats, are still firmly rooted in the industrial model of command and control over their service providers, as if the latter were simply extensions of themselves rather than a fundamentally different and vibrant service delivery system. Those operating with the command-and-control mind-set may object to such profound private initiatives as mergers and alliances because they fear that it will somehow reduce their relative position or importance. Officials objecting to these moves need a great deal of handholding and constant reassurance about the motives and competence of the principals involved in the merger. Alternatively, they may try to push what they perceive as distressed organizations into a merger of their suggestion. In both cases, nonprofit managers seeking to arrange a merger need to go well beyond a courtesy call.

At the same time, the government purchaser who has been satisfied with the services provided to date is equally likely to react with no more than wary indifference. Assuming that there have been no issues with the services provided, this stance makes perfect sense. In fact, a common governmental reaction to a private sector merger is administrative. These officials tend to be focused on maintaining orderly housekeeping, and they will be easier to work with as the merger develops. One can presume that such an approach will be characteristic of most governmental purchasers eventually as they learn how to leverage their role as purchasers without getting deeply involved in the operations of their contracted service providers.

The General Public, as Represented by the Media

Happily, or unhappily, depending on one's perspective, the media are not usually very interested in nonprofit mergers and even less in alliances. As a result, managers get a lot of room in which to maneuver before a story becomes interesting to the media. The downside of this fact is that it may be hard to get coverage if it is desired. Without a hook—the media term for a reason to read a story—there is little incentive to pursue the angle.

There are exceptions to this general situation. Big nonprofits in any field frequently attract media interest simply because of their size. Being the first in the area to announce a merger sometimes is enough, although this is getting harder to do. Also, an instantly recognizable nonprofit name generates media interest.

The media business can best be viewed as a gigantic commodity production system. Individual news stories enter the system, get measured against its expectations and the economics available to cover it, and then get processed through to a conclusion. Most nonprofit mergers do not even show up on the large systems' radar screens, so if there is to be any coverage, it will occur in small-market print or radio outlets. In a few cases, the merger will be a large story for its area; that is when media-conscious managers can count on some intense exposure.

The real challenge of an external media campaign related to a merger is not getting a particular amount of coverage but rather how well and how consistently one can control it. This is the central task of external communications management. Reporters will do a certain amount of their own research, but they do not expect to become experts in the field. Rather, they want an easily understandable framework and a clear story line. If the organizations contemplating the merger can provide that, the resulting coverage will tend to conform to it. Merging partners that fail to provide such information risk losing control of the public dialog.

An example illustrates the point. A major teaching hospital and a major municipal acute care hospital decided to merge. Historically in the hospital industry, mergers frequently have been the precursor to attempts to build integrated health care delivery systems. The principals of both hospitals knew this and had the germ of a long-term integrated system in mind, but the political and operational chore of merging two such dominant institutions was overwhelming, and they did not present the longer-term goal in any way.

The result was that opposition to the merger, largely from the two different and competing collective bargaining units involved, focused on the collapsing of the two hospitals rather than on the larger and much more important effort to build a uniquely integrated care delivery system. Had the leaders of the effort used the media to lay out their larger plan and attempted to convince the public of its soundness, two things might have been different:

1. The opposition would have had to target the plan and spend energy showing how it would not work rather than snaring management in the no-win minutiae of layoffs and union negotiations.
2. If the leadership had staked out the higher strategic ground, critics would have seemed diminished in comparison.

Although the merger eventually went through, it would have been much smoother with a more effective communication strategy.

Communicating with Regulators

Communicating with regulators involves different considerations from the type of communications described up to this point. The regulator, who is likely to be the state attorney general, secretary of state, or some such government official, is accustomed to communicating through policies and how-to materials. It should be fairly easy to find out if there is a formal procedure governing the type of merger you envision and, if so, how to make it work. Unless your situation falls outside the preestablished guidelines, regulatory communications should be largely a matter of following instructions.

The one exception to this idea is when the merger involves a unique twist on the usual nonprofit-merging-with-nonprofit route. One of the more common twists is when a for-profit company purchases a nonprofit corporation. Initially common among nonprofit hospitals in the South and West, these so-called conversions had spread to health maintenance organizations and hospitals in all parts of the country by the end of the 1990s. Today there are well over 200 such conversion foundations. The first ones in each state are the most difficult because regulators have yet to work out the legal, financial, and operational procedures needed to monitor them properly. Once established as an accepted practice, conversions are likely to be more straightforward in subsequent transactions even though they will be individually scrutinized.

Creating the Formal Agreement

The timetable required for formalizing the merger agreement illuminates the critical difference between calendar time and process time. Creating a formal merger agreement—also known as a memorandum of agreement or memorandum of understanding—is easily delayed for mundane reasons. Missed phone calls, inopportune sicknesses, forgotten e-mails, unclear minutes—these are just a tiny sample of the things that stretch the calendar time needed to write up an actual agreement.

Tip: The Value of Paying an Outside Attorney

The written agreement process shows the value of using paid outside legal advisors rather than a board member who happens to be, say, a first-rate insurance company attorney. We saw one merger in which just such an arrangement was made, and the attorney—or, to be exact, his partner who was covering for him—forgot to file the merger papers at the appropriate time. The oversight was not discovered for several weeks and led to much avoidable confusion.

There is no universal format for a merger agreement. Nor should there be. Since every merger is unique, the intentions and details will vary. The state oversight entity, such as the attorney general or secretary of state, may have forms for this purpose, or it may require certain material to be covered. This is the point at which participants will be very happy if they have kept careful notes throughout the process. Usually the merger agreement itself will be the first time all the various points have been collected in one place. The simple act of collecting them, documenting them, and discussing the final draft is frequently a wonderfully focusing exercise.

As difficult and time-consuming as the merger agreement may be on a technical level, the biggest time-consuming step can be the two boards' discussion of it. Be sure to leave ample time for prolonged discussion by one or both boards. There should be no surprises at this point, but many times there will be a need to fine-tune the exact written expression of a point that was agreed upon much earlier.

Tip: Rule of Thumb for Estimating Calendar Time

Here is a rough rule of thumb for predicting how long a merger will take:

> The total estimated calendar time for a merger between two non-profits is equal to three months plus a month for each merger subcommittee that is necessary.

To make a merger work, the collaboration committee must first identify the major areas needing focused attention as part of the merger planning process. Each area then gets assigned to a separate subcommittee created for the purpose, as described earlier. Since a certain amount of work needs to be done regardless of the size of the participants, adding three months to the number of subcommittees gives a workable estimate of the overall time frame.

Merger Announcement (Create a Splash)

Once the merger announcement is signed, participants' inclinations will likely be to go back to their respective offices and breathe a sigh of relief. They certainly know that more work lies ahead, but the tendency is to see that work as happening after a small rest. That is understandable, but this is not the time for relaxation because there is a press announcement to make.

How often do most nonprofits get to command attention from the media? This may be a newsworthy moment if there have been few nonprofit mergers in the media market recently. For the first few mergers in a given area, this is the story hook. Collaborative mergers without announced job cuts and Wall Street drama are still man-bites-dog stories. Two nonprofit organizations that merged their operations in a major media market were able to get excellent media coverage largely because it had been two years since the last announced merger, and the local media was accepting of a replacement for the previous story.

Once nonprofit mergers have begun to induce merger fatigue in a given media market, merging organizations will have to develop different hooks. Any merger involving kids, disease remediation or relief, or a unique service will have an automatic edge in appeal. Others may have to be creative about the angle. If a prominent local figure is involved as an officer, donor, or consumer, this may be a way to get coverage ("Why I support this merger"). Personal-story angles also work—media types invariably resort to the marriage metaphor in covering mergers, so if two spouses will be united as employees of the same organization working in the same building for the first time, it might be a good basis for a story. The idea is to find compelling media hooks that might otherwise be overlooked.

This is not just the institutional version of ego gratification. Most successful fundraising nonprofits have developed a knack for offering up easy media storylines on a regular basis. A single exposure with a strong angle could produce spin-off coverage from the same outlet or other ones that pick up the story. Good stories have a multiplier effect and are the kind of things that establish positive name recognition in the eyes of potential donors. Done properly, mergers can do more for establishing name recognition than a string of golf tournaments.

20

Third Phase of a Merger: Integration

This chapter identifies crucial areas for integration. Readers should be aware that the text does not include recipe cards or foolproof formulas for integrating operations after a merger. Instead, these points should be taken as guidance for how to proceed in key areas. Unique circumstances will change both the problem areas and what to do about them, so readers should be prepared to make appropriate adjustments.

Although the legalities of the merger process are black-and-white—entities are either legally merged or they are not—the management aspect is not as clear-cut. In fact, except for the official acceptance of the merger plan and whatever filings are required by the overseeing state official, there is no universal measure of when a merger can be said to be complete. Entities can go on indefinitely with two of virtually everything they began the merger process with, and as long as there is no agreed-upon plan or set of benchmarks for declaring the effort a success, no one can argue. One national airline is the product of seven different mergers over two decades. It still has at least six separate accounting systems, yet no one would argue that the mergers are incomplete.

At the same time, there is a point beyond which two previously separate organizations can be regarded as a single one. Like the point in focusing a set of binoculars when the two images blend suddenly into a single view, there will come a time when participants realize that the merger has taken hold. This is likely to happen when the new entity is called on to make a major decision, such as hiring a new CEO, entering into a new banking or other professional relationship, or any one of numerous other situations that require people to focus single-mindedly on the future without regard for the past. It will happen with both personnel and the board of directors, although where it occurs first is impossible to predict.

The legal requirements for merging nonprofits usually can be fulfilled with a minimal amount of time and effort. Although it is important not to overlook these areas, the major energies should be devoted to achieving the merger's promise. Just as computer software and hardware need to be constantly upgraded, merger integration can never truly be said to be "done." Integrating and empowering nonprofit programs is the goal, and ultimately a merger is simply one way of achieving that goal.

In truth, postmerger integration probably will occupy the nonprofit field for at least another generation. The fact is that we are not even close to being able to fully live up to the promise of mergers and integrated services. We do not have the administrative systems, the management know-how, or the information systems that will allow us to fulfill that promise. In most cases, these things do not exist. In the case of information systems, they may exist but nonprofits in their old forms did not appreciate the need for them, could not use them, and could not afford them anyway. From a historic perspective, mergers and alliances are little more than a massive restructuring effort that will get the nonprofit system to a point where it can make real use of new ways of organizing service entities.

Time Required for Integration

The effects of a merger take a long time to play out on the lower three levels of an organization. We once asked four nonprofit chief executive officers (CEOs) whose organizations had gone through mergers in recent years how long it took before they felt like their organizations were operating like a single aligned entity again. Here are their answers:

1. Three years
2. Three years
3. Two years
4. Four years

The average in this group is the single most common answer we hear when we ask the same question of other nonprofit CEOs experienced with mergers: three years. Although the question may seem to invite vagueness, it actually gets at a multiplicity of changes, the cumulative impact of which is predictable. It reliably takes a period measured in years before a CEO feels like he or she has the right people in the right places, especially in a much larger organization. It takes years before one can sell properties or initiate leases, years before the board of directors sees more of "us" than of "them," years before the back-room systems have ironed out all the kinks and upgraded their capacities. In a fast-paced culture, this timeline can seem like an eternity. But corporate change is best measured in years, not nanoseconds.

Redefined or Reaffirmed Mission

Since the merger process itself is a kind of oversized strategy formulation exercise, a common vision should have been developed throughout the whole time. Still, the process is not always conducive to producing a clear, carefully thought out statement of vision and mission for the new entity. If such a statement does not already exist, the collaboration committee should make devising one a high priority.

Name

As with strategic direction, the choice of a name or names for the new entity (and possibly its programs) may have been implicit in the merger planning process. The two points to remember here are simple ones:

1. You do not have to change any name as the result of a merger.
2. You can change the name if you want to.

Often, merger planners will assume that a name change is automatic. But why? No matter what the name of the new corporate entity may be, the names of the two previous corporations can still continue as program names without the "Inc." after them. This is especially helpful when loss of autonomy and identity are crucial issues in the merger planning process.

Salary and Benefit Discrepancies

It will come as no surprise that, in a field where the single largest cost of most nonprofits is personnel, resolving personnel issues is critical to

Tip: Get Them Involved in Picking a New Name

One pleasant way of getting both about-to-be-merged staff groups in the spirit of the merger is to solicit their ideas for naming any new entity that may arise. This can be done in the form of a contest, an organization-wide brainstorming, or just an extended shared project. One warning, however: This method is likely to produce tame suggestions bordering on the hackneyed. It is not an accident that corporate brand names usually are produced by small creative teams with lots of research capabilities.

the success of a merger. We will also state right at the beginning that there are rarely fully satisfactory answers to the personnel issues that arise. The best course of action is to recognize the inherently unsatisfying nature of this aspect of the merger and strive to set up a process that will secure as reasonable an outcome as possible.

Salary inequities are the hardest of merger issues to resolve. It is not often financially practical to bring the lower-paid employees up to the level of higher-paid ones in the short term, and it is impossible and typically undesirable to cut higher compensation levels in order to create savings. The result is that salary inequities must be dealt with around the margins, often with largely symbolic means.

For instance, managers may choose to soften the worst of the discrepancies. Requiring two people formerly from different organizations to work side by side with very different compensation plans destroys morale. In these limited cases, management might correct the worst of the differences. It may also be possible to compartmentalize the lower-paying jobs—often from the same organization—in a definable way and treat that program or site as a kind of feeder system to the better-paying positions. Doing this requires a fairly explicit statement from management that this is what is being done and that movement from one program to the other is acceptable.

A powerful and more affirmative method for dealing with salary gaps is to use the merger to create new opportunities for staff. Often there is a reason why a group of staff members are paid less than their peers. It may be that their collective skills and experience have less market value. Creating new programming and guiding those employees in that direction, with proper screening and training, can be a way of narrowing salary gaps.

Perhaps the most common way of dealing with salary discrepancies in larger organizations is to leave them in place through vertical mergers. There is ample reason why managers would want to do this, and most of it comes from very practical motivations. For instance, a university that takes over a series of day care centers would almost certainly keep a separate corporate structure for day care rather than pay university wage scales for day care work. Ideological or emotional motivations aside, the financial and legal ground rules are just too strong to do otherwise.

Staffing Levels

Setting proper postmerger staffing levels is critical for eventual success. Saving money through staff cuts alone is never a sufficient reason for a merger. It does not need to be. The challenges facing most nonprofits in the future, and the benefits to be achieved through greater integration, are so enormous as to dwarf the benefits of saving a few dollars through cutting staff. To put a different twist on it, if the only value that two nonprofits can get through merging is to shed a few positions, then it would be a short-term strategy that may not be worth it.

That said, there will almost certainly be an opportunity to create savings by eliminating redundant jobs. If one accepts as a given that nonprofits exist to provide a needed service to the public of some kind, and if that service has demonstrable value, then the core staff group delivering those services will see relatively few reductions after a merger. Most redundant jobs tend to be found in middle management and what we would call generic positions. These are the jobs found in many or all nonprofits and business entities. Nonprofits compete for generic employees in the same labor pool as other employers because those employees' skills are applicable to virtually any setting. A well-trained bookkeeper, for example, should be able to function as well in a foundation as in a bank. Middle managers, however, tend to have more constrained options and therefore be more difficult to handle. Those just outside the CEO's previous inner circle can be the toughest because they will feel most vulnerable. They are also the ones most likely to oppose a merger (in action if not in word), since they have the most to lose.

The tools of choice for working with these middle managers are attrition and long lead times coupled with plenty of signals.

If the job market is at all favorable, some managers unwilling to go through a merger will have found other positions by the time reassignments must be considered. One of the benefits of the subcommittee planning structure described earlier is that participants get to spend some time with each other. During the course of planning sessions, they find out whether they could work with their peer or a potential supervisor from the other side. Everyone develops a shared impression of others' talents and abilities, so by the time the new CEO and management team begin selecting personnel, there may be a collective understanding about who will do what. For those unlikely to get a future position, the planning framework is a way for them to begin getting that signal.

Why not just lay off staff? Why try to accomplish reductions through attrition? This is one of the areas where nonprofits differ almost completely from their proprietary counterparts. In organizational terms, nonprofits are almost pure political entities. To move a nonprofit forward requires substantial agreement on vision and values, all the nonfinancial things that have to substitute for the profit motive. Nothing detracts from organizational commitment faster than a round of layoffs. Needless to say, this is not the most economically endearing characteristic of nonprofits, but it is a reality. Layoffs and firings are always an option to cope with fiscal crises, but it is better to find subtler ways of reducing staff, even if it means having to work harder at it.

Information Systems

Another major area of potential implementation conflicts is information systems. This one is especially vexing because it masquerades as a technical choice when in fact it is more stylistic and cultural. Rarely are there black-and-white or right-and-wrong answers in information systems. Instead, there are newer technologies and older technologies, and there are system choices that make one type of management activity harder and another type easier.

For example, the advent of relatively powerful low-end commercial accounting software packages has made sophisticated accounting horsepower available to many nonprofits that never had it before. These kinds of packages are called horizontal applications because they are widely available and can be used across a variety of industries. They tend to be developed by commercial software companies that also offer other types of software, including software designed expressly for a particular industry, such as nonprofits. They are called vertical applications and usually are developed with a particular industry in mind. Organizations trying to integrate vertical and horizontal software will face a difficult stylistic choice between the greater precision and sophistication of the vertical software versus the less powerful but easier-to-master horizontal packages.

Either choice can be effective. Ultimately it comes down to a question of management preference; since no package is universally satisfying, what strengths in the software does the organization seek, and what disadvantages is it willing to put up with? Merger implementers should be aware of this central question and not just assume that the choice of one package over another is a matter for the technicians.

The other major aspect of information system choices to keep in mind is the economics of merging the systems. In this regard, merger planners must keep an absolutely relentless focus on the future. Often one organization will protest that it just invested thousands of dollars in a new computer system or that it recently upgraded the wiring in a building slated to be sold as a result of the merger. This is a frustrating by-product of mergers, but it is not a reason for choosing one alternative over another. Financial analysts have a useful concept called sunk costs. The term means that an outlay of money made in the past cannot be retrieved, nor can the decision be altered. The money is gone no matter what one may do today; it has been sunk and nothing that anyone can do is going to change that. Certain information system investments are going to be sunk costs during a merger, and acknowledging as much will help everyone move on from there.

Programming

Integration challenges abound in the area of programs and services. One of the strengths of most nonprofits is that they have something unique to contribute to the fulfillment of their mission. This is also one of their weaknesses, and it shows up when one attempts to integrate programs and services after a merger. Achieving mission-based impact should be the ultimate goal of the merger, yet it is precisely in this area where integration efforts often stall. Largely this is because often there is no widely accepted way to judge program effectiveness, and therefore there can be no universally agreed-upon standard for integrating two or more versions of the same service. Moreover, program staff tend to be emotionally attached to the way their particular services are delivered and to feel that their model is demonstrably superior to those of others. The end result is very likely to be resistance and denial to any attempts at integration. The answer is patience, firmness, and time. This area is one of the reasons that integration can take so many years to complete. The process is likely to take multiple subcommittees, lots of talking, staff changes, and slow cultural shifts.

Common Sources of Resistance

Every merger encounters resistance. A merger is a big idea, and big ideas are rarely accepted unanimously by any group of thinking individuals. Resistance can take many different forms, be active or passive, and will come from a virtually unlimited number of people and institutions. The important thing is not whether the merger encounters resistance but how that resistance is handled. And the key to handling resistance is understanding it. Most resistance to the merger proposal and its implementation will come from one of the two big Es: ego or economics. These two big Es are large indeed and require a clear-eyed response. This section explores some of the more common sources of resistance, why the resistance probably is occurring, and what to do about it.

The idea of economics in this context is probably self-evident: Fears of job loss and salary or benefit reductions are natural companions of the merger process. Ego as a term is normally associated with individuals, and that form of ego is absolutely a factor in resistance to a merger. The biggest and most effective source of ego-based resistance is likely to be the CEO, who does not want to have to send out Christmas cards announcing a demotion to assistant executive director. Close behind is the board member whose pride would be wounded at the thought of being "taken over."

But there is another type of ego at work here as well, and it is a more group-oriented phenomenon. Most commonly it gets expressed as pride in a group, such as a department or even the whole organization. It can also be expressed as a strong preference for a certain management style or an ideology, concern for "the community," the vague assertion that "Their services aren't as good as ours," or even an impatience to "Get this process going." Whatever the exact expression of this kind of ego, it can be a powerful source of resistance. (Note that impatience paradoxically may lead to resistance by creating it on the part of the other organization.)

Ego-based resistance can be dealt with only symbolically. The smaller organization in a merger may feel less like it is being taken over if a majority of meetings are held in its office, if the name is retained, or if the new entity adopts the smaller organization's original name. The time and place of the collaboration committee meetings may be symbolically important ("Our board always meets on the third Tuesday of every month"). The enduring point here is that, like it or not, much of the richness of the merger dialog occurs on a symbolic level. Participants who are not aware of this or who operate as if the symbolic level does not exist run the very real risk of slowing the merger and possibly scuttling it altogether.

Board Members

The first source of resistance is likely to come from board members themselves. Given that nonprofit board members should have no routine financial interest in their organization, their resistance will come from matters of ego. Since board membership is inherently an act of giving, it may seem strange to say that board members operate egotistically. But, as any veteran nonprofit manager can attest, they do. In this case, ego often means the institutional identification that board members feel, although it can also refer to the raw personal ego stake that some develop. Here are some paraphrases of the way board members operate from ego:

> This organization has been around for 112 years, and it's going to be around for another 112 years.
> If we merge with them, the quality of our services will go down.
> I refuse to be known as the last president of this organization.

Ego expressions can be negative too:

> We'll get swallowed up if we merge with them.
> Why would they possibly want to merge with us?

Several things make board member resistance easier to work with than almost any other kind. In general, one will not find a more sincere group of well-meaning people than board members of nonprofit organizations. Whatever their personal styles or ideologies, they usually want to do the right thing for the people and the community they serve. Most are keenly aware of their fiduciary responsibility. In many types of nonprofits, the board members are conceptual and analytical, tending to make decisions on the basis of rational arguments rather than impulse or emotion. At the same time, boards can be difficult to deal with. Most often this takes the form of a kind of genteel totalitarianism in which a single cogent opposing voice can stop the majority from taking a particular course of action. These boards desperately want not only consensus but unanimous agreement. Unable to incorporate differing opinions into a strategic direction, they choose no direction at all.

Pitfall: Board Members' Conflicts of Interest

He was a former mayor, a local businessman, and a tirelessly public-spirited citizen. As president of the local domestic violence program he knew that his program was much too small to survive on its own and needed to merge with a larger entity. Unfortunately, he was also the program's landlord, and he had lost a sizable amount of money modifying and maintaining the building. Seeing the larger merger partner's enviable cash balances up close for the first time, he sensed an opportunity and went after it. Enlisting the help of a local politician and friend, he mounted a campaign to get the new entity to reimburse him for his uncovered building expenses. Through sheer persistence and careful maneuvering, he ultimately won some money from them.

Mergers create the potential for conflicts of interest where none existed before. The case just described was a clear conflict of interest even before the merger and for political reasons probably could not have been avoided. The mayor/landlord's role was a form of hidden cost, and the main thing the larger nonprofit could have done differently is understand from the beginning that it was being set up and that this was a price of the merger.

The upshot of all this is that boards need to be sold on the idea of a merger. And why not? They are the ones with the legally constituted authority, and they have every right to consider such a major decision carefully. Someone needs to present the facts to them.

They may need and want guidance in interpreting those facts, and they will certainly want to debate the idea. If the initiators of the merger—usually management or perhaps a subset of the board—have made their own decision on the merits of the case, the full board can reasonably be expected to come to the same conclusion. If the board members do not do so after a careful, nonpressured review, then the proposal may deserve at least a rethinking if not tabling.

Tip: The Reluctant Board Member

Occasionally, one or two board members will be unalterably opposed to the idea of a merger. To deal with their resistance, determine whether the individual is opposed to the proposed merger or to the *idea* of merging in general. Be forewarned that the individual will almost always say that it is this particular merger they oppose, not the idea itself. If that is true, and if the opposition is rooted in principle rather than a conflict of interest or some other hidden agenda, it is worth spending some additional time with that person. If it is ultimately impossible to gain the board member's support, ask that he or she at least not actively oppose the process. Identify the person's concerns and make an attempt to incorporate them, but make it clear that dissenting opinions are valued and that the process will go on.

If the opposition is more general but cloaked in concern about the proposal of the moment, the director may be able to be politically isolated from the rest of the board. Sometimes the person's personality will accomplish that anyway; sheer stubbornness rarely builds strong coalitions. If not, wavering supporters might be turned away or neutralized by carefully accommodating their individual agendas. This method is not pretty, but it works.

Unions

It is an unfortunate and ironic trend that organized labor, which began in the twentieth century as a force for social change, is passing into the twenty-first century as an increasingly defensive and reactionary political movement. Often this posture grows starkly clear during a merger. Unions are potentially rich sources of resistance because they have both ego and economic reasons for opposing many kinds of collaboration.

Many nonprofit managers are fundamentally sympathetic to labor unions even if they are angered or disillusioned by some of the day-to-day realities of a collective bargaining environment. This fact leads to a quiet ambivalence on the manager's part, which can play itself out in erratic behavior in union relation matters. It can also lead to a downright hostile environment if both senior management and union personnel let personal feelings get in the way of business-like dealings.

Unions have economic reasons for opposition to mergers because many are struggling to survive, and anything that threatens to reduce income from dues threatens the union itself. It would not be unrealistic to expect that, in medium- to large-size nonprofits with sizable unions, losing a few hundred members might translate into losing one or more positions at union headquarters. Of course, a merger alone rarely results in a union being decertified. Rather, the threat comes when two nonprofits proposing a merger have comparable staffs represented by different unions.

Again, the preferred strategy is straightforward, merits-of-the-case negotiation. Realistic managers and board members will not go into a merger hoping that it will get rid of a nettlesome union. In fact, the merger may end up expanding the number of unionized staff. A more practical expectation is that a sensitively handled merger process may improve the overall level of union-management relations.

Middle Managers

In mergers as in life, there is no group more conservative than the newly arrived. Those who have just recently made it according to the old rules do not want them changed. This is the ego aspect of manager resistance. The economic motivations come from the fact that people who have been smart enough to earn a management job are smart enough to figure out that it is their ranks that are the most redundant and therefore the most susceptible to job cuts.

The ticklish part about manager resistance is that it is rarely explicit. Many times there is little or no verbal resistance at all, perhaps because reluctant managers realize that it would be foolish to directly oppose the merger process once it gets started. Instead, the ostensible verbal agreement is subverted by inaction, delay, and diversion. After a while, resistant managers usually stamp themselves as such by the fact that they never actually accomplish the things they are assigned throughout the merger process.

About the only positive thing that can be said about resistant managers is that they help make certain choices clearer. Managers who passively resist the merger process practically guarantee that they will have no meaningful role in it or in the implementation phase. Moreover, they risk branding themselves as expendable in the future, thereby accomplishing exactly what they tried to avoid by derailing the merger—job loss. This is not to say that reluctant managers should simply keep their mouths shut and go along. Sincere, principled resistance actually can be constructive, but ultimately the smart manager will try to lead the parade, not keep it from starting.

Funding Sources

Government funding sources act as a proxy for the open market in many nonprofit arenas and so are instrumental in forcing the conditions in which mergers are advisable (even if they rarely do so explicitly). For this reason, higher levels of government funding agencies usually do not resist a merger. In addition, it is legally and politically wise for them to maintain official neutrality anyway. They are rarely in a position to demand or block a merger, and a statement of neutrality from them is as close to approval as one is likely to get.

The story is different deeper in the bureaucracy, however. Field office managers, in-house attorneys, and even financial analysts sometimes feel threatened by the prospect of a merger, as they should be if they see their job as one of maintaining command and control authority over the groups they fund. Strategic mergers consolidate power in the private nonprofit sector, and in return for giving up a measure of short-term control, the government official gains the ability to profoundly shape and influence the future. This should be an appropriate trade-off for government work in the new information age, but not all officials see it that way. Happily, these freelance control efforts usually extinguish themselves, although a little careful exposing of them may be needed to hasten the process.

Banks

Banks can have a great deal to say about a proposed merger, although it is a bit unfair to call them a source of resistance. Any proposal that potentially can change the ability of a customer to repay a loan—for better or worse—will attract banks' attention. Usually they will have written into the terms of the borrowing the requirement that they be notified of any impending merger or change in the borrower's corporate status, so complying with this clause triggers a discussion. (It is a good idea to do it earlier if possible.) Fortunately, banks' interests are straightforward. Prove to them that the merger will have either no effect or a positive one on the banking relationship and the ability to satisfy covenants, and wise bankers will accept the merger with little objection.

Regulators

Regulators seem to intervene in nonprofit mergers only when there is a proposal to sell nonprofit assets to a for-profit firm, often in the hospital industry. These situations usually are triggered by antitrust considerations, which are rare outside of the health care industry. These conversions, as they are known, have created some large foundations in recent years. As of this writing, only about 15 percent of all hospital care is provided by for-profits, so there is plenty of room for future conversions. Assuming investors' continued interest in health care, this will be a future trend to watch.

Tip: Set Effective Dates at the Beginning of a Quarter

Partners in a merger or alliance need to establish effective dates for various milestones up to and including the effective date of the formal restructuring itself. When setting such dates, keep in mind that the underlying rhythms of all businesses tend to be divisible by quarters. Nonprofit fiscal years are likely to begin on July 1, October 1, or January 1. Certain tax reports are due each quarter. Insurance policies often are renewed as of January 1 or July 1. Special provisions in a loan or other banking agreement often are written to take effect at each quarter, and so on. Collaboration planners should consider setting any dates over which they have control to be either shared fiscal year-end dates or shared quarters.

CHAPTER 21

The Seven Stages of Alliance Development

Unlike mergers, alliance activity occurs only on the Operations, Responsibility, and Economics levels, or below the corporate line in the C.O.R.E. continuum. Whereas mergers of nonprofit organizations usually have some type of strategic purpose (including survival, the most strategic purpose of all), successful alliances will produce tactical advantages, such as economic savings and streamlined services.

By their nature, alliances are far more open-ended and inherently ambiguous than outright mergers. In the latter, a defined number of parties work toward a clear-cut goal, and they either achieve it or they do not. The product of the effort is the end result, and the most intense period of the merger process has a beginning, middle, and end.

For practical reasons, alliances are difficult to organize, motivate, shape, and maintain. But the thing that makes them even more difficult is that leadership in an alliance derives not from an assigned position or role but rather from a delicate mix of personality, organizational identity, and resources. This same mixture is true of internal leadership in any nonprofit, but at least there the leaders have a predefined position and role to reinforce their credibility. Alliances have no such positions or roles and so must depend on the political skills of their members.

Alliances are not new ways of conducting business. It just seems that way because they tend to operate out of sight of the average consumer. In the for-profit sector, there are examples of alliances created for very mundane purposes that have grown to be highly successful. Decades ago, a group of cranberry growers on Cape Cod in Massachusetts got together to find ways of getting their crops to the market. The eventual result was the Ocean Spray company, a very successful cooperative that evolved from being a harvest management tool to a well-known consumer products company. The VISA credit card was the product of a network of credit processors. And professional service firms, such as accountants and attorneys, create national and even international networks of local companies that agree to share referrals and fees when client needs demand both local and global service provision.

Categories of Alliances

We categorize alliances based on their purpose. There are task-oriented alliances and process-oriented alliances. Task-oriented alliances come together for a specific purpose, such as the development of a proprietary software package or to submit a joint proposal. Process-oriented alliances, however, have no end product. Value is derived from the process itself and whatever victories it achieves along the way. There may not even be a set of clearly defined parties involved in the project, and there is not likely to be any strong legal bond between them until they achieve a sophisticated level of operations.

Tip: Alliances Can Be "Premerger" Experiences

Even if alliances create no other value, they can serve as preparation for full mergers. The kind of close cooperation and mutual learning that occur during the building of an alliance lays crucial groundwork for a full merger. No matter what the stated purpose, a successful alliance will help build trust between participants and open communication that would not have existed before.

The other side of this dynamic is that it can be manipulated. Consciously or not, one or two major nonprofits in an alliance may use it to position themselves as logical merger partners for some of the other participants. Usually, however, participants will see through such manipulation, and it may actually backfire on the empire builder.

Seven Tasks of Alliance Development

We see alliance development as consisting of seven tasks. This model is offered not as a prescription for how to develop an alliance of nonprofits (although it could be useful in that regard) but as guidance about the nature of the collaborative challenge facing alliances of nonprofits. The seven are tasks are:

1. Initiate, explore, and analyze
2. Synthesize and plan
3. Establish shared objectives
4. Develop a working committee structure
5. Gain quick victories
6. Institutionalize buy-in
7. Implement and evaluate

Since alliances may involve a number of nonprofit organizations, they are considerably more complex than mergers to start and focus. Because they do not have to involve loss of corporate prerogatives or chief executive officer (CEO) positions, they tend to be popular as an alternative to mergers. It can be expected that, in the future, many nonprofits will participate in at least one major alliance. Already, many such collaborations are forming for a variety of purposes.

Unlike many other things in nonprofit management, alliances are market-driven. When alliances are formed but never quite get anything done, the market is saying that there is not a demand for what the alliance can provide. This is ultimately why alliances fail to get organized, although it is usually blamed on disinterest or a general inability to "get our act together." In these instances, the alliance's focus is usually not sharp enough or its focus lacks a compelling argument.

Alliances are not a way to be just a little bit pregnant. Smaller nonprofits tend to like the idea of an alliance because it seems to offer an alternative to what they perceive as the distasteful option of merger. Alliance's strengths lie below the corporate line in the C.O.R.E. model, meaning that they can most readily affect Economics, Responsibility Distribution, and Operations. However, be warned that rarely can improvements—even dramatic ones—in these areas substitute over the long term for the power of a merger.

Alliances are at their best in helping members find new and better ways of doing what they are already doing.

This chapter examines the seven different aspects of alliance formation. Again, there is no linear sequence of events intended, nor is it necessarily desired. Different objectives can and should be accomplished simultaneously. For example, an alliance may very well achieve a quick victory even before it has completed its planning and analysis. This is likely to happen incidentally, as when the process of planning together coincidentally identifies an objective that can be achieved outside of the alliance process itself. Operations personnel may identify a joint venture that can be put together quickly, such as a response to a request for proposal (RFP). Or perhaps a foundation grant could be submitted jointly. Properly conceived and managed, the process of alliance development itself can produce synergies and pleasant surprises at any time.

The intention of the next material is to offer some concrete suggestions for designing and maintaining nonprofit alliances. It would be presumptuous to suggest that it is comprehensive, but the hope is that it will cover enough key points to make the concept plausible and the effort worth considering.

Task One: Initiate, Explore, and Analyze

Someone has to speak first. An alliance will get started only when one or more individuals take the initiative. In many ways this may be the hardest part of alliance development. Suggesting collaboration may seem like a risky act: What if the colleague is offended? Uninterested? Steals the idea? As the pace of formal collaboration among nonprofits quickens, managers are more likely at least to be familiar with the idea, and this should help facilitate the initial discussions. Still, someone needs to take the lead. Who should it be?

A few characteristics often are typical of a nonprofit executive who initiates an alliance development project. The first and most important is personality. It takes a certain kind of person to make the first move. In addition to being comfortable with what others see as a risky situation (a perception they do not always share), alliance initiators in our experience are often innovative thinkers with a great deal of initiative. They tend to be young or, if older, relatively new in their field. Either characteristic helps them avoid seeing things in predictable ways.

Closely related to personality type is that alliance initiators almost always have to be respected by their peers. This respect is what gives them credibility that they can share with the idea. It also makes them more likely to be trusted by otherwise skeptical or disinterested administrators.

As a practical matter, alliance initiators tend to be associated with larger organizations. Managers of smaller nonprofits tend to be unable to spare the time to devote to such a highly speculative, long-term project. Representatives from larger organizations are also well positioned to do the little things that make a difference, such as hosting meetings, dedicating secretarial time, or copying documents. Although there is no reliable definition of large or small measured in dollars in this context, it might be said that organizations in which the CEO has two organizational layers between herself and program workers are about the smallest ones capable of subsidizing alliance development.

Finally, the alliance initiator needs to have internal "permission" to start alliance discussions. Even though alliances do not change corporate structure or lead to job restructuring, the executive's staff needs to be supportive if only to permit him or her to spend the time necessary to get the effort under way. Similarly, the board of directors needs to be attuned enough to the environment and willing to allow the time investment necessary.

So far, we have spoken of the alliance initiator as a practicing nonprofit executive. And it is usually an executive who initiates an alliance—managers usually do not have the purview for creating external alliances, but executives do. People in other positions, however, can play the same role. One of the most interesting of these alternatives is the trade association. For many years, nonprofits have been joining together in membership organizations with the explicit intention of accomplishing broad goals as a group that no single entity could accomplish on its own. These trade associations, although nonprofit themselves, have as their explicit goal the betterment of their members.

The roles of the traditional trade association are fairly standard. They include lobbying relevant governmental units, educating members and the public, publishing, running conferences, and creating joint purchasing arrangements. In some fields today, as a result of significant restructuring, traditional trade associations are beginning to consider including the creation and maintenance of alliances

---

Tip: Decide Who Is In, Who Is Out

An early fundamental problem of alliances with more than a handful of members is that it may be very difficult to tell which organizations count themselves as a member and which do not. Inevitably some early planners will want to be highly inclusive and free-flowing; others will want structure. In any event, different participants will go through their internal decision-making processes at different times and in different ways. The question of who is in and who is out may be answered quite differently at different times depending on where participants are in their decision-making processes.

The best way of resolving this problem is to devise a symbolic way of indicating membership. Have participating organizations sign an agreement. Issue a public document with everyone's logo on it. Issue certificates of membership. Or—the most symbolic and the most real—spend the same amount of money on something for the alliance. This could be a membership/capitalization fee, a consultant's report, or any number of things. Nothing makes an abstract idea more real than spending money on it.

---

and networks of members in their services. There are two reasons why this is happening:

1. Associations' classic role as packagers of information is being undermined by the explosion of telecommunications. Today, it may be possible for nonmembers to be informed of changes in the environment just as quickly as association members, which diminishes one of the strong arguments for membership.
2. Associations' methods and successes in areas such as joint purchasing and newsletter production are being copied and improved on by for-profit competitors, so they must seek new revenue sources. What organization is better positioned to facilitate collaboration among a group of nonprofits than an association of them?

Some associations, particularly those with too few members to afford a large association management staff (such as in rural or small states), are turning to professional management consultants to be part-time executives. Assuming ethical considerations are not an issue, these individuals are well situated to act as catalysts for alliance development among their membership.

Funders may also encourage the formation of alliances. Although their interests are not typically as nitty-gritty as those of their recipients, visionary funders can be a good source of support, advice, and money for formal efforts at collaboration. Sometimes they can go even further. One foundation, for example, responded to a change in state law encouraging the formation of health care provider collaboratives by helping to create an alliance of several long term-care providers. Another association collaborated with two others to create a three-association multiyear alliance for the explicit purpose of lobbying for key pieces of legislation. In one community, an unsightly abandoned railroad-bed-turned-junkyard was the impetus for a community-wide collaboration between various groups to build a nonprofit shared services building.

Deciding on a Purpose

The next logical question after the matter of who initiates the collaboration is to whom it should belong. This question is best answered after clarifying the alliance's purpose. The inevitable tension is between an open membership policy in which anyone who wants to join can do so and an invitation-only group. The discussion is likely to have ideological overtones. Nonprofit managers as individuals tend to have highly egalitarian instincts and a strong dedication to the public good. Typically this philosophy leads to an open membership policy. The counterargument is to limit membership in order to keep control of one or more aspects of the alliance.

The C.O.R.E. model offers a guideline. Planners should consider how high up on the continuum they ultimately want the alliance to reach. If the alliance has strictly economic goals, an open membership policy is best. At the other extreme, if participants can envision doing joint marketing at some point or even considering mergers with each other, they will be well advised to be selective about who participates. Holding the alliance out to the market as one entity for marketing purposes means that quality has to be reliably defined as the minimum threshold standard. To ensure that quality standards are easier to enforce in the future, the alliance will want to be selective in the present.

Models of Alliances

The characteristics and intent of the organization initiating the alliance will have a great deal to do with the shape that it takes. This is not to say that alliance planners should consciously try to replicate a particular model but rather that a given set of circumstances will tend to play out in the same ways each time. When a strong and stable nonprofit acts as the alliance convener, using its own staff to coordinate and support the work of the group, the alliance will tend to look like a hub-and-spoke model. Here, the initiating nonprofit will be literally at the center of the effort, and the major relationships will be the ones between it and the other participants instead of those between participants themselves.

In this model, the convening entity becomes something like the anchor store in a shopping mall. It should be noted that just being stable and fiscally strong does not automatically make an organization an alliance leader. Instead, it is the combination of these characteristics with a more intangible commitment to leadership that makes an organization the pivotal entity in the development of an alliance. Ultimately, the drive to assume this role comes from some combination of personal and organizational characteristics that cannot be predicted reliably.

This model obviously encourages paternalism, a trait that rankles managers of smaller organizations. There is little sense pretending otherwise. The best hope is that ultimately a swallowing up of the others can be forgiven if the lead entity sincerely uses its resources to advance the common good—*and* the CEO can successfully communicate trustworthiness, credibility, and restraint. It also does not hurt to incorporate people as well as ideas from the smaller organizations if the lead organization merges with its former colleague groups.

A second model of alliance structure is the loose confederation. This is more likely to happen when at least some of the participants are similar in size and strength, or when the alliance is initiated and nurtured by an outside force, such as an association or consultant. It can also take shape when some of the organizations' managers have known and trusted each other for a period of time and decide to turn that relationship into a more formal one. This model can also come into being when the members share a common trait, such as nonprofit status, religious or other affiliation, or simply geographic proximity.

Mutual Learning

Once the initial members of the alliance have been identified, they need to begin sharing critical information with each other. This is roughly equivalent to the due diligence stage of a merger, with a few exceptions. The proper goal of this part of the process is to learn as much as possible about each other. The same is true in a merger, except that, in an alliance, the learning should be focused more below the Corporate Structure line in the C.O.R.E. model and less on corporate matters. Program compatibility and the possibilities for integration, for example, will be more important at this stage of alliance building than will the state of each member's by-laws (although they are of secondary importance).

Another difference between a due diligence investigation and the mutual learning phase of an alliance is that the learning can be broader and more qualitative than quantitative. What is the stated vision and mission of the entity? What are the values of the respective participants? What are their strengths and weaknesses? How will the alliance fit with the established management style? Is it a valued initiative or just another set of meetings?

At the same time, many quantitative areas are appropriate for exploration:

- One of the most important of these is the nature of the members' market areas. All concerned should have a good understanding of the programs and services offered throughout the alliance. A good way to display this information is in a matrix format so that it can be read at a glance. A representative sample of program marketing material can help show how organizations have positioned their services.
- Information about how services and programs are organized internally, such as organizational charts, is necessary, as are descriptive information about board members and senior managers.
- If the service requires a significant physical site, such as a private school campus, some overview information about it would be helpful.

- Any quality benchmarks or indicators in the organizations' field are extremely useful to present.
- Financial information, especially in the form of an analysis, is a must so that all members can see and understand their individual and collective financial pluses and minuses.

All of this information should be in writing, and the body of work becomes the background for group discussion on one or more occasions.

Note that task-oriented alliances will go through the same kind of process as listed, except that they will focus intensively on one particular area to the exclusion of almost everything else. For example, an alliance whose major task is to create or modify software for use by the group will need to explore the capabilities and limits of each member's information management systems, including hardware, application software, and personnel competence.

A persistent question in a process alliance is whether representatives of each organization should visit the others. If the group is too large, or if a consultant has been engaged to develop the alliance, this may not be necessary. But if there are a small number of participants, it may be practical to introduce each individual to the other participants' programs. One way to do this is to hold meetings at each member's location on a rotating basis, planning time for a tour the first time each site hosts a meeting.

Board Involvement

It is wise for each organization to involve its board of directors during this stage of alliance development, if only on a for-your-information basis. Since the work of alliances will involve noncorporate change, managers may be tempted to avoid early discussions about them with boards on the grounds that exploratory discussions do not need board approval. Not only is this missing the point of CEO/board relations (boards exist to do more than just "approve" projects), but it also misses an opportunity to build support that will be useful later on.

An inescapable reality of nonprofit management today is that virtually all boards of directors—not to mention managers—will need education about collaborative relations, including alliances. There are many myths to dispel, and the collective need for education alone is a logical way to involve boards at an early point. Ideally this education will occur either before a specific alliance is proposed or as part of the early stages of considering whether to join it.

Task Two: Synthesize and Plan

Alliances need to take the results of the first stage and fashion out of them the broad outlines of a direction. At this point, the direction need not be concrete or even highly specific, and usually it is not. If the first stage has confirmed that their purpose seems feasible, task-oriented alliances may be able to eliminate this step altogether and begin committee structure planning.

Alliance participants may feel the first stabs of frustration at this stage. For one thing, membership may still be fluid. Alliance leaders may not have emerged yet, or those who are emerging may not be acceptable to the group as a whole. Another source of frustration is that objectives probably have not been identified. Yet another frustrating aspect of the synthesizing step is the persistent and often unspoken skepticism that this whole effort will even work. In response to all of these legitimate concerns, one must counsel patience.

Task Three: Establish Shared Objectives

Just as a single nonprofit functions best when it has a vision and clear-cut tactics for achieving that vision, an alliance needs agreement on broad themes and objectives. Articulating a common vision could be relatively easy because it is what brought the entities together in the first place. In many areas in which nonprofits are active today, the shared idea is to find ways of coping with reduced funding. Many organizations need to find solutions to rising economic size requirements and reduced government and corporate support, especially in the wake of the 2008 decimation of state revenue sources. Social service providers face declining support and a demand for less expensive models of service delivery. Such challenges tend to forge agreement over what needs to be done well before an alliance is attempted.

With general agreement over strategy in place, the alliance can begin designing ways of getting there. Again, the C.O.R.E. model can help. In a brainstorming session, based on the mutual learning already done, alliance members will almost certainly be able to identify dozens of potential ways to collaborate. Although the brainstorming should be done without regard to the C.O.R.E. model so as to make it as innovative and unconstrained as possible, the next step is to categorize the objectives on the four levels. The actual objectives identified could be endless, but we present some possible ones in the language of the model:

Operations

Seek funding for joint programs

Run programs jointly

Devise shared quality standards and benchmarks

Train staff jointly

Seek accreditation together

Agree to provide assistance in the event of program emergencies

Share equipment or temporary staff needed to run operations

Responsibility

Agree on common information exchange standards

Share key administrative staff

Agree to share job postings

Use common job descriptions

Implement a wide area computer network

Collaborate on disaster recovery plans

Economics

Purchase goods and services jointly

Share office space

Borrow money together

Run transportation systems together (buses and vans, etc.)

Two things are important about alliance objectives:

1. They will almost certainly change several more times in the coming years as conditions change and objectives are accomplished.
2. More important, in a sense it does not matter what the objectives are at this stage. What is of lasting value is not so much

the individual objective but rather the process through which it was created. The more subtle but ultimately long-lasting work here is to build a foundation of mutual trust and understanding beginning with the topmost layers of participating nonprofits.

Discuss a Timetable

Although process alliances are inherently open-ended, they still need the discipline of a general timetable to shape and monitor their progress. Experienced managers know that timetables established at the beginning of a project are worth about as much as yesterday's newspaper, yet the exercise of discussing the expected time frame will help mold future efforts and prevent misunderstandings.

Usually there is no external reference point for determining a time frame. This is why process alliances need to impose a time frame on themselves, either through mutual agreement or as part of an outside consultant's work. Even if the deadline is privately regarded with skepticism, at least it is a way of holding everyone minimally accountable.

Board Involvement

Once the alliance members familiarize themselves with each other and begin discussing future direction, participating organizations that have not already done so should engage the board of directors in the process. This would be a late start for a board, but it can still fulfill its responsibilities and make a contribution to the effort. Moreover, involving the board now helps ease the task of securing institutional buy-in later on. Managers should make sure to do some catch-up education and show how the alliance would fit with overall strategy. For their parts, board members must be careful to keep an open mind about the alliance taking shape. Their overriding responsibility is to make sure that management is entering into an arrangement consistent with previous discussions about the organization's future.

Pick a Name

Perhaps the single most important thing that alliance planners can do at this juncture is to establish momentum by picking a name for the blossoming project. Having a name for something gives so many obvious benefits that it is easily overlooked. Because it gives outsiders a way to refer to the project—no small benefit considering that an alliance is an abstract process rather than a building or even a corporation—it marks the beginning of an external identity.

Picking a good name is not easy. There is a reason why large national firms pay millions of dollars for research into potential brand names. Nonprofits historically do not have those advantages and so must operate by collective intuition. In all likelihood, the choice of a name will be ad hoc and a matter of divided opinion. It does not matter. It can always be changed, and the real point of selecting a name is that it gives everyone something to hold on to.

Tip: Whom to Look to for a Name

Already, certain words are getting overused as nonprofits form alliances. Words such as "choices," "partners," "network," "care," and even "alliance" itself are creeping into names. When choosing a name, try to be smart and forward-thinking. Early alliances can afford to try using some of these obvious choices because there is little competition. Later alliances in a given market area will need to be a bit more creative.

Also, be aware of the nature of group dynamics. As in mergers, it may be fun and trust-building to involve all participating organizations' staffs in the hunt for a name. But name picking is a creative activity, and creativity flourishes more readily in individuals and small groups. The trade-off is that getting the name from all of the alliance members' staffs will probably result in a bland, safe choice with wide buy-in. A name from a small group or individual consultant may prove too unpopular to be used.

Note: Less Charisma in Alliances

Single nonprofits sometimes can go far on the strength of a single charismatic leader. In fact, some nonprofits are implicitly organized to take advantage of strong individual leadership—a rubber-stamp board, small or at least simplified operations, an intensely private orientation—and they operate best this way.

Alliances, however, rarely succeed solely on the strength of a single leader. By nature, they disperse decision making, take a longer time to achieve their goals, and resist concentration of authority in any one place. Charismatic leaders tend to avoid such situations, and if they get involved at all, it is usually as a noteworthy but definitely part-time participant.

Task Four: Develop Working Committee Structure

In the first two stages of alliance development, it is natural for a single group to handle most of the planning tasks. This group is analogous to the collaboration committee described in the section on mergers, and for convenience we will refer to it this way. Generally the membership will be the CEOs or other high-ranking administrators of the member organizations, and there should be some continuity among them. This committee must assign, delegate, and coordinate alliance functions for all activities relating to Operations, Responsibility, and Economics. The committee has to be extremely clear about when it is acting in a coordinating role and when it expects direct results from itself.

Governance

In the very beginning, there is not likely to be much of a concern with formal governance, mainly because the members of the collaboration committee will be too preoccupied with getting to know each other and exploring what the alliance might accomplish. If there is any single decision to be made at this stage requiring a more or less formal statement of position it will probably be the hiring of a consultant or part time staff person. Still, regular decisions have to be made by the group, and the way they make them says a great deal about the nature of the collaboration committee as a governing body. Three principles can be deduced from those alliances already in operation:

1. Resistance to creating "bureaucracy"
2. Sophistication and formality reflect the membership
3. One organization, one vote

Resistance to Creating "Bureaucracy"   Many managers will be acutely aware of the inherent tension in their attempt to get the benefits of being a larger organization without actually becoming part of one. No matter how large the member nonprofits may be, usually there will be a tacit expectation that formal operating policies and procedures will be kept to a minimum. To do the job, after all, members need to be able to control their alliance directly without a lot of intervening layers of management or procedure.

Sophistication and Formality Reflect the Membership   Organizations usually prefer doing intercorporation business with other organizations that think, act, and look like they do. This is not a reflection of a mindless club mentality but of simple economics. The independent auto mechanic will do business with individuals and small local businesses because that is the nature of who he is equipped to serve. The multinational agricultural combine needs to do business with large companies because it is not designed to serve individual farmers.

As a result of this tendency, alliances will look like their members. Universities will use skilled specialists from a variety of disciplines to create a formal, legal entity with staff of its own and possibly even capital assets too. A dozen day care centers will use no paid staff and will try to put the alliance together without incorporating until it is absolutely necessary.

One Organization, One Vote   For practical reasons, alliances tend to be determinedly egalitarian in their decision-making process: one member, one vote. Why not? What other basis exists for making decisions? Even if endowments or revenue size counted for much in the nonprofit world, few nonprofits would get involved with an alliance partner that insisted on judging their balance sheet rather than the organization.

It is a wise idea for the collaboration committee, in its role as the corporate collaboration planners, to have its relationship with the subcommittees clearly defined. It can be expected that the collaboration committee will operate like a board of directors. This would mean that it has at least technical veto power over the subcommittees and that their work is framed as a recommendation to the collaboration committee. At the same time, the alliance needs to find ways of either making decisions with lightning speed (not a strength of any group) or of delegating sufficient authority to ad hoc committees that they can make a certain level of commitment without getting explicit clearance from the planning group. Otherwise, the process will get bogged down in approval requests and authorizations.

Characteristics of Subcommittees

Although subcommittees will vary according to each situation, three characteristics in the C.O.R.E. model are reliable enough to guide alliance planners. These are not goals for a system of subcommittees

Tip: Forget *Roberts' Rules of Order*

Some nonprofit board members and a few managers feel that meetings should be conducted according to *Roberts' Rules of Order*. These durable rules of procedure were initially created for large parliamentary bodies, not smallish groups of managers or board members. For that reason, they generally do not get used beyond the usual motion/second/discussion/vote of most board meetings. Alliance boards are problem-solving bodies, not public entities. If *Roberts' Rules* are needed to keep order, the atmosphere may be too stilted to get anything done anyway.

or even necessarily desirable characteristics. What they do represent are traits that alliance leaders are likely to see emerge as the process unfolds.

Operations   One of the quiet realities of nonprofit management is the sense of isolation that many professionals feel. The size and nature of many nonprofits often mean that there is only one or two of many types of professionals in each organization. Properly designed and communicated, a subcommittee focusing on some area of program operations can be a welcome experience for many of these professionals. The key is to establish that participation in the alliance is not expected to cost people their jobs—they will not, in short, be downsizing themselves out of existence.

Tip: Continuing Education for Operations Professionals

Many types of professions commonly found in nonprofit organizations require their members to get continuing education in their field, and most licensing programs have explicit requirements for continuing education. One way to motivate and reward program personnel for participation in such planning would be if their professional societies would accept such work toward their continuing education requirements. Although month-to-month committee meetings are unlikely to be eligible for credit, the education sessions that should be part of the early stages of the process may very well qualify.

As noted earlier, unless there is a ready-made opportunity for collaboration, operations subcommittees are likely to be slow to act. There are three reasons for this:

1. Program people—whether they are curators, librarians, therapists, performing artists, or teachers—usually have chosen to concentrate on what they do because it is what they enjoy doing. Asking them even to participate on a subcommittee may seem so unnatural that it takes time to adapt.
2. Successful subcommittees are administrative task-focused, and this is different from what program people are accustomed to doing.
3. Many program-oriented people are deeply ingrained in the intricacies of their normal funding stream, sometimes without even knowing it. Arts people have National Endowment for the Arts grants, community development program managers have the Community Development Block Grant, social service types have a variety of federal and state funding streams, and health care personnel are used to the dictates of Medicaid, Medicare, and private insurance.

Giving them the chance to rethink and redesign their own systems of services without a lot of education and support is likely to produce disappointing results. As a consequence, program subcommittees are more likely to focus on doing what they already do better, faster, or in greater quantity. For instance, one alliance's program people decided to pursue accreditation as rehabilitation facilities jointly because they discovered that most of the members happened to be planning to seek accreditation individually anyway.

Depending on the size and complexity of the alliance, there could be several program subcommittees. Health care facilities and some social service organizations bring together so many diverse professional and paraprofessional program service staff members that their opportunities for collaboration are often easier to handle in logical groupings of professionals, although the problem then is to establish an overall coordinating mechanism.

Responsibility By contrast, administrative personnel are likely to spawn only one or a handful of subcommittees. Largely this is because financial and administrative staffs in nonprofits tend to be much smaller compared with program staffs. Also, administrative matters are usually easier to centralize or to control through a small group of people. One budding alliance of developmental disability service providers pondered with some surprise the following insight. Owing to the fact that 3 to 5 organizations out of the 40 in the area provided services to well over 70 percent of the consumers, a subcommittee composed of just one individual from each organization could effectively set dominant standards for the exchange of computer information.

The most difficult issues for these types of subcommittees often will be the ones involving things over which participants have little control. In particular, many individual nonprofits must work within a reimbursement system, and more often than not that system is controlled by government authorities far removed from participants' day-to-day operations. Any attempt at standardization must somehow take these realities into account. In the end, some activities may need to take place on a different level—such as statewide—or not at all.

The subcommittee on administrative matters could easily turn out to be a permanent thing. There is always more that can be done and individual members will speak each other's language, thereby making communication easier and more pleasant. (Administrative staff can suffer from the same professional isolation that program people frequently feel.)

Economics Because economic collaboration is so unique to specific goods or services, collaboration on this level may tend to occur through a series of ad hoc task forces. Administrative staff members may know a great deal about how to buy copier paper, but they will almost certainly be at a loss when it comes to purchasing industrial paper supplies, such as sterile paper goods and paper examining-room gowns. Fortunately, the process of economic collaboration is straightforward and can be applied to almost any product or service.

Once the alliance planners have identified a product or service for economic collaboration, they can follow these eight simple steps:

1. Identify which members currently purchase what products or services from what vendors.

2. Exclude any existing vendors from the list if they are currently not performing satisfactorily; add vendors that may be appropriate but that do not happen to service any member organization at present.
3. Identify the list of most common items the alliance wishes to purchase. Consolidate items as much as possible, and be sure to compare similar specifications. Be sure to identify non-quantifiable specifications, such as service requirements.
4. Send the information gathered to the selected vendors, asking them for a written quote.
5. Compile the responses and analyze.
6. Select a manageable number of finalists for an interview.
7. Choose a vendor on the basis of the written quote and the interview.
8. Notify all alliance members of the choice, detailing a target date for the changeover.

The economic subcommittees have the power to be highly successful and influential. One alliance of seven nonprofits identified opportunities to save as much as $50,000 collectively just on the basis of issuing joint RFPs for dairy products, bread, industrial paper, and plastics. Moreover, because economic subcommittees can involve a full range of personnel from all levels of participating members, they are an excellent way to build support for the overall project. Once formerly passive or possibly disillusioned staff members

Pitfall: Watch Out for the Cherry Picker

Sooner or later—and for a successful alliance, it will be sooner rather than later—a losing vendor will attempt to cherry-pick the group. It will do this by, for example, belatedly undercutting competitors, by offering special deals to certain members, or appealing to the board of directors of a former client that just decided to go with the winning vendor. The best way of dealing with this attempt is to warn members ahead of time that this may happen and by constantly reminding them that they will find true clout only in tight unity. Failing in that, the second-best way is simply to shine a spotlight on the vendor's actions (quoting the salesperson, sending around copies of proposals for sweetheart deals, etc.). Often the group's members will react negatively enough that the vendor's attempt at cherry-picking will be self-defeating.

have the chance to participate in a meaningful and straightforward joint purchasing exercise, they can readily become champions of the process among their peers. In this way, the economic subcommittees have value well beyond measurable dollar savings.

Task Five: Gain Quick Victories

At this point, the notion of integrated services and strategic collaboration may seem awkward and untested to many, including some of the participants themselves. At the same time, some of the promise may be evident by now. Consequently, the concept must be continually sold. Board members need to be reassured that collaborating in some way is worth exploring even though there can be no guaranteed return on the effort. Even among the participants, not every CEO will be comfortable with the prospect, nor will all of their management staffs. Once done, a merger cannot easily be unwound, while an alliance can fall apart (or dissolve into a sea of apathy) at just about any time.

The solution is to shoot for some quick victories. Anything positive and traceable to the alliance that occurs within about 90 to 150 days of the official beginning of the project is a quick victory. These could be savings from a very focused joint purchasing project or the importing of a highly regarded speaker made affordable by all members' helping to defray the costs. An early victory may happen when members collaborate on a joint proposal submission or share the cost of acquiring a valuable piece of software.

Quick victories prove the usefulness of the concept. They show that something of value is feasible in the short term so that members can see that longer-term benefits are even more promising. They also create a sense of momentum. Staff members actually involved in the early success can feel justifiable pride, while those who were not involved may begin to see the possibilities in their own areas. But most important of all: Quick victories get people's attention. This is no small feat in most organizations. Those early victories act like little billboards attesting to the success of this previously abstract and vague process of an alliance.

Often the quickest victories are economic ones, for reasons similar to why economics is the lowest level of collaboration. Different participants discover they share the same supplier and that combining their business gets them a lower price.

Or they realize that the same vendor has given each participant a vastly different deal, which can be standardized to everyone's benefit. It is difficult to analyze purchasing patterns and carry out a rebidding process within a short time span; planners would be well advised to stick to one or two clearly definable areas (e.g., dairy products, or copier paper). Still, just identifying the possibilities can be considered a victory.

Tip: Getting Vendors' Interest Is a Victory Itself

Most vendors figure out that an alliance can mean new business very quickly, so it does not take much to capture their interest. Whether they knew it or not, their previous success with participants may have depended on keeping them fragmented. They understand the prospect of greatly expanding their share of business by bringing in the other participants even if it is at the risk of losing what they have now to another vendor that captures the full group.

Economic victories tend to be attractive to boards of directors as they consider whether to join an alliance or for foundations potentially interested in funding the transaction costs of collaborating. Sometimes a less direct and quantifiable benefit will appeal to management. Ironically, program managers, who often are most resistant to any collaboration that appears to affect their

Tip: An Idea for a Foundation Proposal

The reality of alliance development is that, to be successful, participants almost always have to spend money in the beginning. This can be particularly painful for organizations hoping to see savings up front. One solution is to approach a willing foundation with a proposal to fund the start-up costs of the alliance, especially an economically focused one. The central idea is that the foundation money could be leveraged: If $20,000 spent now to get the alliance up and running leads to a process that offers collective savings throughout the alliance of $50,000, the funder can be pleased to have created $5 in savings for every $2 donated. This can be a very powerful argument, and it is perhaps more compelling for alliances, where the savings are likely to be less visible.

professional autonomy, may embrace an alliance readily enough to offer some quick victories in a nonthreatening area such as training. Administrative staff members, who may be tentative or actively resistant later if the collaboration ever threatens to reduce administrative positions, tend to accept early collaboration if it involves new projects. Seeking new software or pursuing a type of professional accreditation that no member currently holds are examples of this less intimidating type of alliance activity.

Task Six: Secure Institutionalize Buy-in

No matter how well intended or stable some participating organizations and their managers appear to be, an alliance must move aggressively beyond its formative stages to ensure lasting institutional buy-in. Of necessity, the early days can involve only one or two individuals from each organization, but once the outlines of collaboration have been set, the budding alliance needs to create widespread support within each member organization.

To understand what needs to be done to gain widespread institutional acceptance of the alliance as a way of getting things done, it is helpful to examine the barriers to institutional acceptance and what can be done to lower them. We can identify several predictable barriers:

- Lack of understanding of the concept of alliances
- Lack of communication about the specific alliance being proposed
- Interruptions in leadership
- Lack of demonstrable benefits

We discuss each in turn, along with suggestions for how to deal with them.

Lack of Understanding of the Concept of Alliances

Board action could conceivably prevent the participation of some potential members in an alliance. Halfhearted support for participation can often be traced to lack of knowledge on the board's part, which in turn derives from inadequate preparation. The solution is for individual boards of directors to have a basic understanding of alliances, how they differ from mergers, and what they can reasonably be expected to accomplish. This is knowledge of the head; the next section deals with knowledge felt with the heart.

Ideally, several months before the management of each participating organization proposes membership in an alliance, it will begin a process of education with the board of directors. This might take the form of special mini-courses embedded in board meetings or outside speakers at the meetings. It could be done through disseminating written material, sending board members to conferences and seminars, and so on. The exact format of the presentation is not as important as the fact that the material gets presented and that board members have a chance to consider it as an option for the future. No binding votes need be taken at this time. Nonmanagement staff members can be informed through existing communication vehicles, such as newsletters, staff meetings, and the like.

Lack of Communication about the Specific Alliance Being Proposed

Board members and others connected with the entity may have intellectual knowledge of alliances, but what will really make a difference to them is to know how it will affect their own organization. This is knowledge of the heart, and it is equal parts calculation and inspiration. Without a shared vision of the alliance's benefits, it will be seen as just another quirky idea of the CEOs.

Although at this stage the alliance probably will not have a plan in place, it is quite reasonable to communicate a broad overview of the alliance's direction. If the previous type of preparation was successful, the various constituencies of the nonprofit will be able to fill in the blanks between concept and execution. The problem here is that likely not a large amount of material is available about the alliance except the initial analyses, which may be too unwieldy for broad audiences. Fortunately, the same communication vehicles mentioned in the last subsection will help get the message across.

Interruptions in Leadership

Few developments can destroy a growing alliance's momentum faster than leadership turnover. Not surprisingly, the most critical leadership disruptions occur among the planning group. Departures from some of the subcommittees often can be overcome once the groups are accustomed to working together. The alliance is most vulnerable at the point when the original leaders have begun to coalesce but have not achieved widespread acceptance of the alliance at all the necessary levels in their own organizations.

There are a few solutions to leadership interruptions. The strongest grows out of accomplishing institutional buy-in. When managers and staff are accustomed to participating in planning sessions, when they have experienced victories firsthand, they will be among the first to orient a new CEO to the alliance. Prior to the point of achieving such widespread organizational interest, key people, such as the board president or senior managers, need to be sure to pass on the oral tradition of the alliance. Finally, other alliance members will need to assume responsibility for conducting at least an informal orientation with new CEOs and other senior managers.

Lack of Demonstrable Benefits

Board members will be particularly quick to want to pull the plug on an alliance that does not seem to be offering any clear-cut benefits. And if after a reasonable time the alliance is not fulfilling its promise, that is what should happen. But before individual boards withdraw or the membership as whole decides to disband, it should be determined why the alliance is not working and what, if anything, could be done to make it work.

If it is not working because planners misread the possible benefits or because structural obstacles to collaboration were uncovered late in the process, then termination makes sense. However, a more likely explanation is that the process itself is flawed. When members themselves try to provide the alliance's staff support work, the

---

Tip: Consider a Mega-Board Meeting

At a point in the early stages of alliance development, it is a good idea to consider some type of meeting involving the boards of directors of all participants. A full board meeting probably will be unwieldy, so the meeting may have to be done on a representative basis (e.g., two representatives from each board). It also needs to be facilitated very carefully lest it become counterproductive. (A single unfortunate remark in the mega-board meeting of mixed religious faith health care institutions set their alliance development process back a full six months.) Still, the advantages of people seeing and hearing each other as leaders of their respective organizations are hard to match any other way.

result can be a drifting, unfocused process. Before concluding that the alliance has no value, be sure that the process of making it work is not the culprit.

Task Seven: Implement and Evaluate

Task-oriented alliances have it easy when it comes to planning the work. By selecting a single focus point for their efforts, they efficiently narrow the choices available to them. Knowing where they start from and what they want to accomplish, they can fill in the blanks with sensible steps. If they do not know what those steps should be, they can consult an expert.

Process alliances, however, do not have the benefit of a road map style of operating. Even though they can and should identify areas on which to focus, half of their work consists of going through a process of mutual discovery and applying the lessons they learn on the fly. They have to build the bus as it takes them on the journey.

Most managers in a start-up operation devise a business plan, and lenders and investors usually insist on seeing a business plan before putting any money into the venture. Typically a business plan contains an overall statement of the new organization's purpose and mission, research into potential markets, a plan for introducing the product or service, and some financial projections. Being aware of this practice, alliance members—or their own boards of directors— often expect a business plan from the alliance. It is an understandable conclusion but often an impossible demand.

Process alliances are really a series of small business undertakings, each of which could legitimately have its own plan (assuming the task is complicated enough to warrant it; even if it is not, the principle still holds). The ambiguity comes from the fact that often the specific tasks are not identified until well after the whole process has begun, and then they usually relate to something already accomplished.

Still, in spite of all these uncertainties, it is possible to outline a multiyear work plan for an alliance. Using the C.O.R.E. model will help determine what comes first and to what extent individual tasks should be pursued. Exhibit 21.1 illustrates a simplified plan for a hypothetical alliance of a group of elder care facilities. The narrative interprets the plan.

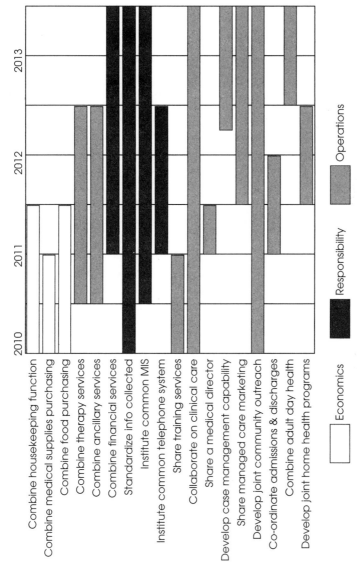

Exhibit 21.1   Timing of Collaboration Activities

Notice that, consistent with the time continuum implicit in the C.O.R.E. model, the alliance plans to pay early attention to Economics collaboration. In this case, planners have identified three areas of focus that can be done right away.

Of the Responsibility areas for collaboration, the alliance will plan to concentrate on standardizing their information systems first. Considering the complexity of this area, it is no accident that standardizing the information they collect and manage is expected to be a multiyear effort. Operations people usually find it easiest to integrate training activities early, which is why it is one of the first Operations-related tasks to be attempted.

Developing a case management capability, although it is expected to be a major benefit to the alliance, simply cannot be done until much later in the process. Integrating around such a sensitive function will need a foundation of trust and organizational comfort in working together that will take years to build. Also, from a purely practical perspective, developing a case management system (meaning an administrative system capable of assessing consumers' needs and placing them in the most appropriate setting) needs to be preceded by a lot of work in information systems management and in determining clinical standards.

Tip: Joint Marketing on the Cheap

How does a self-defined alliance, existing only in the minds of its planners, go about introducing itself to the public? One such group came up with a quick and inexpensive idea at its very first meeting. A related community group was having a special event and selling ads in the program book. For a fraction of the cost of a full ad, each member of the budding alliance contributed its share of a single ad, which was signed with the names of all the member organizations—instant joint marketing.

A final word on the chart. What is not shown here—and is extremely important—is serendipity. It will not take long before people at all levels of the member organizations will catch on to the power of the alliance. One idea will lead to another and another. Paths that seemed to make sense at the beginning fade in comparison to more exciting and valuable projects that were conceived only because of some other success (or failure). Whole new directions and opportunities open up, while others close down or seem less appealing based on experience. As long as participants are prepared to incorporate these happy discoveries, the true work plan will be essentially a framework for opportunism. This is what management thinkers refer to as learning organizations, and experiencing it is a treat for anyone connected with the project. The fact that it is accomplished by a network of organizations collaborating voluntarily makes it that much sweeter.

Alliance Operational Structures

An alliance of this sort could create a limited liability company (LLC) or other vehicle. This would be an extremely light level of activity because becoming a partner in an LLC does not change the structure of the participating corporation. Many alliances will never need to create a formal operational structure. They will stick to lower-C.O.R.E.-level collaboration, or perhaps they will fade away over time. Some, however, will grow to the point where they need to form at least one legally sanctioned vehicle, and others may spin off initiatives that themselves will need to incorporate. (This has been true mainly in the for-profit sector to date.) The guiding principle for alliance structure should be the same as for mergers: Let form follow function. This means that members will need to pay careful attention to their shared objectives because these will tell them how to shape the organization.

Groups of CEOs collaborating via a process alliance for the first time are likely to respond emotionally to the question about formalizing a structure for the process. Some will prefer a legal entity from the beginning, while others may want to keep things informal as long as possible. In the beginning, this is a stylistic matter to be resolved jointly. At a certain point, however, the question stops being one of style and starts being one of substance.

For example, some alliances will be able to operate within the existing corporate structure and operations of one or more member organizations. These sponsoring nonprofits initially may donate or lease office space and provide supplies and equipment and maybe even staff time. It is the same model frequently used for small trade associations, where a large member of the association temporarily acts as an administrative parent of the association itself. As long as the sponsoring organization is comfortable with this type of arrangement and the members are satisfied with the services, there will be no problem.

It is probably more likely that alliances will persist in keeping matters informal too long rather than the reverse. Even if a few members want to incorporate or set up a formal partnership right at the beginning, there is a good chance that it will not happen. Formalizing a structure takes time, thought, competent legal advice, and at least a bit of start-up capital. Unless there is a strong reason for the members to come up with all of those things, it is easier to manage alliance affairs on the back of an envelope.

The things that will push an alliance away from the informal stage tend to be economic forces or legal requirements so strong that a single entity cannot respond satisfactorily. These forces or requirements tend to be powerful enough considerations that they can greatly influence the choice of structure even in the absence of any other forces.

Capital Investment

Having to put a sizable sum of money into an alliance can be a catalyst for developing a legally recognized structure. This is similar to the initial investors in a start-up enterprise. The organization will need to purchase equipment, hire staff or consultants, make deposits on supplies and services, pay incidental fees, do research, and so on. Or the alliance objective simply may call for acquiring a single piece of equipment, a marketing study, or some other one-time-only purchase. Members will insist on having a record-keeping system capable of keeping track of their money and being able to show the linkage between what they are putting in and what they are getting back (even if it is not expected to occur for a few years).

Tip: Prepare to Make an Investment

It will be virtually impossible for an alliance to make broad and effective improvements in operations over a long period of time without each member making a capital contribution. How much? The answer to that question depends on the alliance's goals, objectives, and strategies. Expect it to be more than petty cash. And do not expect to get it back soon.

Liability

Liability is always a consideration. If members expect to engage in activity that puts them at risk collectively or individually—and it is hard to imagine any activity of consequence that does *not* put organizations at some risk today—then they will need to settle on a structure accordingly. Factors influencing liability are often driving forces behind choice of corporate or other vehicle. Partnerships, as described earlier, inherently determine the nature of participants' liability. Corporations will have more or less liability depending on local laws. One of the reasons for formalizing an alliance structure is not so much to escape liability—if that were even possible—as much as it is to make the nature of the liability clear and predictable.

> #### Note: For-Profits for Nonprofits (and Vice Versa)?
>
> In alliance structure, there is a paradox. For-profits will not trust a competitor with responsibility for the collaboration structure, so they need trust and accountability from their alliances. This is why real estate companies established Multiple Listing Services as nonprofits.
>
> Nonprofits, however, may be well advised to establish for-profit alliance vehicles, for several reasons. The lower the alliance operates on the C.O.R.E. Continuum and the larger it is, the more difficult it is to claim that it is consistent with charitable purposes. But a larger reason is that dollars flowing back to the participants in the form of profits or shared revenues are unrestricted funds, the most valuable kind of dollars a nonprofit can have.

Market Advantage

Finally, participants may find that they gain important credibility in the market by forming a single joint vehicle. For health care nonprofits, the ability to negotiate as a block with payers could be vital. Aside from the administrative ease of committing a variety of organizations with a single signature, the designation of a vehicle sends symbolic messages of continuity and commitment to the long haul. Alliance members could find that the advantages of this move far outweigh the complexity and additional cost.

CHAPTER 22

Postscript and Conclusion

As this edition was being completed, the nonprofit sector was witnessing the biggest and most spontaneous burst of interest in collaborations in its history. Conventional wisdom portrayed this upsurge as caused by the recession that began in December of 2007 with the implosion of the subprime mortgage market and deepened rapidly in the fall of 2008 with the suddenly tottering banking sector. On some level, this interpretation is accurate, but it misses a larger point. The economic downturn was nothing more than a catalyst that revealed the underlying economic and programmatic weaknesses of substantial numbers of nonprofits. Moreover, the nonprofit sector usually lags recessions by about two years. For example, the last recession began in March 2000, but the number of nonprofits reporting a deficit did not peak until 2002. There is every reason to expect that the same pattern will hold true this time, perhaps with a slower recovery period.

Ultimately, this cycle will also end. When that happens, it is our hope that the collaborative impulse in the nonprofit sector will have transformed from an afterthought to an enduring way of achieving mission. Enough organizations will have combined to create newer, stronger entities capable of accomplishing even greater things than before, and parochial self-interest will have receded at least a bit. American society needs the nonprofit sector to take an unprecedented leadership role in solving a vast array of problems. If this book can contribute to that transformation in some small way, it can be judged to have been a success.

About the Author

Thomas A. McLaughlin, M.B.A., is Vice President for Consulting Services at Nonprofit Finance Fund and a member of the faculty at the Heller School for Social Policy and Management at Brandeis University. He has 35 years of nonprofit management experience as a consultant and executive. He is a contributing editor for the *Nonprofit Times* and is the author of *Streetsmart Financial Basics for Nonprofit Managers* and *Nonprofit Strategic Positioning: Decide Where to Be, Plan What to Do*, also published by John Wiley & Sons.

Index

31901047616885